Promoting Quality in Learning

Also available from Cassell:

S. Acker, *The Realities of Teachers' Work: Never a Dull Moment*

D. Ager, *Language Policy in Britain and France: The Processes of Policy*

A. Pollard and P. Triggs with P. Broadfoot, M. Osborn and E. McNess, *Policy, Practice and Pupil Experience: Changing English Primary Education*

M. Osborn, E. McNess and P. Broadfoot with A. Pollard and P. Triggs, *Policy, Practice and Teacher Experience: Changing English Primary Education*

A. Pollard and A. Filer, *The Social World of Pupil Career*

Promoting Quality in Learning

Does England Have the Answer?

Patricia Broadfoot, Marilyn Osborn, Claire Planel and Keith Sharpe

CASSELL

Cassell
Wellington House
125 Strand
London WC2R 0BB

370 Lexington Avenue
New York
NY 10017–6550

First published 2000

British Library Cataloguing-in-Publication Data
A catalogue record for this book is available from the British Library.

ISBN 0-304-70684-1

Typeset by Paston PrePress Ltd, Beccles, Suffolk
Printed and bound in Great Britain by Creative Print and Design Wales, Ebbw Vale

Contents

For Dr Albert Osborn
of the Graduate School of Education, Bristol University

To whose memory this book is dedicated, in recognition of his outstanding qualities as a researcher and as a colleague and in appreciation for all the help and support that he gave to the QUEST project.

Acknowledgements

All books reflect the efforts of many different people and this one is no exception. First and foremost we would like to thank our colleague, Brigitte Ward, who was one of the researchers on the project. We acknowledge here our deep appreciation of her contribution to the QUEST team and of her many skills. We thank her for her commitment, her enthusiasm, her ability to remain cheerful in the face of problems and her invaluable insights into French culture. Vikki Davies, as project secretary, coped magnificently with a mass of data in two languages and remained unfazed by the complexity of the project. Mike Taysum, Oz Osborn and Maggie Shapland provided invaluable technical help with data-analysis. To them we express our sincere gratitude.

We acknowledge our debt to the members of our Consultative Committee: Professor Kathleen Hall at Leeds University, Professor Rosamund Sutherland and Dr David Johnson from Bristol University, and Mrs Beryl Webber from Canterbury Christ Church College.

In France, Arlette Brucher provided invaluable help in facilitating access to schools in Marseilles and in providing advice about French education more generally and we thank her most warmly. Mme Françoise Rossignol, of the IUFM in Arras, provided expert guidance throughout the project. Thanks too are due to André Segard, Inspecteur de L'Education Nationale for Calais and to M. Hory, his counterpart in Marseilles, for facilitating our work there.

Many colleagues in the host institutions of the QUEST project – Bristol University and Canterbury Christ Church College – gave willingly of their time and expertise to support and guide our work; Jan Winter provided expert guidance in relation to Maths testing and David Johnson and Pat Triggs in relation to language testing. Andrew Pollard provided expert advice in relation to English primary schools. Stephanie Burke and Sue Cottrell contributed their very considerable secretarial skills to the later phases of the project and Jan Archer and Sheila Taylor have provided invaluable assistance well beyond the call of duty in the production of this book. We thank them all most warmly.

We take this opportunity too of thanking the many other individuals who have helped us in our work: Dick King-Smith, Pie Corbett, Jean Haigh and Christopher Robinson who provided advice on the assessment of aspects of language; Catrin Meredith, Ian Gathercole and Steven Osborn who provided help with field work in France; 'Auntie Peggy' (Mrs Mason), who allowed us to meet in her home in London; Carol Jubb and colleagues at ALLEF who greatly facilitated our 'movers' study of children who had been to school in both France and England.

Every educational research project depends for its success on the willing cooperation of partners in the education system. In the case of the QUEST project which sought both pupils' and teachers' involvement in two different countries, this dependence was particularly marked and we are delighted to take this opportunity of formally acknowledging the great debt we owe to the many different individuals who helped us in what we hope will prove to have been an important and valuable study. To the pupils, teachers, headteachers and inspectors in Marseilles, Calais, Rouen and Alpes-Maritime in France we offer our sincere appreciation for allowing us access to a significant number of their classrooms and for so actively cooperating with us in the process of data-collection. Equally, we would like to thank our English colleagues in Bristol and Kent where also local officials, headteachers and teachers were most willing to allow us access to schools and to pupils in them who provided such perspicacious insights into their school experiences. We would particularly like to thank the many hundreds of pupils who voluntarily undertook extra testing in order to provide us with crucial data for this project.

Finally, to the ESRC who funded the QUEST project and to The Qualifications and Curriculum Authority who funded further analysis of the maths and language assessments, we extend our grateful thanks.

Note: Extracts from children's comments recorded in this book retain their original spellings.

Chapter 1

Why Compare? The Fashion for International Comparisons

THE OBSESSION WITH ASSESSMENT

We live in an increasingly international world. A world in which the impact of new, global technologies and the activities of multinational companies is weaving an increasingly influential global culture. But, while increasing possibilities for international trade are associated with a greater mobility of labour and the transferability of qualifications, the provision of education which will equip individuals to take advantage of these opportunities is still very largely the preserve of the individual nation state – a modernist institution which owes much of its current influence to its association with the era of nineteenth-century colonial expansionism. Individual countries are increasingly recognizing that their future prosperity is closely linked to their capacity to compete on the international stage – and all that goes with this in terms of political and social change, such as the growing influence of the European Community: the current UK debate concerning the desirability of European Monetary Union is typical of this tension between traditions of national sovereignty and the growing recognition that economic union is vital to future successful competition on the global stage. However, it is to the national education system that policy-makers continue to look for the production of a working population equipped with the necessary skills and attitudes to take full advantage of new economic possibilities.

Many nation states too, some long-established such as France (Sharpe, 1998), others of relatively recent origin such as Sri Lanka (Little, 1997) or Malaysia, faced with the pressures for political and cultural disaggregation that are a feature of an increasingly global, post-modernist society (Cowan, 1996) are also looking to the education system as a source of national unity, a state institution that will meld diverse ethnic and cultural traditions into a united and powerful whole and diffuse political unrest. Still others, such as Britain and the United States, faced with the social and moral fragmentation that is a symptom of change, and the need to curb problems of violence, drug-taking and other manifestations of social inequality and anomie, are seeking ways to address these problems through the education system. In many countries too, governments are increasingly having to respond through their education systems to issues concerning equity and access in terms of, for example, gender, ethnicity and disability which are being raised by diverse pressure groups.

Thus, economic, social and political pressures – albeit in different proportions in different countries – are typically combining to produce a powerful cocktail of pressures on national education systems that is making the relative success of those systems a matter of increasingly high stakes. As such pressures mount, policy-makers are increasingly concerned to reassure themselves that this key state institution, the institution on which rightly or wrongly so much of the nation's future prosperity and health is seen to rest, is being effective in achieving the goals set out for it.

Thus assessments and comparisons of educational standards have become fashionable because governments around the world are becoming increasingly convinced that achieving their educational goals – whatever they are – has never been more important. In particular, many are convinced that high levels of knowledge and skills in the working population are the key to future economic competitiveness. Whether this is indeed the case – and there are certainly some who would call such a widespread assumption into question (see Robinson, 1999) – is arguably less important than the fact that governments believe it to be so; that although education is expensive, it is also the key to future national prosperity and so must be made to work efficiently and effectively.

One of the most obvious starting points for ascertaining both the relative and the absolute effectiveness of the system is to establish the level of national standards and to compare these with those of competitor nations. To this end many countries have in recent years set up national assessment systems to generate nationally-specific data concerning pupil achievement. Many have also become involved in one or more international comparative studies such as the recently-published IEA Third International Mathematics and Science (TIMSS) study (Keys *et al.*, 1996) and the International Assessment of Educational Progress (IAEP) studies.

In many countries, such as France, Australia, Canada and New Zealand (Broadfoot, 1992; Masters and Forster, 1997; Anderson and Bachor, 1998; Crooks and Flockton, 1996), these national assessment systems have been designed to generate diagnostic data concerning pupil achievement. Such data both provide governments with information concerning the impact of social, environmental and school level variables on pupil achievement and give teachers information about individual pupil performance that they can use to support learning in the classroom.

In other countries, such as England, national assessment systems, while also being intended to fulfil these needs, are primarily designed to provide summative achievement data as the basis for 'league tables' of institutional performance. Their aim is to encourage the operation of market forces in education. In this latter case, it is assumed by government that providing consumers with information about school standards in this form will provide a degree of inter-institutional competition that will act as a stimulus to the achievement of higher standards across the system – a philosophy which is borrowed from the market-place.

The background to such developments is the relatively recent international recognition of the potential of assessment as a policy tool. Although many education systems have always relied to a greater or lesser extent on external examination systems to control the education system through influencing teachers' and pupils' priorities, it is arguably only in recent years that policy-makers have realized the potential for assessment systems to influence priorities at all levels of activity within the education system through the imposition of formal accountability measures. The result of this realization has been the conscious manipulation of systems to collect and publish assessment data to an ever-increasing extent. Thus, if the 1980s was the decade in which accountability became firmly enshrined as an explicit feature of state-funded institutions, the 1990s may be seen as characterized by the translation of this relationship into a concern with quality – its promotion through quality-assurance devices, and its measurement by a variety of quality control procedures. It is a decade in which the notion of 'performance indicators' has become ubiquitous as the basis for defining and measuring quality. The result has been the development of a 'discourse of evaluation', an assumption that aspects of social and corporate life can and should be subject to systematic, typically numerical, judgements of their quality.

Fundamental to this growing domination has been the development of a discourse rooted in a rationalist vocabulary of scientific measurement – of standards and scales; of objective judgements and comparisons. It is a profoundly modernist discourse, the product of an age committed to a belief in the power of science and rationality to lead to social and economic improvement. Thus, in education, the 1990s saw the rise to prominence of notions such as 'target-setting' and accountability based on calculations of the 'value-added' to a pupil's progress by an individual school. Key performance indicators are used as the basis for 'benchmarking' in which individual institutions compare their performance in relation to others that are broadly similar.

The effects of the pervasive use of performance data to judge the quality of institutional processes are profound. Since these indicators more or less explicitly define the parameters of institutional quality, they exert a powerful influence on how priorities are defined. Those responsible for making policy – whether this be at the institutional or the system level – find themselves locked into systems of quality control which provide both the criteria and the procedures for judging the performance of individuals and institutions as well as passing more synoptic judgements on the system as a whole. Increasingly too, as the 'discourse of evaluation' becomes more and more embedded, the desirability of making such judgements and the possibility of so doing in a way that is useful and defensible is taken for granted. The result of such growing trust in the technology of assessment is evaluations that are matters of increasingly high stakes, in that serious consequences in terms of benefits and penalties become linked to positive or negative evaluations.

The driving force for the increased attention now being given to various kinds of assessment, monitoring and evaluation, appears to be first a desire to 'know': to establish how far the activity in question measures up to a specified or relative level of performance. This concern is linked to the pressure governments increasingly feel to ensure high levels of national educational performance. It reflects a concern with effectiveness and accountability and the ensuing need both to ensure and to demonstrate value for money. To this extent the judgements are essentially standards, or criterion-referenced. However, a second source of motivation behind much of the current emphasis on assessment, notably the reporting of results in terms of a range of 'performance indicators' in comparative 'league tables', is norm-referenced in that it is concerned with relative standards of performance. It is a practice rooted in a belief in the value of competition – between individuals, between institutions or between whole systems – as a valuable spur to improvement.

In short, it would seem that assessment activity of one kind or another is increasingly being regarded as a management 'panacea' – the key mechanism for both monitoring and indeed enhancing quality at every level. Such use of assessment information is necessarily based on the assumption that it is possible to 'measure' quality by applying criteria to the available evidence and, on the basis of this evidence, to form a judgement. It is further typically assumed that it is both appropriate and desirable to express such judgements in the form of grades or marks and of ranks, percentages or levels; that is, in some quantitative or 'categoric' rather than descriptive form, in order to provide a common basis for comparison.

This belief – that it is meaningful to identify objectified *standards* (Resnick *et al.*, 1994) and desirable to use these in order to compare some aspect of national, institutional or individual performance on a common, objectified scale – is arguably an increasingly characteristic and international feature of current approaches to both policy-making and management in a wide range of state and private organizations. Nowhere, however, is this approach more pervasive and sophisticated than in the field of education, where at every level of activity the assumptions of the 'assessment society' (Broadfoot and Pollard, 1999) and its underpinning belief in measurement and scientific rationality find expression in systems for collecting, analysing and interpreting data which are deemed to provide a dependable representation of the quality of the whole.

As this book is intended to reveal, such a belief has the most far-reaching consequences for the nature of the decisions that are taken concerning education and for the practices that follow. Its very pervasiveness should challenge us to question first whether such data are sufficiently reliable to justify the weight put upon them as the basis for key decisions. Secondly, if indeed such data can be shown to be reliable and dependable, are they meaningful? What is the effect of using them on the individuals, institutions and systems in question? In what follows, we explore these questions in more detail. Given the assumption that educational policy and practice can potentially be enhanced by lessons learned from comparisons with other systems and settings, we consider the various factors that are likely to be relevant to any such comparison. We consider, briefly, the strengths and weaknesses of different methodological approaches in terms of both their technical features and their capacity to influence what is being studied.

One of the key purposes of this book is to explore these issues; to demonstrate not only the limitations, but the very real dangers, of an uncritical belief in decontextualized measures of educational quality which may be both technically flawed and spurious in their underpinning assumptions. Our aim is to demonstrate the desirability of a very different approach to identifying quality and promoting improvement, one that is more qualitative: that is, more in the spirit of the integrative and comprehensive approach of total quality management, and which embodies the respect for cultural integrity which is the hallmark of post-modernist perspectives.

Thus, in this introductory chapter, we raise a number of key questions concerning the current fashion for identifying and, particularly, for comparing the quality of different aspects of education. The first section offers a brief introduction to the rationale for comparative studies in general and the recent spectacular growth of interest in one particular genre within this broad field – international comparative studies of academic achievement. This is followed by an exploration of some of the important questions that the powerful influence of such international studies makes it urgent to raise.

- How far, for example, do test results from international surveys provide a valid representation of what is being learned in a given country?
- In terms of their construct validity (Wiliam, 1998a), what is the washback effect of such tests on the curriculum and teaching styles?
- Is the current preoccupation with international comparisons of pupil performance globalizing test-taking skills rather than achievement?
- How far is it possible to make valid links between classroom practices and subsequent results in international league tables?
- Why is the learning of some groups of pupils apparently more effective than that of other groups?
- What is the balance between home and school, cultural attitudes and experiences versus the nature of educational practices in influencing learning outcomes?
- How far are insights generated in this respect relevant to other countries and to what extent might their generalizability be constrained by issues of legitimacy and cultural traditions that limit both the acceptability and the potential value of particular practices?
- Can such international comparisons of achievement be a means to improving the quality of learning and/or the standards of performance (not necessarily the same thing) and if so, how?
- Are there any absolutes in terms of good practice that will work regardless of (national) context?

These are some of the pressing questions prompted by the increasing international obsession with comparing relative national educational performance. As a research community whose efforts should ultimately be concerned with guiding policy, we urgently need to establish how best we can meet policy-makers' legitimate need for reassurance concerning both the absolute and the relative effectiveness of national education systems and provide them with guidance concerning what can usefully be learned from such comparisons about how to improve the level of pupil achievement.

WHAT IS IT TO COMPARE?

'Comparison is the basis for almost all forms of enquiry' suggest Bray and Thomas (1995: 472). To compare is to conduct 'studies that inspect similarities and/or differences between two or more phenomena relating to the transmission of knowledge, skills or attitudes from one person or group to another' (Ibid: 473). This very broad definition encompasses systematic comparisons ranging from the level of the individual to that of the classroom and school, to those of districts and regions and states, to that of the nation as a whole and to those between nations. It also potentially includes demographic groupings and aspects of education and society such as curriculum or labour markets. In each case, the core rationale is the same: the comparison of two or more parallel entities with a view to eliciting insights. It is an approach that lends itself particularly well to the study of education since it is an important policy field that is subject to all the conflicting messages about cause and effect that so bedevil the relationship between research and social policy as a whole.

However, comparative studies take many different forms with the various traditions suffering from a lack of integration. Bray and Thomas (1995: 472) argue that

> the chief focus in comparative education literature has been on countries and world regions, and that this has tended to lead to unbalanced and incomplete perspectives. On the other side of the coin, we have noted that much research in other fields of education has been undesirably localized in focus. In many of these studies, unbalanced and incomplete perspectives have resulted from the lack of an international dimension.

It is possible to cite many examples of comparative studies that belie this criticism. Both quantitative and more qualitatively-oriented comparative thematic studies have been undertaken on a wide range of topics including, for example, text books (Sutherland, 1998; Crossley and Murby, 1994), teaching styles (Whitburn, 1996) and retention rates (Steedman, 1999).

As Fletcher and Sabers (1995) suggest:

> international comparative studies in education provide alternative perspectives on early childhood educational practices, school curricula, school policies, student backgrounds and other socio-cultural variables that affect teaching and learning. . . .

But they go on to argue:

> Researchers have compared levels of academic achievement cross-nationally and attempted to draw conclusions and advance hypotheses to explain why certain groups surpass others [see Stevenson *et al.*, 1985]. Such studies frequently arouse political and public interest when results suggest the superiority of one country over another in one or more specified academic domain [see Bracey, 1993] (Fletcher and Sabers, 1995: 455).

Although policy-makers are increasingly interested in all kinds of international comparison, it is relative levels of pupil attainment – arguably the key outcome measure for any education system which associates final level of education achieved with national prosperity – that has captured the attention of both policy-makers and the public at large.

The argument of Bray and Thomas (1995) for a more integrated and comprehensive focus for comparative education studies in terms of levels of analysis, topics and populations does not address the (arguably) equally pernicious problem of the lack of a well-developed theoretical rationale. The significant impact of a number of key 'comparative' theories in recent years such as 'world systems theory' or dependency theory and more recently, for example, 'social cartography' (Paulston, 1996) and 'post-modernism' (Rust, 1991; Cowan, 1996), has tended to increase the specialist nature of the field in such a way that comparative studies remain uneasily linked to other core social science disciplines as applied to education – such as sociology, psychology, policy studies and history.

If, as has been argued, it is a context rather than a discipline (Broadfoot, 1998), it is a field that deserves a fuller integration with the methodologies and theories of broader social science perspectives so that they can be enriched by its unique possibilities; and so that comparative studies, in their turn, can be subject to the methodological and theoretical rigour and integrative focus of such studies. The attempts currently being made within the field of comparative education to redefine itself in the light of major new international trends such as globalization reflect a recognition both of the need for a change of focus by scholars working in the discipline and of the very significantly increased potential for this kind of educational research in an increasingly international world (Alexander *et al.*, 1999).

If there has never been a greater willingness on the part of national governments to learn from other countries, there has by the same token never been a greater opportunity for comparative educational studies to demonstrate their worth. But opportunities also mean responsibilities, and there is an urgent need for scholars to encourage governments, the media and other users to apply the discipline and rigour of the comparative tradition – notably the respect for context – in their interpretation of international performance data that was the hallmark of the early pioneers of international surveys of achievement such as Husen and Postlethwaite in the 1960s.

As it is, the ready availability of 'performance indicators' in the shape of test and examination performance data, as well as other outcome measures (such as employment rates in relation to input and process indicators such as resources, teacher qualifications, and truancy rates), means that education lends itself to comparative studies aimed at elucidating the strengths and weaknesses of a particular system. Thus, for example, the OECD has for many years been engaged in a project to define an internationally relevant battery of education indicators that provides for detailed statistical comparisons of a wide range of aspects concerning the inputs, processes and outputs of particular national education systems (OECD, 1994 Education at a Glance). Significantly, it is now engaged on a new international project which involves a similar methodology as the INES project to identify an international set of Student Achievement Indicators and it has identified 597 national education indicators which are valid across all the countries involved (Harlen, 1998).

However, in the context of the prevailing influence of an evaluative discourse the very measurability of such performance indicators has fuelled the development of a highly quantitative, often decontextualized, approach to international comparisons. But the seductive positivism of such data frequently conceals the absence of the equally crucial *qualitative* data that are necessary to the proper interpretation of the meaning and implications of such indicators.

Thus if, in recent decades, policy-makers have been quick to grasp the potential of using pupil performance data as a key quality indicator, they and the media have typically been rather less willing to engage with the dangers and shortcomings of many such comparisons. Headlines such as 'British Pupils and a Maths disaster' which appeared in the *Mail on Sunday*, 4.2.1996, are typical both of the media's desire for provocative stories and the typically high-profile impact of comparisons based on pupil achievement. Yet it is these same studies, the tip of a much larger iceberg of less salacious but often more scientifically defensible comparative studies, which are arguably the most technically contentious. The section that follows provides a brief review of some of the key themes in the methodological debate surrounding the validity, reliability and utility of such international studies.

THE TECHNICAL PROBLEMS OF CONDUCTING INTERNATIONAL COMPARISONS OF ACHIEVEMENT

International tests cannot, by definition, be context sensitive. There cannot be the same degree of matching between the structure, content and approach to learning of any one international test and the different curriculum and classroom learning of each of the participating countries. It thus challenges the meaningfulness, the validity and reliability of any one test which is administered to pupils from different national educational systems (Planel *et al.*, 1998: 13).

For users, it is important to be able to distinguish *real* differences between student performances when compared cross-nationally and those that are the product of methodological weaknesses. In this latter category may be located problems associated with sample comparability, with test design, with data analysis, and with opportunity to learn. The extent to which any comparison is defensible on any or all of these key factors will determine the extent to which it is 'comparing like with like' and hence producing valid and potentially useful data. In many studies, despite efforts to match pupil samples in terms of age, gender and socio-economic characteristics, significant differences undoubtedly remain in, for example, the numbers of children who have repeated years in different countries and are thus older than the putative sample (Brown, 1998) and in those with 'special needs' who are included or excluded. Stedman (1997), for example, argues that student achievement in the United States has been represented unfairly because results for a whole age cohort have been compared with those of small elites in other countries.

Student motivation and attitude towards test-taking has been identified as one of the factors that may impact differentially on performance in cross-national studies of achievement. Murphy (1997) argues that for an assessment to be valid it must have a clear purpose and meaning for the student and involve a problem that is seen as significant. She argues that students' confidence and their level of interest in a task may well affect their motivation to engage with it. For some students, metacognitive strategies that lead them to try to make sense of the question in a particular way may inhibit their ability to give the correct answer. A revealing example of this is provided by an experiment in which English graduates were asked to take the Scottish O-Grade examination for 16-year-olds. A significant number did not 'pass' the comprehension section because they 'read' too much into the questions. These problems are further compounded by the interaction between gender and culture, for example, especially where an attempt has been made to give meaning to the problem in question by creating a 'real life' context for it. The problems of cultural bias in test items of all kinds, even apparently 'culture-free' tests (Kincheloe *et al.*, 1997) are now well recognized in the testing literature but have yet to be overcome in international comparisons of achievement. Thus apparent consistency of scoring does not necessarily represent consistency of meaning in terms of what the test reveals. Murphy concludes that such studies 'have immense impact but very little meaning'.

Moreover, as Secada (1998) has argued, the more or less deliberate misinterpretation of international comparisons such as TIMMS has, in some contexts at least, been misused to create policies and laws that are more harmful than beneficial to children's education. The meaning of such test results needs to be recognized as essentially phenomenological in that the significance of the results is capable of potentially different interpretations depending on the location and stance of the interpreter. To the extent that a particular interest group can succeed in imposing a particular interpretation at the expense of others concerning both the meaning of the results achieved and their apparent causes, it is likely to exercise a very powerful influence on national educational policy. Such influence can go well beyond the making of specific decisions to impact on the discourse of education itself and the way in which both ends and means are defined.

Current policy debates in the UK provide one good example of this, since the apparent finding from the recent TIMSS international surveys that English and Scottish children achieve much less well in Mathematics than their Asian and East European peers (Burghes, 1996) has been the stimulus not only to defining key policy concerns in these terms but also the impetus to adopt teaching strategies which appear to be instrumental to the success of these other countries.

Later in this volume we discuss in detail the demands made in French and English national tests of 11-year-olds. We highlight the significance of pupils being familiar with a particular type of test item including its layout. This suggests that what may appear to be relatively superficial differences in test-design are related to fundamental national differences in the ideology of schooling and the messages that pupils have therefore received about the kind of performance that will be valued and how they should set about responding to test items. A pupil trained in the Cartesian tradition to value conformity and the ability to reproduce existing knowledge will approach an item requiring a measure of independent problem-solving quite differently from pupils whose national educational culture has taught them to be bold in giving their opinions and in using their own problem-solving strategies. We contrast the French approach with that of children in England who were found to outperform their French counterparts in some areas of Maths even though the TIMSS study had ranked them lower overall. Perhaps more importantly, as we explore in Chapters 7 and 8, their learning strategies were, in some respects at least, markedly different from those of French children.

Curriculum content will also clearly affect pupil learning outcomes both in terms of the emphasis within a particular subject and in terms of the number and range of different subjects studied. As Winter (1998) has shown in a study of Hong Kong pupils' performance, the 'allocated instructional time (AIT) for a particular subject such as Maths can vary substantially both within schools and across countries, with very significant effects on learning outcomes'.

The importance of such conceptual and methodological issues is well illustrated in a study by O'Leary, Madaus and Kellaghan (1997). Their comparison of the results of two international Maths and Science surveys – IAEP and TIMSS – which were conducted four years apart, shows significant differences in the rankings achieved by several countries. Not only do such variations make it very difficult for policy-makers to know what action to take, they also call into question the reliability of the data themselves and hence the utility of the whole exercise. They raise what must be very real concerns about both the equity and the utility of international comparisons of educational standards and indeed of similar intranational, inter-institutional comparisons based solely on the comparison of test scores (Brown, 1998; Goldstein, 1995, 1996).

An equally important and closely-related concern is the extent to which national profiles of performance are a valid representation of a particular country's overall quality and the extent to which emphasis on national aggregates obscures significant *intranational* disparities in levels of pupil achievement and the causes that lie behind them. For example, recent evidence of rising levels of achievement in England may obscure the fact that the gap between the best and worst schools in England is widening (Ofsted, 1998). As Hollen Lees (1994) points out, the variation within both France and England in terms of pupils' levels of performance on the 1992 International Assessment of Educational Progress study was greater than the overall difference between them.

In Chapter 10 we discuss the scale and significance of these differences in both France and England. Such differences were found to be less significant than the international ones – a finding that reinforces the importance of conducting national comparisons to elicit the influence of national culture and institutional practice. However, the fact that there were significantly greater differences between the performance of pupils from high and low socio-economic status areas in England and those in France, in terms of both their attitude to school and their attainment levels, highlights the importance of combining inter- and intranational comparisons in order to explore the significance of particular policy approaches.

If it is the case, as *Le Monde de l'éducation* (1996, June: 26, 27) claims, that equality is a myth even in a country that is characterized by a tradition of homogeneity and a strong commitment to it, how much greater are such differences likely to be in countries where there are significant local variations in funding and provision, curriculum and school ethos, teacher expectations and parent support such as the United States or the UK?

SO WHY DO SOME COUNTRIES DO BETTER THAN OTHERS?

Even if it were possible to overcome the technical problems associated with such international comparisons to achieve data with demonstrably high validity and reliability, simply to know how a particular country is performing, either in absolute terms in relation to its own targets and goals or in relative terms in relation to the achievements of other countries, would be of limited use to the policy-maker. Two further steps are needed if such data are to be the basis for a positive influence on practice. The first of these concerns *explanations*, generating hypotheses to explain the differential performance, and the second concerns *resolutions* about what is likely to prove effective in addressing any perceived area of weakness.

As has already been suggested, the scope for both national and international comparative attainment data to be the basis for intense media attention has tended to result in a good deal of hand-wringing, scapegoating and jumping to conclusions about causes, instead of a careful and informed analysis about cause and effect: the relationship between inputs, processes and outputs which is essential to the effective use of comparative performance data. Coupled with the scope for making political capital about apparent weaknesses in national educational performance, it is all too easy to see why so much more attention has been given by the research community to the design, administration and reporting of such surveys and by policy-makers to the results.

The amount of attention given to *explaining* the outcomes in a careful and systematic way has arguably been much less. In the United States in particular, where there has been a great deal of high-profile concern expressed over apparently poor 'national' standards in Mathematics, scholars are now arguing strongly against what some see as simplistic interpretations of the data and stressing the need for a much more careful analysis of what the findings show as well as the need to contextualize them in terms of a subtle teasing-out of the impact of various influencing factors in the very variable education provision of different localities and states (Bracey, 1996).

Relatively unusual, therefore, is the UK-based Kassel Project, for example (Burghes, 1996), which involves a careful study of approaches to Maths-teaching in thirteen countries, together with other educational variables, with a view to distilling recommendations for good practice in the UK. The project recognizes many of the arguments against de-contextualized, simplistic assumptions concerning 'what works' that have been made in this chapter:

- that it is impossible to compare like with like because there are too many variables, including setting and streaming; the curriculum being taught; time spent on Maths tuition, teaching style and so on
- that the impact of such variables is further compounded by the difficulties involved in equating the tests used in terms of the contexts used for item design, language issues and student familiarity with particular kinds and layouts of items.

Thus Burghes recognizes that:

Although international comparisons can highlight problems, they cannot easily give us solutions. The best we can do is to use the data as indicators of performance, then observe, interview and use our experience and common sense to formulate recommendations.

In this vein, he suggests that the roots of underachievement in the UK, for example, may be traced to an education system in which, in contrast to other countries, pupils are not typically keen to be educated and do not accept the need for hard work. He contrasts a confrontational system which emphasizes fragmentation, school inspections, competition between schools and national testing, in which 'everyone seems to be at war' with the vast majority of other countries in which 'there is a real sense of purpose with pupils, staff and parents all working together to achieve success'. As we discuss in Chapter 3, it may well be that it is the foundations of English education as an essentially voluntary network of provision that underpins its continuing emphasis on differentiation between schools and between individual pupils and hence, the difficulty of making a reality of a common set of expectations for all pupils. Even the current emphasis on target-setting appears to have run into this problem once again with concerns that the emphasis on A* to C passes at GCSE risks ignoring the needs of lower achievers, and similarly, at Key Stage 2, the emphasis on numbers achieving level 4 which is likely again to draw attention away from the weakest pupils and hence widen the gap between high and low achievers (Brighouse, 1998).

Hughes (1997) makes a rather similar case in highlighting the relative success of Maths teaching in Japan, emphasizing both the pedagogic concern that *all* pupils should succeed and the close cultural link between education and the wider society in which learning is very much valued and teachers have high status. Many other commentators on the apparently outstanding success of the Japanese educational system have identified this potent combination of input and process factors including parental concern and active support; culturally-based, high levels of pupil motivation; teacher expectation that all pupils will achieve the basic standard, plus a teaching community which is expected to have a very professional approach to the active development of supportive and engaging pedagogic strategies (Green, 1999; White, 1987; Woronoff, 1996).

But at the same time, it is important to look beyond the issue of standards *per se* and to consider the kinds of learning that are being encouraged. Many Asian countries are currently deploring their inability to wean pupils off rote learning and to engage them in more creative thinking.[1] Schools in many countries are increasingly being marred by pupil violence, and student suicide rates are rising. Cousin (1998) gives a damning critique of French junior secondary schools.

One of the central arguments of this book is that learning outcomes are a product of a complex mixture of factors – such as, for example, the perceived importance of qualifications or the stage in industrial development – and that it is important to understand the resultant synthesis *as a whole* before trying to draw any lessons for another system. Education plays a different role in different societies and this is likely to affect pupils' motivation. Little (1997), for example, suggests that in Tanzania the lack of modern sector jobs has dampened the enthusiasm for pursuing educational qualifications, and in Egypt too, the disintegration of the previously close link between qualifications and elite jobs is influencing the role of the education system as a whole and the motivation of pupils within it (Hargreaves, 1997). In Malaysia, until recently, the buoyancy of the job market discouraged pupils from seeking further qualifications.

But such structural factors are only one sector of a mass of explanatory variables. For example, the fact that many immigrant pupils from high-achieving countries do outstandingly well in United States schools – and indeed in those of many other countries – points to the salience of culture as another influence, particularly that of family values.

Thus the core theme of this book is the way in which cultural, structural and educational variables *combine* to influence pupil achievement and hence, the need to study the relative success of different national systems in this light. To illustrate the importance of this argument, we may usefully consider a brief illustrative example. The country chosen is Taiwan since it is one of the 'Asian tiger' economies and the one most often cited admiringly by educators in the West for the level of its students' educational achievements. Historically, as Jacques suggests,

> The original Asian tigers – Taiwan, South Korea, Hong Kong and Singapore – were amongst the poorest countries in the world in the 1950s with agrarian-based economies and little industry. They were confronted with the problem of how to 'take off' when conventional economic wisdom suggested it was virtually impossible (Jacques, 1996).

Yet Taiwan's economy, since that time, has typically grown at 10 per cent a year. There are a number of reasons for this, including

> import substitution, an aggressive export strategy, a powerful international orientation, a highly active state. Relative income equality and a strong emphasis on the importance of education. From the outset, Taiwan recognised the crucial importance of education in a way that other countries such as Brazil and Pakistan, which were at an equivalent level of development in the early 1960s, did not. But it was not just that Taiwan understood the significance of education, perhaps even more important was the kind of education policy it pursued ... Taiwan, like the other Asian tigers, pursued a strongly egalitarian educational policy (Jacques, 1996).

Jacques also suggests that the key ingredients in Taiwan's educational achievements are:

> Firstly, culture. There is an immense desire to learn which is lodged deep in the cultural and national psyche. This is linked to the Confucian tradition, which accords a special place to education and teachers.
> Secondly, the commitment to the idea that every child has the right and the ability to reach a certain level of achievement. Unlike the UK and the US, there is not a built-in assumption that a certain proportion of the age cohort cannot make the grade and therefore must fail ... coupled with this goes an educational approach in these (elementary) schools which ensures that every child makes that grade; classes waiting for the slowest to catch up, special catch-up classes, one to one help, the involvement of parents....
> To sum up, the Taiwanese educational system has two enormous strengths. One a commitment to all children succeeding which means that, unlike Britain, there is no trailing edge of failure. Two the relative excellence of the public system of education which means that private schools, rather than public schools, are second best (1996: 1).

Another view, however, would highlight the fact that Taiwan is a country that has only recently (in 1987) emerged from forty years of martial law. Central to the educational goals of the Kuomintang government that has ruled Taiwan since 1949 has been the desire to promote Confucian ethics and to suppress potential political unrest. Schools have traditionally been very large – one primary school, for example, until recently had 12,000 pupils aged 5 to 12 – in order to facilitate strong central control. There is a national curriculum and teachers traditionally have had little freedom in either what or how they teach, including the use of teaching materials. Textbooks, likewise, have tended to stress respect for authority and patriotism rather than, for example, the development of individual perspectives or potential. Three-quarters of all elementary schools' classes have class sizes of 36 and above, and more than half have 41–49 pupils.[2]

Within this tightly-controlled and in many ways inevitably impersonal system, pupils are subject to intense competitive pressure. Only 30 per cent of pupils pass the Joint Secondary Examination at age 15 to go on to academic high schools and university entrance. The rest must attend the less sought-after vocational schools.

Students are not seen as individuals but as statistics on a conveyor belt of examinations and rote learning. At each stage, narrowing gates push many off the conveyor belt until only a tiny elite reach the holy grail: Taiwan National University (Sharma, 1997: 17).

Once there, the subject studied depends more on exam grade than personal choice because pupils will tend to opt for a less selective subject at 'the best university' rather than go elsewhere to pursue their preference. As in other Asian countries, the intense examination pressure results in a high take-up of places at cram schools (*bushiban*) and more than one million pupils attend such private lessons, although this can disadvantage children with poorer parents for whom the cost may prove prohibitive.

Taiwan does outstandingly well in international comparisons of maths and science achievement. However, underpinning this statement are two of the central themes of this chapter. First is the need for *methodological* caution concerning whether the comparison is being made of similar populations. In Taiwan, at age 15, only the 30 per cent of students in the academic high schools are included in such surveys, many of whom are specialists in science. Second is the need for *interpretative* caution. For example, in the UK much has been made of the apparently high level of pupil achievement in Taiwan (Reynolds and Farrell, 1996) and an hour long 'Panorama' television documentary was devoted to what the UK might learn from their teaching methods such as 'whole class interactive teaching'. Yet in Taiwan, educationalists believe that the 'country's high international scores at maths and science are due to the rigorous exam-oriented training in junior high schools'. In the words of Education Minister Dr Wu Jin, 'we do perform well on international comparisons, but should we be proud of it? We would like to have well-balanced training for students and they are not receiving it. We are only repeatedly drilling them to be professional exam-takers in those subjects' (Sharma, 1997).

Thus, while it is indeed possible to ascribe Taiwan's high level of apparent achievement to a particular teaching style or curriculum emphasis, it is also possible to attribute to it a number of other factors such as the intense pressure on students to achieve; a culture that promotes high levels of motivation among students; a willingness for higher-achieving students to help their weaker colleagues; and the very considerable extra time spent learning for the many students who attend cram school, as well as doing substantial amounts of homework. Other more subtle factors are relevant too, including, as Baumgart (1997), Watkins and Biggs (1996) and others have argued, the much more subtle relationship between culture and cognitive style which challenges simplistic assumptions concerning what is an apparent emphasis on rote learning. Teasing out what other countries might learn from the Taiwanese experience thus requires careful, in-depth, qualitative study of the kind reported in this book, research which gives due account to the influence of both culture and structure as well as to educational methods and opportunity to learn.

WITH WHAT EFFECT?

Finally, important as these issues are for understanding the factors that influence the apparently greater levels of educational success in some countries relative to that in others, in the end they are arguably less important than the most fundamental questions concerning the *goals* of education. As discussed above, the first question that faces policy-makers is quite simply, what do we want the young people of tomorrow to know and be able to do? As governments around the world grapple with the challenge of rapid social, political and economic change and its implications for education, they are faced with deciding the *relative* importance of different aspects of educational achievement.

At the most profound level such questions include the desired balance between academic study – for long the core of schooling in most countries – and other potentially increasingly important aspects such as personal, social and moral education;[3] work-related, vocational and key skills which are shortly to be a requirement of all post-16 certification in England; health, physical and leisure education. However, debates about educational priorities are likely to become wider still as the impact of information technology and other generic international developments bring about profound changes in all aspects of life.

In such a context, if it is indeed the case, as Hollen Lees (1994: 65) suggests, that 'school children today represent not only themselves and their families in an imaginary nationwide competition but also their countries in an international race for superiority', the ground on which that competition is played out, and hence the focus for such international comparisons, is likely to become ever more important. In particular, the issues of whether current assessment practices are tending to globalize test-taking skills rather than the kinds of achievements relevant to the twenty-first century, must become a central concern.

Our aim, in this chapter, has thus been to challenge the current hegemony of one particular type of comparison – large-scale, quantitative international surveys of pupil performance – and so to lay the foundations for justifying a very different approach to such concerns, an approach which embodies those qualitative methodological traditions which have impacted so powerfully on social science research in recent decades; an approach rooted in a more interpretive theoretical perspective that gives due weight to individual and cultural phenomenology as a determinant of national educational achievement.

The next chapter in this volume provides a more detailed elaboration of this argument in providing an account of the rationale for the Quality of Primary Education: Children's Experiences of Schooling in England and France (QUEST) project on which this book is based. This project, which was funded by the Economic and Social Research Council from 1995 to 1997 is one of a programme of comparative studies which, since 1989, have used the empirical focus of comparing aspects of educational organization and practice in France and England, to develop and demonstrate the potential of a more qualitative comparative methodology. In its central concern with establishing relative levels of educational performance among pupils in England and France, the QUEST project engaged with one of the pressing educational issues of our time. In adopting an unorthodox testing methodology for this purpose, which is rooted in the understandings and methodological traditions of comparative education itself rather than in psychometrics, the project illuminated new possibilities for comparative assessment studies.

Through an account of the rationale, conduct and findings of the study that forms the core of this book, we seek to demonstrate the need for a fundamental reappraisal of how comparative studies of educational 'quality' may most fruitfully be conducted.

On the one hand, we argue for the adoption of a socio-cultural theoretical approach in the tradition of Bronfenbrenner (1979) and, more recently, Bruner (1990) and Wertsch (1991) which takes the interaction between the individual and their 'cultural tools' as the starting point for understanding the processes of teaching and learning, and hence educational outcomes. On the other, we argue for new 'micro-comparative' methodologies to be developed and applied on a wide scale involving an in-depth comparative scrutiny of the activities of teachers and learners in different national systems or cultural settings, particularly the strategies and understandings demonstrated by pupils as they respond to given tasks. In focusing on the link between pupils' perspectives, classroom processes and the differences in educational outcomes that characterize these two countries, the project raises fundamental questions concerning the source of such differences and where we may most fruitfully seek to effect change.

A third introductory chapter provides the necessary overview of the two national education systems – of England and France, so close geographically but separated by so many differences of ideology and tradition – that form the empirical focus for this book.

Part 2 of the book supplies the rich contextual data so often missing from 'the quest for quality'. It provides data on the attitudes and aspirations of pupils in each country; their views of themselves and their national culture, their ambitions, their classroom experiences and their responses to the very different educational worlds that they encounter.

The results of these different experiences are documented in Part 3 of the book which explores in detail both the relative levels of success of a matched cohort of pupils in each country on the same Maths and language tasks, and also the nationally-idiosyncratic factors that influence that success in terms of how pupils go about responding to the tasks set and the misunderstandings and weaknesses that the pattern of errors on different items reveals.

In the light of these findings the book raises the consideration of whether, after all, the focus on national differences in achievement is not obscuring other more fundamental and important patterns of difference in achievement that ought to be the major focus of concern. Its conclusion offers a powerful challenge both to comparativists and to measurement experts to recognize the significant potential of micro-comparative studies and the importance of a more holistic understanding of context, culture and ideology as the basis for effective policy-making.

NOTES

1. See, for example, *South China Morning Post*, Friday March 5th 1999, 'Exam culture is failing our students'.
2. *Times Educational Supplement* citation of Ministry statistics, 7.2.97, p. 17.
3. Chinese Premier's speech, March 1998, reported in James, M. and Broadfoot, P. (report on visit to Shanghai concerning Personal, Social and Moral Education, British Council, Shanghai, 1998).

Chapter 2

The QUEST Project: Its Rationale and Approach

WHY THE QUEST PROJECT?

What kind of educational provision is most effective in promoting learning? This is the question that lies at the heart of all educational research activity. The answers to it are the basis for both teacher ideology and educational policy. It is known, of course, that just as there is no one model of the 'good' teacher, so there is no one answer concerning the best way to promote learning – not least because this is so much a function of the *kind* of learning goals in question. However, as we argued in Chapter 1, the growing interest in international comparisons of educational standards in recent years has encouraged a tendency for governments to look abroad in seeking answers to questions concerning how to improve their education systems. It has also encouraged the introduction of national assessment systems which reflect the increasingly general concern among governments with raising standards. However the very rapid development of interest in the comparative assessment of learning outcomes has arguably not been matched by equivalent efforts to achieve a better understanding of how and why the various policies adopted are likely to achieve their intended goals, of how pupils can be helped to learn more effectively. Yet, ultimately it is on such insights that the achievement of higher standards in education will depend.

In Chapter 1 we described this growing international interest in raising educational standards and in comparing national levels of achievement. We discussed some of the pitfalls associated with both collecting and interpreting such data and the dangers associated with the all too ready assumption that 'what works' in one country to produce high achievement will work in another. The Quality of Educational Systems Transnationally (QUEST) project was conceived as a response to these concerns. Its overall aim was to examine the interrelationship between the various factors which potentially affect learning. It was designed to investigate the relationship between pupils' learning and performance strategies and their educational experiences and attitudes to school in view of significant variations in teaching approaches and curriculum emphases. In this chapter we describe the rationale for the project in more detail. Why were England and France chosen as the focus of this study? What kinds of data can legitimately be used to link perspectives, practices, inputs and processes with the outcomes of education? How are these outcomes most usefully measured? What are the problems associated with undertaking integrated comparisons of this kind?

These and other related methodological problems are addressed in the pages that follow. The first part of the chapter briefly rehearses the socio-cultural theoretical rationale which underpinned the study in the light of some of the key differences between French and English educational traditions. The second section describes the process of data collection in relation to pupils' perspectives and their classroom experiences. The third and final section focuses on the comparison of learning outcomes in the two countries which constituted a major part of the research. It documents some of the steps that were taken to construct, administer and mark an internationally valid assessment instrument which would overcome some of the limitations of more conventional international comparisons of achievement.

Rationale: exploring the ingredients of educational success

Theories abound concerning how teaching may be made more effective. Often they are contradictory. In the two countries that form the focus for this book, for example, recent years have seen sharply contrasting, but equally significant, policy initiatives aimed at raising standards. Thus in England, the passing of the 1988 Education Reform Act marked a commitment on the part of the British Government to a combination of stronger central government control of the content of the curriculum coupled with a freer rein being given to individual institutions to allow them to respond to the demands of the market, as the most likely way to raise educational standards. In France, by contrast, the passing of the equally momentous 'Loi Jospin' in 1989 marked a commitment on the part of the French Government to strengthening the autonomy of individual schools and teachers and to extending teachers' professional skills as the most likely way to raise educational standards.

As we discuss in Chapter 3, these diametrically contrasting policy initiatives reflected the different political stances currently prevailing in England and France. They are mirrored by a range of similarly-targeted policy initiatives currently taking place in other countries as governments seek to respond to the perceived challenges of the twenty-first century. The existence of significant differences in the policy responses being made to common international pressures reflects the fact that education is a cultural project. It takes place against a background of national, institutional and ideological traditions, as well as other influences such as race, gender and the local environment. (Bonnet (1998) highlights the key role played by variations in national culture in either encouraging or inhibiting both motivation and achievement in the learning of English in the EU Countries.)

Motivation to learn emerges from research findings as particularly subject to cultural influences. The six-country Student Learning Orientations (SLOG) project (1987) for example, found between the different countries studied considerable variations in what motivates pupils to learn. Particularly relevant to this study was the finding that there are significant variations in the way in which assessment motivates pupils to learn. All too often, it seems, policy-makers assume that the examination 'carrot' will motivate learners to try harder. In fact the extent to which this is true varies from culture to culture and as Kellaghan *et al.* (1996: vii) point out, 'current assumptions about the role of examinations in motivating students fail to take into account differences in the personal characteristics of students and the contexts in which they live'.

In the same way, it is also assumed by policy-makers in countries such as the UK and the United States that 'naming and shaming' by means of national and international 'league tables' of performance will motivate institutions to try harder. But the apparent failure of 'high-stakes' institutional assessment to have an effect on standards (Stake, 1991) is further testimony to the fact that the link between effort, learning and performance is considerably more complex than most policy-makers believe (Firestone, 1998). Thus, attempts to put in place policies aimed at improving performance are only likely to be effective if they are informed by an understanding of the culturally-specific relationship between motivation, intervention and outcomes for both individuals and institutions.

It is the argument of this book that comparative studies of learning outcomes, like other policy initiatives, are only a useful policy tool if they are contextualized within an analysis of the national culture, pedagogic traditions and educational priorities of a particular country. Even if de-contextualized comparisons can be developed to a point where they are *technically* defensible in that they are indeed comparing 'like with like', it is hardly equitable or useful to judge the quality of the educational provision of either individual schools or countries as a whole in terms of pupil achievements without reference to the broader social context. Indeed it may well be that differences *between* schools *within* countries are a much more valid and pressing source of concern. However, to the extent that international patterns of differences in pupil learning outcomes can be established reliably and validly, we argue that it is nevertheless still vital to take culture as the starting point for analysing the association between particular pedagogic procedures and pupil learning outcomes. The key to enhancing pupil learning, we suggest, lies in understanding the different meanings of what are often apparently similar educational perspectives and practices in different cultural contexts (Alexander, 1999).

The fundamental rationale for our study can thus be traced to Bronfenbrenner's (1979) argument that what matters is not necessarily the 'objective' features of a learning situation, but the ways in which these are construed and interpreted by subjects within that culture and setting. Subsequent writers, such as Bruner (1996) and Wertsch (1991), have developed this socio-cultural approach in arguing that forms of meaning and intellectual capacity have to be located within the social context from which they derive. Vygotsky's work (1978, 1986) has also reflected a similar emphasis on the key role of culture as a mediating force in learning. His work on thinking and learning highlights the development of higher mental processes through the mediating effect of tools, signs and patterns of action which are embedded in different cultures. A central place too is given to the role of social interaction in shaping the particular way in which learning is provided for in different cultures.

The importance of this perspective is well-evidenced by a number of studies of children's learning in different cultures, including, for instance, the influential collections of Richards and Light (1986) and Whiting and Edwards (1988). However, much of this work is small-scale and anthropological in character and does not link pupil perspectives to teacher practices in classrooms or to learning outcomes. This was a unique feature of the research forming the basis of this book.

This book is also very different in its comparative approach to that of more conventional and well-established studies of national differences in pupil achievements – the more familiar approach of large-scale, quantitative surveys. This is because the QUEST project was designed to link a detailed and careful comparison of pupil learning outcomes with related data concerning culture and classroom practices. In what follows we explore in more detail the rationale and associated methodology for this much more qualitative approach to international comparisons of pupil learning outcomes.

Subsequent chapters demonstrate the potential of such a comparative approach by presenting a range of empirical insights which illuminate the link between pupil attitudes to school and education, the pedagogy they experience and the ways these impact on their learning as demonstrated in a variety of assessment tasks. Perhaps even more significant, however, are the insights presented in Chapters 7 and 8 which illuminate differences in *how* pupils set about solving the assessment problems with which they were presented and the associated insights these data provide into the impact on learning styles of the different curricular and pedagogic emphases which are rooted in national educational traditions.

France and England: similar but different

The focus of this book is on two countries – England and France. These two countries are closely linked in many ways – not least, as one of the founding fathers of comparative education, Sir Michael Sadler, argued in 1906 (Higginson, 1979), through their history, their common link to the classical tradition, the Enlightenment and religious traditions as well as their geographic proximity. More recently they have become even more closely linked within common institutions such as the European Union. This reduces the potential impact of broader political and economic differences on any comparison, and hence highlights the specific role played by differences in culture and educational practices in the learning outcomes being studied. The powerful influence of national culture in shaping both educational traditions and participants' perspectives, despite such historical communalities, had already been clearly demonstrated in previous studies of teachers (Broadfoot and Osborn, 1993). The 'Bristaix' study had revealed that the *national* differences between English and French primary school teachers were more marked than any intranational variations based on either the personal characteristics of the teacher, such as age and experience, or the location of the school.

This earlier research had also explored the construction of primary teachers' professional identity in England and France. It showed that teachers' priorities, and what they define as their responsibilities, are a function of the national culture and the national educational traditions in which they work (Broadfoot and Osborn, 1987, 1993). This research suggested that French teachers had a narrower, more 'restricted' and more classroom-focused conception of their role which centred on academic objectives, while English teachers saw themselves as having a more 'extended', wide-ranging and diffuse set of responsibilities and goals. These included responsibility for children's social and personal development as well as their academic progress. It also involved perceived responsibilities to colleagues, headteacher, parents and the local community.

Striking differences in teaching methods, in classroom organization and in teacher–pupil relationships were also observed in the course of this earlier research (Osborn and Broadfoot, 1992). At the time of the first study in the mid-1980s, French classrooms were often characterized by a didactic, highly authoritarian teaching style in which children sat in rows of desks facing the front of the class while the walls were dominated by teacher displays. Most French primary school teachers seemed to stress the 'product' more than the 'process' of learning. Strong emphasis was placed by the teacher on reaching the correct answer as quickly as possible. Neatness, attractive well set-out exercise books and meticulous pieces of finished work were highly valued. In England, more stress was laid on the learning process and less on the finished product, with teachers differentiating according to the perceived needs of the pupil, arranging different levels and types of work according to what they believed their pupils were capable of. By contrast virtually all the French teachers had as their main aim that *all* pupils should achieve the same basic standard, in order to meet the set objectives by the end of the year. Work was paced to conform to the level of the middle group. Those who could proceed faster were unlikely to be allowed to undertake work at a higher level.

In England the approach was more active. Children were allowed and encouraged to work co-operatively some of the time and were often free to move around the room, while in France they were expected to work either alone or in a whole-class situation and movement around the room was strongly discouraged. Teachers' efforts in France were typically directed towards leading children to one correct answer rather than encouraging them to think independently or divergently as was often the case in England. In France all children were typically engaged in the same activity whereas in England there was a greater variety of activities taking place, a more differentiated pedagogy, more emphasis on teaching for understanding and more positive feedback given to pupils.

However, as suggested earlier, the education systems of both countries have recently been the focus for major policy changes. In France, the reforms have been aimed at helping teachers to focus more on the learning needs of the individual child to create 'une école moderne, mais à la française' in that it remains a central instrument of the State (Charlot, 1997). In England, by contrast, the reforms have been aimed at implementing a common National Curriculum and a much greater measure of homogeneity and central control.

In France, further research at this time (Broadfoot, 1998; Osborn *et al.*, 1998) revealed more diversity in teaching styles and in classroom settings than in the past, with some classrooms seating children in small groups, displaying pupils' work on the walls and being characterized by a more relaxed and informal relationship between teacher and pupil. However, the formal *leçon* continued to predominate. Teachers used the blackboard to present ideas to children and then worked extensively with individual pupils at the blackboard at the front of the class. Other children in the class were asked to comment on the work being done by the pupils at the board. Children then went on to work individually at the tasks set. Although pupils had more freedom of movement, choice of activity and resources available to them than when the earlier study was conducted in the mid-1980s, the overwhelming emphasis on French language and Mathematics had not changed, nor had the dominating authority of the teacher.

In England, likewise, these more recent studies revealed that there had been significant changes in teachers' classroom practice and ways of working which included a more collaborative approach, more whole-class teaching, a more coherent approach to curriculum planning and progression and much more emphasis on formal assessment (Pollard *et al.*, 1994; Croll, 1996). But here again, the fundamental values of teachers concerning the purpose of education and their role within it had not changed and were still clearly different from those of their French counterparts.

Thus, prior to the current study, there was evidence from relatively large-scale systematic studies of teachers over an extended period that there were major differences in priorities and practice between primary teachers in England and France. Secondly, there was evidence that such practice was changing and becoming more similar in the two countries partly in response to the common social and economic developments which were impacting on them. Thirdly, there was evidence from small-scale qualitative studies (for example, Sharpe, 1992a) that pupils' attitudes to school, their ability to manage their own learning and the learning outcomes themselves were very different in these two countries, largely reflecting, it seemed, the different teaching approaches they experienced. But what we did not have, prior to the QUEST study, was any sustained relatively large-scale comparative study which had been specifically designed to explore the nature of these differences in pupils' classroom experience and their significance in relation to the achievement of particular learning outcomes.

Previous research has revealed that the traditional formal didactic style of teaching, characteristic of French primary schooling, was based on an instructional philosophy of education. This tended to foster a passive, authority-dependent style of learning among pupils. In England, the variety of teaching styles employed by teachers in English primary schools was more focused on a developmental philosophy of education, which promoted a more autonomous and individualistic style of learning among pupils (Sharpe, 1993a). As a result, it might be hypothesized that French pupils would typically perform better on tasks requiring the careful application of learned formulae and procedures, whereas English children would typically perform better on tasks requiring problem-solving skills and creative independent thinking.

In addition, previous research had suggested that French pupils had a stronger sense of their own and other pupils' location within the familiar nationally-defined levels of schooling (the *cours* and the *cycles*) but less of a sense of belonging to a particular school (Sharpe, 1993a). It might therefore be expected that because of the decentralized administrative structure and the ideological commitment to diversity of provision characteristic of education in England, English pupils would have a stronger sense of belonging to a particular primary school, but a relatively weak appreciation of their own and other pupils' position within the nationally-defined levels of schooling. Similarly, because of the strong Napoleonic tradition, and because of the more overtly nationalistic content in diffuse programmes of study, especially for language, history, geography, and above all, civic education, it might be anticipated that French pupils would have a much stronger sense of national identity than English pupils. In contrast, because of the greater recognition given to multiculturalism in the English National Curriculum, English pupils might be more likely to place emphasis on multicultural issues.

It is clear from this that the pedagogic regime in France is characteristically one geared towards the concept of the child as 'future citizen' to which universalistic values apply, whereas the pedagogic regime in England is one which celebrates the child as 'an individual' and which is impregnated with particularistic values (Broadfoot and Osborn, 1988). It is arguable that in neither country have recent major reforms so far changed this fundamental difference of value orientation. In France, the Loi Jospin introduced the notion of *pédagogie différenciée* but this referred essentially only to the different *rates* at which pupils progress through the same sequence of development. Although the terms used echo those of English child-centred education, their meaning is very different (Broadfoot, 1998).

This profound difference in the educational assumptions underpinning the two systems – assumptions which are rooted in the very discourse itself – is well illustrated in the English 1988 Education Reform Act. This Act, which was designed to introduce an unprecedented degree of homogeneity of both provision and outcome into the traditionally anarchic English educational system by introducing a national curriculum, also emphasized what was in many respects a differentiated and child-centred approach to learning (Coulby and Ward, 1990). Moreover it introduced other measures such as local financial management of schools which were likely to have the effect of making schools more heterogeneous. As we explore in more detail in Chapter 3, subsequent revisions of the reforms in France such as Education Minister François Bayrou's 24 propositions (Ministère de l'Education Nationale, 1994) and in England the Dearing review (1993), set up to simplify the National Curriculum and Assessment procedures, can be seen as reassertions of these traditional cultural values.

In this book we argue that such enduring and fundamental differences in pedagogic traditions are likely to create different pupil identities, with associated contrasts in attitudes, perceptions and styles of learning. To the extent that this is so, it is likely to have very significant implications for policy. We also felt that an

National Culture and traditions
⇓
Pupil attitudes, characteristics and expectations
⇓
Classroom processes
(curriculum, teaching and assessment)
⇓
Learning outcomes

Figure 2.1 *The QUEST hypothesis*

empirical exploration of the nature and scale of such cultural differences would help to reinforce the argument that to be both valid and reliable and hence, useful, international comparisons of pupil achievement needed data to be properly contextualized in a broader understanding of the educational and cultural context. This core hypothesis is summarized in Figure 2.1.

It was in recognition of the need to understand how these various national differences impact on learning that the QUEST study was undertaken. One of its central goals was to respond to the need for more contextualized comparisons of pupil achievement; to compare, in considerably more detail than is possible in large-scale international surveys, the strengths and weaknesses of pupils at the end of primary school by assessing their performance on the same set of tests in the core subjects of Language (English or French) and Maths. By conducting a detailed examination of the links between learning outcomes, classroom processes and pupil attitudes in these two countries, it was hoped to explain any national differences identified in terms of both pupils' attitudes to learning and characteristic classroom approaches on the part of teachers.

The project set out to examine the previously documented differences in French and English teachers' priorities and pedagogy which have been referred to in this chapter, to determine their significance for children's attitudes to school, their motivation to learn and, most importantly, their learning outcomes. It was hypothesized that if there are significant international variations in teachers' practice as a result of national cultural influences, this is also likely to be true for pupils. It was anticipated that, as products of a different national culture with all its associated traditions and institutions, children in England would come to school with attitudes about themselves, about school, and about their country significantly different to those of their counterparts in France. As a result, their expectations for themselves and of their teachers were also likely to be different.

It was further anticipated that any such differences in attitude to school would be further compounded by the impact of the very different pedagogical practices and styles which are characteristic of these two countries; and that as a consequence of these differences, ostensibly the same pedagogic intervention by a teacher might have a very different effect in England than it would in France. We wanted to explain, for example, why French pupils, even those in inner-city schools in deprived areas, appeared to have surprisingly positive attitudes to school even when faced, as they typically still were, by an apparently irrelevant and often negative learning environment? Was it because pupils were motivated by the long-standing existence of a clear and publicly well-understood learning pathway in the French education system? Or was it rather the clear separation in pupils' minds of 'work' and 'play' which allowed them to accept the discipline of classroom life more readily than English pupils who expected to be interested and even entertained (Sharpe, 1992d)? How far was the provision of explicit and immediate feedback to pupils a significant factor in motivating them to learn?

This kind of contextualized comparative approach arguably provides a sounder basis on which to make judgements about the relative quality of different systems, and hence a more useful one for policy-makers. By the same token, not to do so is both unfair to the efforts of those involved in the education system and, potentially, seriously misleading.

The QUEST project therefore represents an important new approach to the comparative study of pupil achievement, which is one of the most rapidly growing aspects of contemporary comparative education research. It brings to bear the methodological and theoretical insights which have been built up in the field since Michael Sadler's work at the turn of the century drew policy-makers' attention to both the potential and the dangers of international comparisons and associated 'policy-borrowing' (Crossley and Broadfoot, 1992). In the light of a growing international obsession with simplistic and often deeply-flawed international surveys of student achievement, the QUEST project is a response to the clear need for a sustained comparative study specifically designed to explore national differences in pupils' classroom experience and to establish new, more productive, ways of comparing the outcomes of very different educational experiences.

This broad ambition translated into a number of specific questions which form the basis for this book:

- In what ways did the performances of pupils in Language and Maths differ in France and England?
- How significant were these differences?
- What factors underpinned any perceived pattern of differences in learning outcomes? How far could these differences be traced back to different teacher perceptions, pedagogical approaches, and curriculum content?
- Were there other patterns of differential performance which were more significant than those between the two countries? (e.g. gender, social class)
- What appeared to be the main effects on pupils' learning experiences of current policy reforms in both countries?
- What could an exploration of both the scale and the nature of such differential performance reveal about the factors that influence learning?

This was the rationale for the study that forms the basis for this book. It was designed both to *compare* primary school learning outcomes in France and England and, more importantly, to *explain* the source and significance of these in terms of the different classroom practices which the pupils studied had experienced. It built on what was already known about characteristic styles of curriculum *delivery* in England and France in order to investigate the *effects* of these differences on the processes of curriculum *reception* by pupils. Its central concern was to establish the relationship between culture, the pedagogic regimes of the classroom and the levels and types of pupil learning outcomes which these combine to produce. These aims led us to adopt a range of different approaches to data-collection which were capable of illuminating in some detail the fine grain of the factors which appeared to be influencing pupils' learning in the two countries. A description of the approach adopted forms the basis of the next part of this chapter.

HOW WERE THE DATA FOR THE QUEST STUDY COLLECTED?

Studying pupils' perspectives and experiences

The aim of the current study was to collect both nationally representative data about attitudes and performance and to explore in depth some of the reasons for any differences between the two countries being studied. This required a combination of quantitative and qualitative approaches to data-collection. The approach we used built upon the strengths of the previous comparative studies referred to above which we had conducted of teachers. In these studies we had been able to show clear national differences in the patterns of response to a questionnaire survey which supported the validity of generalizations about national differences. At the same time, more detailed classroom studies had enabled the processes which underlay the differences identified in the questionnaire findings to be explored in greater depth. Given the focus of the QUEST project on learning outcomes the design of the study also included some novel comparative features, including the assessment of learning outcomes and 'focus group' interviews with pupils.

A sample of 800 children aged 9 to 11 (400 in each country) formed the basis of the research reported in this book. Children in the last stages of primary schooling were chosen for study because in each country they undertake national assessments at this age. Although no sample of this size can be truly representative, the spread of schools chosen – four in each of two contrasting regions in each country – represented a socio-economic and geographic mix, and each school was matched as carefully as possible in size, location, and socio-economic catchment area with a counterpart in the other country. Care was also taken to have a roughly comparable proportion of ethnic minority children in the two samples. The regions in which the schools were located – Kent and Avon in England, Pas-de-Calais and Bouches-du-Rhône in France – were chosen because the use of existing contacts made access to schools easier, and the regions were seen to be broadly comparable in terms of geographic, economic, and demographic factors.

Questionnaires in English and French were developed simultaneously by the bilingual, bi-national team. We made great efforts to ensure conceptual and, as far as possible, linguistic equivalence. The difficulties of creating research instruments that are equally valid for different cultures and languages are well recognized in the comparative literature and great care needs to be taken to ensure that they are as comparable as possible. The lengthy experience of the project team in conducting this kind of study led us to recognize the importance of working with French collaborators in order to enhance validity and of the need for the questionnaire to be extensively piloted. The administration of the questionnaire in person in each country by a trained researcher also helped to ensure maximum response rates and uniformity of administration as well as minimizing misunderstanding. The questionnaires contained both fixed-response and open-ended questions covering each child's perception of teaching and the curriculum, his or her understanding of the purposes of schooling, his or her views of an 'ideal' pupil and school, and his or her perspectives on national identity and citizenship.

In order to pursue in more depth the insights on pupil perceptions of schooling generated through the questionnaire study, the project also included a more qualitative element involving interviews and observation of a sub-sample of children in each country. In order to ensure the inclusion in the sub-sample of children from contrasting socio-economic backgrounds, we selected two matched schools, one from an affluent and one from an inner-city catchment area in each region in each country for more intensive study. Three pupils were chosen at random from the schools identified and were interviewed as a group of three in order to encourage them to talk more freely and to exchange ideas about schooling.

In each of these schools, we also carried out both qualitative and quantitative classroom observation. Open-ended field notes were used to provide a rich account of classroom interaction and to record theoretically significant events, dialogue or activities. For the systematic observation we used a schedule developed for the ESRC Primary Assessment Curriculum and Experience Project (PACE) in which two of the present authors had been involved (Pollard *et al.*, 1994). This schedule was explicitly designed to quantify different types of pedagogic strategy and curriculum context as well as pupil engagement and interaction. Each child's behaviour was recorded over a ten-minute period. Six minutes of systematic observation at ten-second intervals was followed by four minutes of contextualizing field notes. These more quantitative data were designed to complement the more qualitative data in providing overall national comparisons of the amounts of different teaching approaches such as whole-class teaching and group work in the two countries. They also made it possible to note the time given to different subjects and activities, the level of pupil engagement and the range of different types of interaction which were taking place. In addition, other qualitative data in the form of photographs, teaching documents, and examples of children's work were collected to provide background contextual information.

Another novel feature of the research was the inclusion of a small exploratory study of the experiences and perspectives of ten children in each country who had experienced both English and French primary education. These interviews, which were largely conducted by telephone, have provided some rich illuminative insights to confirm those from other sources.

All these different sources of data are woven into the account of pupils' different perspectives on themselves, their lives at school and their aspirations, which form the subject of some of the chapters that follow. They are woven into the descriptions of the classroom life that our children were experiencing; they highlight the very real differences in educational reality that can separate children going to school within a mile or two of each other, as well as those which are governed by the English Channel.

But what is the significance of these differences? This is the ultimate question that we have sought to answer in our study and which this book addresses. In order to do so, it was necessary to collect carefully-matched data on the achievements of the pupils in our study. The account of how this challenging task was undertaken in the unique context of the QUEST project forms the final section of this chapter.

Comparing learning outcomes

A central element in the QUEST study was the collection of data which compared pupils' learning outcomes in France and England. As already suggested, only by so doing would it be possible to fulfil one of the central aims of the project which was to compare national patterns of strengths and weaknesses in pupils' achievements and, just as important, in their approach to different aspects of Language and Maths work. A further goal was to try to trace the connection between any national differences in the pattern of pupils as learners with differences in their attitudes and experiences identified through the questionnaire, interview and observation parts of the study. We anticipated that both the tests themselves and the curricula on which they were based would reflect the distinctive ethos of the two systems. It was further anticipated that the profile of pupils' strengths and weaknesses, which we would be able to document in the light of their performance on the tests, would similarly be a reflection of such national differences in approach. As such our interest was less in comparing the relative *level* of pupil performance, which is the focus for most international comparisons of achievement, but rather was more focused on exploring in a more qualitative way *the nature* of such international differences. A further objective was to compare the scale and apparent significance of any international differences identified with those between schools in different socio-economic settings in the *same* country.

As a small-scale but multi-faceted study which combined a range of different data sources in an effort to build an *explanatory* picture of the strengths and weaknesses of two different education systems, the QUEST study is arguably unique and represents an important methodological development in the search for more general insights concerning how standards can be improved. Not only does it show how a comparative study of national assessments can be used to illustrate the fundamental educational and cultural values that underlie national educational systems, it also highlights some important implications for the conduct both of international surveys of student achievement and of national assessments. In the latter case it can highlight discrepancies between the aims, content and ideology of national tests on the one hand and prescribed curriculum content and classroom pedagogy on the other.

Thus in what follows we explore in some detail the steps adopted by the project team to produce an assessment instrument that would be capable of being used in both England and France to identify the different strengths and weaknesses of pupils' learning. The account is essentially a methodological one, designed to highlight some of the difficulties involved in realizing such a goal. It is divided into five sections which document different aspects of this process – the scrutiny of curriculum content; the selection of questions; the administration of the tests; marking procedures; and, finally, the kinds of analysis that were conducted. However the analysis of the results of the tests are reported later in the book in the section entitled 'Learning Outcomes'. First, however, it is important briefly to put in context the two national assessment operations on which the QUEST assessment study was based.

French and English national assessment arrangements

The national assessment systems in England and France, from which the tests studied originate, have only recently been introduced and have very different aims. The French 'Evaluation' is designed for two purposes: as a diagnostic tool to locate an individual pupil's level in each subject and as a national monitoring device to assess the overall profile of pupil achievement (Broadfoot, 1996a). By contrast the aims of the English SAT tests are much broader: to gain a national picture of pupil achievement and to compare school and teacher effectiveness as well as to assign individual pupils to different levels.

Thus, in England, three years after the 1988 Education Reform Act, testing was initially introduced for 7-year-old pupils in 1991 in Mathematics, Science and English. Pupils are now tested at the end of each Key Stage at ages 7, 11 and 14 in these three subjects. The Key Stage 2 tests for 11-year-olds are taken by English pupils two months before they leave primary school. (English year groups are organized strictly on the basis of age, which means that some pupils with summer birthdays are still not quite 7 or 11 when they take the national tests in May.) Then results for all schools with more than ten pupils in the year-group have to be submitted for local and national 'league tables' which are published and widely disseminated through the press, as well as being a required element in school prospectuses and annual reports to parents. The results thus constitute a common language for comparing schools (Broadfoot, 1996).

In France national tests were introduced as part of the 1989 reforms 'Loi de l'Orientation sur l'Education'. Pupils have been tested nationally since 1989 in Mathematics and French at 'Cours Elémentaire 2' level, which is at about the age of 8, and again after primary schooling and during their first few weeks at secondary school – 'Evaluation à l'Entrée en Sixième' – when they are aged about 11 years. In contrast to the English system, French year-groups refer to a level reached and not to the age of the pupil. This difference between the two systems has important consequences for both the tests themselves and for pedagogy. It results in increased homogeneity of levels in French year-groups, though pupil ages may vary by as much as three years. But in the English context where the criteria for the year-group is pupil age, there can be as much as a seven-year difference in Mathematical levels (Cockroft, 1982: 100) and this has important implications for test design. Furthermore, the differences in class organization make it difficult to establish that the pupils being compared constitute similar samples in that the French group is likely to be more homogeneous on the basis of ability and less in age, with the reverse being true in England.

However, in the QUEST study these differences were less of an issue than is normally the case in international comparisons since the focus was more centrally on the different strengths and weaknesses of the two national cohorts rather than in differences in their levels of achievement *per se*. For this reason too, differences in the two countries' approach to providing for pupils with special educational needs and their policies for withdrawing such pupils from testing, while addressed in the study, were not of critical importance to its value.

In search of international validity: content and approach

The necessary first step in constructing the type of assessment instrument required was a careful scrutiny of the content of the two different national tests. Each test reflected the emphases of the national curriculum which it was designed to assess and the overall purpose such tests were designed to serve. In Maths this analysis revealed that the English national test in Maths – the SAT – was wider in its curriculum coverage. The test papers included questions on graphs, pie charts, nets, map scales and conversions between metric and imperial measures, all of which were absent from the French 'Evaluations'. The SATS also dealt with fractions at a higher level than the Evaluation.

By contrast the French Maths 'Evaluation' paper, though narrower in breadth, had greater depth in terms of difficulty. This was particularly noticeable in the areas of arithmetic. There were questions involving long division and multiplication with decimal points. The geometry questions required a good working knowledge of practical geometric drawing and geometric terminology. In England the curriculum included negative numbers (Level 3), rotation and reflection, means and averages, probability and the use of letters in algebra (Level 5), but it did not in France. In France, by contrast, the curriculum included proportionality (only for Level 5 in England); area formulae in geometry (Level 8 in England); more emphasis on mental arithmetic; more depth in operations with decimal points; more depth in units of measurement; more depth in geometric drawing skills and more depth in fractions (Level 8 in England).

In terms of approach the French Maths Evaluation test was more 'closed' in the sense that the questions were straightforward and involved fewer mathematical skills at once. By contrast the SATS questions required more open-ended thinking. For example a sum which looked like a multiplication sum in fact required division. The tests also seemed to be testing a different type of mathematical thinking. Even computational sums which might have been thought similar revealed such differences. The French tests had sums set out horizontally or vertically, which tested pupils' methods of computation. These included decimal points. The English tests favoured sums which had missing numbers so that pupils had an extra stage of having to work out what to do before carrying out the actual computation. This analysis led to the conclusion that the SATS were conceptually more difficult. It seemed easier in the French tests to define the area of knowledge being studied and the skills required than in the SATS tests. English questions were more complex, sometimes including several different aspects of Maths in the one question. One question, for example (Test A no. 8), involved reading from a table, completing a graph and working out a computational problem. Another question involved pie charts, estimation, fractions and percentages. This made comparison difficult since the English computation tended to be easier but required a wider range of understanding for success. The only solution was to include both English and French types of arithmetic question in the QUEST assessment.

Similar differences in content and approach were apparent in the Language papers. The French Evaluations reflected the importance attributed to the possession of a knowledge and understanding of grammar, and the choice of reading texts from the French classics reflected the importance that is given to French literature in the French curriculum. There was a similar difference to that in Maths between an 'open' and 'closed' approach to learning. The French reading comprehension questions required straightforward factual answers (con-textual). The SATS reading comprehension questions encouraged pupils to 'read between the lines' (co-textual) and make inferences with leading questions of the 'What do you think ...?' type. A similar difference in approach was also evident in the different test instructions for story-writing in the two tests. The French tests stipulated that pupils follow a method to structure their stories – 'tu respecteras ces consignes ...' (see p. 6 of 'Français'). The SATS, by contrast, gave suggestions that might be helpful to the pupils and provided a sheet on which to record ideas as well as offering a guided plan for those pupils who wished to use it.

Such differences of both curriculum content and approach embodied in the national tests illustrate the difficulty that attaches to any international comparison of learning outcomes; of comparing like with like in terms of opportunity to learn.

The difficulties associated with curriculum content and approach were further compounded by differences in the organization of the tests. The tests were set out differently. The SATS comprised three graded booklets given to pupils according to teachers' expectations of the National Curriculum level their pupils would achieve. The Evaluations were all in one booklet but were designed to reveal three different levels – 'compétences de base', 'approfondies', or 'remarquables'. Thus it was very difficult to select a range of questions which would constitute an equally valid test of achievement for both national pupil samples. In Language there were fewer obvious differences in relation to the level of the tasks set than with Maths, which meant that there was less difficulty in constructing a valid common test paper; but, partly in consequence of this, marking proved to be more problematic.

The selection of questions

In the light of these differences, the research team spent a considerable time scrutinizing the two sets of national test papers in relation to the curriculum specification of each of the two countries. With the help of curriculum experts in Maths and Language, the decision was made to abandon the aspiration to create 'value-free' tests by selecting only 'level 4' SAT questions and topics covered in both countries, since this approach would reflect neither the breadth nor the depth of the two national curricula. Given that the aim of the research was to compare 'primary school learning outcomes in England and France', the inclusion of only questions which were common to both contexts would not be representative of the two curricula. Rather, it was felt that key features of both systems – such as the use of different levels of test in the English context and differences in depth and breadth, as well as the age at which a particular topic was scheduled to be covered in each of the two countries – all needed to be taken into account. It was therefore decided that the questions should represent the *breadth* and *depth* of each curriculum, and that in Maths, the questions should avoid high levels where the curriculum area had not been covered by the other country, so that all questions were at least attemptable by both sets of pupils (see Figure 2.2).

For Language the same approach was taken as for the Maths tests – that the tests should represent the two different national approaches to the subject, e.g. that the more closed types of French reading comprehension should be matched by those requiring more inference which are characteristic of the English questions. It was also felt to be important to include a grammar section in order to try to compare the effectiveness of the English and French approaches to the teaching of grammar. In order to allow more time it was decided to make two Language papers (see Figure 2.3).

All the tests were then translated as necessary so that each existed in a French and an English form. They were then checked for validity by teachers/advisors in England and in France. However, it was very difficult always to maintain both comparability and validity in the process of translation.

When these stages had been completed, the Maths and Language tests were given to children in each of the classes in the presence of both the researcher and the teacher. Children in both countries completed both types of question, thus ensuring that they were all exposed to forms of assessment characteristic of both countries.

MARKING

In a pilot of the French and English versions of the Maths and Language tests, a post test debriefing session with the pupils based on specific questions revealed interesting insights into how pupils had perceived the different questions they had been asked to undertake. Minor changes to the timing and order of the tests in the two countries were designed to maximize the opportunity for all of the pupils to perform as well as possible in all of the tests in which some of the questions would inevitably be unfamiliar in terms of either content or approach, and possibly both.

Due to a time limit on the tests we decided on 18 questions for the Maths test, 8 from the French national assessments and 10 from the English SATs. Following the syllabus for each context this resulted in:

QUEST Maths B (based on English SATs papers A and B)
– Using and Applying – 2 questions: Probability (A no. 13, pp. 10–11) QUEST Q7
Number problem (A no. 16) QUEST Q8.

Number – 4 questions: Equivalence of multiplication and division (A no. 5) QUEST Q2a
Equivalence of addition and subtraction (B no. 11) QUEST Q2b
Multiplication (A no. 19) QUEST Q3a
Multiplication and subtraction (A no. 10) QUEST Q3b

Decimals and fractions (C no. 7a,b) QUEST Q10a, Q10b

Number patterns (A no. 14) QUEST Q4

Shape, Space and Measure – 2 questions: Symmetry (B no. 10) QUEST Q9
3D/2D shapes (C no. 7) QUEST Q6

Handling Data – 2 questions: Tables and graphs (A no. 8) QUEST Q5
Averages (B no. 14) QUEST Q1

QUEST Maths A (based on French National Assessment Papers)
Nombres et Calcul – 4 questions: (Ex 15) QUEST Q1a
(Ex 16b) QUEST Q1b
(Ex 21b) QUEST Q1c
(Ex 25) QUEST Q1d

Multiplication and division by 10s and 100s (Ex 18c and Ex 18) QUEST Q2a, 2b

Géometrie – 2 questions: Geometric drawing (Ex 30) QUEST Q3
Terminology (Ex 27) QUEST Q4

Mesure – 2 questions: Area (Ex 38) QUEST Q5
Area (Ex 12) QUEST Q6

Problèmes – 2 questions: Multiplication problem (Ex 4) QUEST Q7
Choice of operation to use (Ex 34) QUEST Q8

Time: Maths B: 30 minutes; Maths A: 25 minutes.

Figure 2.2 *Contents of QUEST maths test*

Language 1 (25 minutes)	Reading Comprehension A (French)
	Reading Comprehension B (English)
	Punctuation
	Use of alphabet
	Grammar
Language 2 (30 minutes)	Narrative writing (English 'A Door Opens')

Figure 2.3 *Contents of QUEST language test*

It was decided that marking for Maths A and B and Lang 1 and 2 should be based on the criteria of the national tests in question. This proved difficult, however. Even if in the case of Lang 2 the stories were marked twice, once according to each system, it was difficult to apply the French scheme as it was not aimed at a piece of 'creative writing' but rather was designed to reflect how far a pupil had followed the instructions for a specific narrative structure.

It was apparent, however, even from the team's first training session in use of the English national test's mark scheme, that there were methodological problems in reliability and validity when this scheme was applied to French children's scripts. The English mark scheme was designed to assess written productions in the English language and written productions that were set in an English learning context. Thus first there were problems in adapting the mark scheme to be applicable to the French language. Secondly, it was found that the mark scheme, as a product of English educational values, was not a valid tool with which to assess written scripts from a different culture. The mark scheme tended to mask cultural differences between the performances of English and French children. For instance, French stories were generally much shorter than English ones. This was particularly the case with the weaker French scripts which tended to consist of a few short and fairly well punctuated sentences. For example:

'L'histoire se passe ...' (ESRC seminar).

The weaker English scripts were, in common with most of the English scripts, longer. In structure they were, unlike the French scripts, more likely to be in the form of a continuous stream, with little or no punctuation and also little content. For example:

Tosh my best friend came around today I like tash shes funny and she allways weres cool stuf I used to have a difcerent friend but she went of with Helen cooper. Only way wher tash came over we were about to go to the park when my mum finn asked me to B.f the washing away I hate putting the washing away becaus I have to go down to the creepy celler I don't like the celler thores a door that no one since we've moved in has gone into but tash said she would help me We went down I clang on to tasha's arm "don't be a babby" She said we got down there I looked at the creepy door it burst open like somone was there I didn't think belived in ghosts tash said the dont open to we both went in "See its

'Tosh my best friend ...' (Frankfurt or York paper).

Not only did the English mark scheme tend to mask cultural differences but it could also distort the children's performance levels. In applying the criteria of the English mark scheme, the weaker French stories invariably achieved higher scores than it was thought they merited.

In the Maths A and B the national criteria were not sufficient for the kind of detailed analysis of national strengths and weaknesses in pupils' performance in the subject that we sought. Thus further QUEST criteria were added, to reflect the more diagnostic aims of the research.

This detailed account of the QUEST project methodology illustrates the very different emphasis of international comparisons of pupil achievement when the primary goal is to explain, rather than simply to document, national differences. The assessment data are limited in scale and a sample of this size cannot claim to be nationally representative in a formal sense. However, as Chapters 8 and 9 make clear, the results provide a powerful insight into differences between the two countries in terms of what is being learned, how, by whom and why.

Chapter 3

Primary Schooling in England and France: The Importance of the National Context

The development of primary schooling in England and France clearly illustrates the importance of historical and cultural factors in shaping the institutional structures in which teaching and learning are embedded. Between 1833 and 1870 systems of elementary education emerged on both sides of the Channel largely in response to changing economic needs, but equally as part of a concern to provide appropriate moral education for the growing urban industrial working classes. But whereas the French state assumed overall responsibility for the education of 'the people' into a common national culture built around republican values, in England the government funded local initiatives to supplement what was already provided privately. These contrasting approaches reflect long-established differences in political, social and religious practices in the two countries.

PRIMARY EDUCATION IN FRANCE

In France the characteristic 'universalistic' approach to organization and social provision – the same for everyone – had been mediated by the Catholic Church for decades before the French Revolution and the Napoleonic era with which the Revolution tends to be associated. Indeed the primary school system was not set up at the time of the Revolution, as it had already been flourishing during the last century of the Monarchy. Schools were from the very beginning seen by the Catholic Church as an instrument for controlling the masses socially and intellectually (Furet and Ozouf, 1977). However, it was with the passing of the much-celebrated 'Jules Ferry laws' in the 1880s that legal endorsement was given to the replacement of religious universalism in French education by the markedly secular universalism which had been ushered in by the Revolution. The three key principles were henceforth to be, and remain to this day, that primary schooling should be compulsory for every child, free and entirely secular, *obligatoire, gratuite, et laique.*

Elementary education was and is widely perceived as the vehicle through which republican values should be officially proclaimed and transmitted to succeeding generations. Schooling was to be, and continues to be, a public service controlled and delivered by the State through civil-servant teachers following official instructions and programmes of study issued centrally by an appointed government minister. Religious education was and is seen as part of the private domain, the responsibility of individual families, and no business of the State. The wearing or display of any religious insignia in schools has always been illegal in France. The national crisis that was recently precipitated by a female Muslim pupil's desire to wear a headscarf in school provides clear testimony to the enduring strength of this tradition.

The formal structures of this strongly national system of education have remained recognizably the same over the decades since the Ferry laws. The system is hierarchically organized with direct lines of official accountability, explicitly referred to by those involved in it as '*La Voie Hiérarchique*', down from the Minister of Education through the *recteurs* of each *académie*, the regional inspectors for each *département*, and the local inspectors for each area who are responsible for the primary teachers working in their *circonscription*, as shown in Figure 3.1.

The system is based in principle on an unbroken line of command from the office of the Minister of Education straight into the classroom of each primary teacher. However much individuals in the hierarchy in practice use their position and influence to exert a local and personalized authority, the formal structure does not provide for local independence at any level. There are no local education authorities as such, individual schools have virtually no autonomy in an Anglo-Saxon sense, and headteachers have little real power. They play no part, for example, in the selection of the staff who work in their school. This is now a computerized process whereby teachers make a number of choices on an official form if they wish to move. Choices made by teachers with the greatest seniority, defined in terms of years of service and an inspection mark given by the *inspecteur départemental*, are automatically given precedence.

Throughout the 1980s concern was expressed about the rigidity of the system in the context of rapid social and cultural change. In 1989 the then Education Minister, Lionel Jospin, introduced a '*loi d'orientation*' which was intended to promote greater flexibility. The system is, however, extraordinarily resilient in the face of attempts by policy-makers to bring about change, and the history of French education to date provides a fairly unarguable case in point of the maxim, *plus ça change, plus c'est la même chose*. Structural principles have survived several reforms, and research on teaching in French primary classrooms carried out by QUEST team members five

Ministre	–	Ministère	(Nation)
Recteur	–	Académie	(Region)
Inspecteur d'Académie (IA)	–	Département	(County)
Inspecteur de l'Education Nationale (IEN)	–	Circonscription	(District)
Instituteur	–	Classe	(Class)

Figure 3.1 *L'Education Nationale – La Voie Hiérarchique*

years after the implementation of the 'Loi Jospin' found that 'fundamental teacher values and practices remain substantially unchanged, English teachers' perceptions of education still emphasizing individual development and the whole child, French teachers' perceptions of education still focusing on the acquisition of skills to standardized national levels' (Broadfoot *et al.*, 1995: 6).

This systemic obduracy is ironically both widely recognized, generally supported, and yet commonly lamented among educational professionals in France. 'We've been trying to get more flexibility into the system for 10 years, but no one will let us,' says M. Delaquis, the French deputy chief inspector. 'Everyone believes that you must have the same programmes, the same number of hours devoted to subjects, the same kinds of textbooks, the same training for teachers ... a common programme is integral to the concept of equality of opportunity. It's entrenched by history. It's natural' (*TES*, 6.3.87, p.19). And, as an exasperated Minister of National Education, René Monory, recently exclaimed in the Assemblée Nationale, 'In this country, as soon as you touch a single comma in education, you have a revolution on your hands!' (Weiler, 1988: 252).

PRIMARY EDUCATION IN ENGLAND

The traditional emphasis in England has by contrast been precisely on local autonomy and independence. It used to be said that England had 'a national system locally administered', but some have disputed that there has been anything constituting an English 'system' of education at all, so great has been the stress on the 'rich tapestry of variation'. Historically, there was a great diversity of independent providers of schooling in the late eighteenth and early nineteenth century. Gradually social changes consequent upon industrialization and urbanization prompted governments to reflect on the need for mass elementary education, but the concern was essentially with 'filling in the gaps' left by voluntary provision rather than with constructing a full national system offering a unified school experience for all. The 1870 Forster Act set up state-funded school boards to provide for sound and cheap elementary 'instruction to all classes of the people' in areas where there were no other schools available. In 1880 it was made compulsory for all 5–10-year-olds to be in a school whether controlled by a school board or by an independent or voluntary organization.

The origins of the English system of education are thus grounded in an ideology of 'grass-roots' autonomy which was already deeply embedded in English institutional history (Archer, 1979; Johnson, 1980; Simon, 1960). The idea of a highly bureaucratized, hierarchical and centrally controlled education system was anathema and an offence to English sensibilities. The long struggles over the years between rival groups for control over education created an anarchic 'ideology of teacher autonomy and governmental interference as a monstrous entity to be resisted at all costs – a situation in which central government was typically happy to concur' (Salter and Tapper, 1981). Local Education Authorities were set up in the early part of the twentieth century, but in practice individual schools, headteachers and teachers enjoyed for most of the century what was, by international standards, an extraordinary degree of professional autonomy. Until recently, the actual exercise of authority over the system by the centre, in the shape of the Ministry of Education, later the Department of Education and Science, was limited to resource allocation and the monitoring of local authorities. The role of the central inspectorate, HMI (Her Majesty's Inspectors), was predominantly advisory. The concept of the 'partners' in the educational process was a key idea, with schools, LEAs, parents, the 'community', teachers and headteachers all assumed to be working together in some vague collaborative effort for the educational benefit of children.

What has been characterized as the 'Plowden' era, because of the landmark government report, 'Children and their Primary Schools' published in 1967 which was chaired by Lady Plowden, might be regarded as the apogee of this situation. The establishment of comprehensive schooling and the widespread abolition of the eleven-plus selection examination freed primary schools in the late 1960s and early 1970s from one of the few external constraints over teaching and the curriculum, and gave a major impetus to the emergence of 'child-centred education'. The traditional concern in England with individualism was translated into an educational philosophy based on the theory that because every child is unique and develops in a particular, individual way, teaching should be essentially about the facilitation of learning and the provision of opportunities for discovery and investigation. Key concepts of progressivist child-centred primary education were 'meeting the needs of the child' and catering for the 'whole child'.

During the 1970s and 1980s, however, increasing concern was expressed about the consequences of the adoption of this philosophy and through a variety of means 'the Department of Education and Science gradually assumed a more assertive role in educational policy' (Litt and Parkinson, 1979: 15). These measures culminated in the Education Reform Act of 1988, which dramatically increased the number of powers available to the Secretary of State for Education. This Act is commonly seen as constituting a radical break with the 'national system locally administered' tradition because it imposed a National Curriculum which required schools to follow statutorily defined programmes of study.

It is important to note, however, first that this same Act, which significantly increased centralized control of the system, also introduced other measures which reinforced aspects of decentralized control, such as open enrollment, local management of schools and increased responsibilities for school governors. Moreover, the subsequent fate of the National Curriculum as it passed through revision after revision 'watered down' very considerably the original intentions of the policy-makers to exert a very direct form of control. It continues to be impossible to draw up a simple diagram of authority and organization within English primary education comparable to that presented in Figure 3.1 above for the French system. A wide range of agencies exert influence: the Department for Education and Employment, the inspection agency OFSTED, Her Majesty's Inspectorate, the Teacher Training Agency, the Qualifications and Curriculum Authority, Local Education Authorities, voluntary organizations including the churches, governing bodies, headteachers, parents and teachers.

This is not to say that fundamental changes have not taken place. The reforms have introduced a whole new discourse carrying with it a raft of novel concepts into the everyday experience of teachers and pupils, Key Stages, reporting procedures, core and foundation subjects and the like, and more recently the 'literacy hour' and the 'numeracy hour'. Nevertheless all of these changes have of necessity been interpreted by teachers and other educational professionals according to frameworks of thought and value through which they make sense of their professional lives (Pollard *et al.*, 1994). It is essentially through these frameworks of understanding that characteristic differences between teachers in England and those in France are sustained. The values which undergird them are also shared by national policy-makers, and it is therefore unsurprising that other aspects of the reforms reinforce deeply-rooted traditions and dispositions. For example, the emphasis on choice and diversity in education, the keenness to promote competition between schools offering different kinds of ethos, the stress on the importance of the headteacher as a charismatic personification of any particular school's values and beliefs are all associated with basic value orientations in the English tradition of education. In both countries these bedrock values of the national context continue to be extremely influential.

THE CONCEPT OF NATIONAL CONTEXT

Ten years ago, in reporting the results of a study of French and English primary teachers' responses to an open-ended question: 'what does professional responsibility mean to you?', Broadfoot *et al.* (1988: 265) concluded that 'the national context within which teachers work deeply influences their professional ideology, their perceptions of their professional responsibility, and the way in which they carry out their day-to-day work'. In this and subsequent papers it was argued that teachers in the two countries had distinctively different professional ideologies, notably in four key domains:

- extended (England) versus restricted (France) professionality
- problematic (England) versus axiomatic (France) conceptions of teaching
- process (England) versus product (France) conceptions of learning
- particularism (England) versus universalism (France).

In discussing these very clear differences between the two national groups, the concept of 'teachers' professional ideology' was developed to explain why

> major differences in the pattern of systemic control from one country to another could not be directly translated into equivalent differences in teachers' classroom practice; rather they appeared to be an *independent dynamic* operating at the latter level, bound up with teachers' ideology and how this was relatively related to more objective constraints upon their practice (p.268); [and] it is the ideology, or to put it another way, the conception of their professional role, which plays the most fundamental part in determining what teachers do (p.283).

This would suggest that policy formulation which does not take teachers' professional ideology into account is unlikely to be effectively translated into practice. It explains what may appear to be the 'systemic obduracy' in both countries which was referred to above. As suggested above, it is certainly arguable that the fate of the National Curriculum in England since its inception ten years ago, which subsequent to the 'Dearing Reforms' has now been diluted into a form not so different from the unwritten broad consensus which preceded it, bears testimony to the power of this independent variable. Broadfoot *et al.* also used the concept of 'teachers' professional ideology' to account for the puzzling failure of French primary teachers to use their freedom from external surveillance and accountability. As explained above, French primary teachers enjoy the almost total employment security of civil-service status and are not directly accountable to anyone within the school where they work. They are 'inspected' every few years by the local IEN (see Figure 3.1 above), but this is a rather 'ritualized' procedure (Sharpe, 1993b) and teachers actually have the right to refuse it and still proceed, albeit more slowly, up through the national salary scales. Thus the 'Bristaix' research project found that 'French teachers are actually relatively free institutionally to identify their own teaching strategies but are constrained by an ideological tradition of commitment to central control' (Broadfoot, 1985: 267).

In the course of an ethnographic study of two primary schools in Northern France (Sharpe, 1993a) the Bristaix research questionnaire concerning teachers' perceptions of the influences on their professional practice was used with another small sample of French primary teachers. The similarities with the Bristaix results were striking, adding to the impression of a clear national consensual professional ideology among French primary teachers. Particularly significant again, however, were the responses to questions about teachers' professional ideology. The French teachers did not think that their teaching practices were much influenced by 'professional ideology', yet this is the very factor research indicated influenced them most. How can this seeming contradiction be explained?

The answer appears to be that the divergent frameworks of thought which characterize the different professional ideologies of English and French teachers are not just associated with two different professional groups; they are characteristic of two different *national* professional groups. The attitudes, values and beliefs, the implicit philosophies and epistemologies embedded in them are national and reflect shared national identity as well as shared professional identity. In this sense it might be contended that the argument that French teachers' professional ideology constrains their practice is valid because *that ideology is a specific, applied instance of national ideology* and it is for this reason that it is so much taken for granted by the teachers themselves.

Conceiving of teachers' professional ideology in this way helps deal with the conceptual problem of cause and effect in explaining teacher behaviour. If the 'cause' is located in the national context which includes national ideology, rather than in the notion of professional ideology as some kind of independent factor exerting an influence on practice, there is less difficulty in accounting for why the 'effects' continue when institutional surveillance is weak. It is then possible to argue that French primary teachers' apparent failure to take advantage of such weak institutional surveillance and adopt innovative and diverse professional strategies simply reflects what Durkheim (1968: 18) described as: 'the very authority of Society, transferring itself to a certain manner of thought ... a special sort of moral necessity which is to the intellectual life what moral obligation is to the will'.

It is even arguable that French primary teachers could be said not to have a characteristic 'professional ideology' as such at all, as they themselves report, but rather that they share a generalized bureaucratic, people-processing, occupational ideology common to many employees of the French state. In their career trajectories French teachers have experiences similar to those of all other civil servants. For example, to be '*nommé sur un poste*', allocated to a post, by the impersonal mechanical (now completely computerized) procedure described earlier is a quite different experience from that of enjoying personal individual success at an English-style interview, and arguably predisposes those so treated towards some kinds of teacher behaviour rather than others (see Beattie, 1997).

NATIONAL CONTEXT AND NATIONAL IDEOLOGY

The advantage of emphasizing the articulations between teachers' professional ideologies and national ideological traditions is that in this way the mutual interrelationships between the elements constituting the national context can be recognized. In an early paper Broadfoot (1985) suggested that key among these were:

1   prevailing educational policies and priorities
2   the institutional infrastructure
3   dominant ideological traditions.

By treating these as interacting components of a dynamic network in which each has a historical momentum of its own and exerts an influence on the other two at the same time as being influenced by them, it is possible to trace relationships between republican ideology, centralized hierarchical organization and teachers' moral commitments to uniform provision in French primary education (Sharpe, 1997). It is also possible in this way to distinguish fundamental orientations underpinning actions and institutions, and in the case of English and French primary education, to detect the continuance in secular forms of orientations deriving from earlier religious structures – Protestantism on the one hand and Roman Catholicism on the other (Sharpe, 1997). These fundamental orientations are set out in Figure 3.2.

This analysis may shed some light on the issue of why the Bristaix research study found that French teachers do not believe their practice is influenced by a professional ideology, do not tend to understand the notion of 'teaching style', and conceive of teaching as an axiomatic, unproblematic and obvious activity. This is in contrast to their English counterparts who believe their consciously adopted educational ideology is important, who employ a variety of different teaching styles according to prevailing circumstances and who anguish about the nature of teaching and learning in their pursuit of 'perfection' (Osborn *et al.*, 1992). Universalistic value orientations are by definition monopolistic: they promote homogeneity, they create a

	Roman Catholicism/ French Education	Protestantism/ English Education
CENTRAL VALUE ORIENTATIONS	universalism uniformity equality specificity	particularism diversity differentiation diffuseness
	lead to	
DOMAINS OF SOCIO- EDUCATIONAL PRACTICE *Authority*	monolithic hierarchical universal/national impersonal	diffuse democratic localized personal/charismatic
Accountability	bureaucratic	personal
Environment	formalized transmission teaching focus	flexible reflection/expression learning focus
Action	role-impermeability didactic	role-permeability negotiated

Source: Sharpe (1997)

Figure 3.2 *Value orientations shared by religious and educational systems in France and England*

sense of a socially constructed world as the only conceivable reality. Particularistic value orientations by contrast give a vision of a social world as one among many, where alternatives are built-in possibilities, where decisions about what to do and what to believe are not givens to be taken for granted but to a greater or lesser extent matters of personal choice and individual responsibility.

It is important to stress that none of the foregoing discussion of the concept of 'national context' is intended necessarily to imply a structural–functionalist approach to social analysis in which the coherence of society is viewed as depending on a common value system into which individuals are thoroughly and passively socialized. Some have argued that shared values play little part at all in binding society together (see Thompson, 1990). Nevertheless the empirical evidence concerning national differences in attitude and action among English and French teachers reported above, and among English and French pupils reported below, is striking and unequivocal. In this instance it is difficult to resist the conclusion that there are characteristic national values which are widely accepted by teachers and pupils on either side of the Channel, even if there are other processes also underpinning the continuities identified.

In a recent paper on national identity Beck (1996) suggests that the stability of modern industrial societies rests on three principal factors other than shared consensual normative values:

1   processes of non-normative institutional reproduction – the use of power within and between organizations, industrial, commercial, political
2   taken-for-granted everyday knowledge – the use of interpretive procedures by individuals in order to manage and accomplish orderly social interaction; not so much shared values as shared 'background expectancies' (Garfinkel, 1967) through which members of society take for granted what they know and what they know others know, drawing on this knowledge to construct their own sense of what is happening
3   discourses as technologies of power – the discursive regulation of social action and individual identity in which discourses create regimes of truth, 'normalize' reality and constitute individuals as subjects (Foucault, 1979; Fairclough, 1995).

There does not appear to be prima facie any reason why all of these processes should not be seen as contributing to an overall explanation of how the 'national context' operates to generate the evidence about teachers and pupils being discussed here. It is surely possible to analyse educational structures and actions in terms of institutionalized values, power relations, interpretive interaction and discourses, and treat the results of such analyses as cumulative rather than contradictory. Like the apocryphal four blind men describing an elephant in terms of the part they can each touch, each of these different conceptual perspectives opens up vistas on what is actually happening in different education systems.

A relevant example of how such an eclectic approach might be useful is the common institutional situation of teachers and pupils in the French system of primary schooling, presented in Table 3.1.

It is easy to see how these parameters of life experience are set by the *values* of universalism, uniformity, equality and specificity. Equally, however, both teacher and pupils are constrained by the use of *power*: the teacher's role obligations are specified in legal texts and institutionalized in the huge state bureaucracy which is *l'Education Nationale*. In a real sense pupils are at the bottom of this massive hierarchy and feel

Table 3.1 *Common institutional parameters of life experience between teachers and pupils in French primary schooling*

	pupil	teacher
external expectations	follow teacher instructions	follow official instructions
nature of obligation	specific	specific
	predefined	predefined
	impersonal	impersonal
assessment	marks and grades	marks (*barèmes*)
assessors	teachers	inspectors
basis of assessment	official national texts	official national texts
assessment	reports and dossiers	reports and dossiers
initial institutional allocation	sectorization by académie	sectorization by académie
career path	movement through curriculum levels	movement through civil service grades
eventual institutional location	dependent on marks	dependent on marks

the weight of its expectations of them, through the direct surveillance and discipline (cf. Bourdieu's concept of *la violence symbolique*: Bourdieu and Passeron, 1977) of teachers as agents of the French state, and through the coercion of consequences which ensue if their compliance is not forthcoming – *redoublement* (repeating the year) and eventual withdrawal from the normal cycle. At the same time the whole apparatus functions through innumerable mundane scenes of orderly social *interaction* in which teachers, pupils, inspectors, administrators, policy-makers trade on 'what everyone knows', i.e. what everyone takes for granted, in France. Through normalized *discourse* concerning (for example) curriculum levels, the functions of the Académie, the constituent categories of the curriculum – *lecture, grammaire, vocabulaire, conjugaisons* (reading, grammar, vocabulary, conjugations), etc. and regularized assessment procedures, *contrôles, dictées* (tests, dictation) the social reality of *l'école élémentaire* (the primary school) is constructed and teachers and pupils are constituted as such in a particularly French fashion.

THE ROLE OF 'NATIONAL CONTEXT' IN SHAPING PUPILS' EDUCATIONAL EXPERIENCE

Earlier research on teachers thus revealed clear *national* differences, with most French teachers focusing on the transmission of specific knowledge and the development of specific skills while most English teachers emphasized the development of intelligence and a concern with the education of the 'whole child'. One recent researcher (Vinuesa, 1996) has concluded that '*Les instituteurs français et anglais ne pratiquent donc pas le même métier*' ('French and English primary teachers do not practise the same profession'). Indeed it is possible to argue more broadly that education itself is not the same thing in the two countries.

There is a tendency in some educational discussion to talk about 'education' as if it were some kind of naturally-occurring, single, unitary phenomenon; as if it were possible to remove it from the social context in which it emerges and is lived out daily in schools; as if it were somehow 'neutral'. This might be called the fallacy of neutrality. Education is itself part of the 'national context' and in the terms proposed in this paper can be seen to be impregnated throughout with values, power relations, interactional styles and determinative patterns of discourse. Fourez (1990: 52) comments:

> *Les valeurs, les idéologies et l'éducation à la vie sociale sont partout présentes dans l'enseignement. On peut notamment les analyser dans les contenus, les motivations proposées, les relations, les structures institutionelles.*

> (Values, ideologies and social education are present in every aspect of teaching. They can be analysed through the curriculum, the systems of reward and punishment, relationships and institutional structures.)

And ever since the two systems of primary education can, underneath surface changes, be seen to have promoted divergent but characteristically national orientations through all the various reforms inaugurated in each country under the

	France	England
Power relations	bureaucratic	charismatic/market
	ascriptive	achievement
Institutionalized values	universalism	particularism
	collectivism	individualism
Interactional style	specificity	diffuseness
	affective neutrality	affectivity
Patterns of discourse	objectified	personalized

Figure 3.3 *France and England: national context orientations*

exigencies of social, economic and political pressures up to the present day preoccupation with assessment and accountability. As suggested above, these national orientations can be analysed along four dimensions: power relations, institutionalized values, interactional style and patterns of discourse, as in Figure 3.3 above.

POWER RELATIONS

Bureaucracy (F) – Charismatic/market-based (E)

Power relations within French primary education are bureaucratically structured with clearly circumscribed authority status attaching to particular positions within the national organization, from the Minister down through the *académies*, each with inspectors responsible for constituent *départements*, to the level of a *circonscription* of around 400 teachers presided over by a National Education inspector. In English primary education the authority of actors at each level of responsibility is much more affected by their personal characteristics, and by their 'market situation', teachers competing for posts, schools competing for pupils, local authorities selling their services, inspectors tendering for contracts. Occupational roles are more personal and less positional than is the case in French education.

Ascription (F) – Achievement (E)

In France the pupil's identity is largely an ascribed one: if he or she is in the *cours préparatoire* then he or she will be treated as a *cours préparatoire* pupil, the same as all the others, wherever they are in France. It is predominantly an identity ascribed on the basis of a given social category. Individual characteristics which mark this particular child out as different in personal terms are largely treated as irrelevant. In a real sense this is arguably a preparation for citizenship in that a key principle of republican citizenship is that citizens are, or are treated as, homogeneous with no fear or favour being accorded to individual differences. In England pupil identity (and teacher identity) is a much more open business, with opportunities to acquire a range of positions within the class according to the vagaries of individual behaviour, attitudes and performance. In the absence of clearly defined national educational statuses much more is open to negotiation between pupil and teacher in the particular local circumstances obtaining within the class, the school and the local area.

INSTITUTIONALIZED VALUES

Universalism (F) – Particularism (E)

The goal of French education is to offer the same education equally to all pupils as an entitlement due to them as future citizens of the French republic, irrespective of who they are, where on the national territory they live (including French colonies), and as far as possible irrespective of any disabilities they may have. As Vinuesa (1996: 15) observes:

> *On peut donc suggérer que l'universalité de l'enseignement française est révélatrice de l'héritage républicain et d'une certaine conception de l'éducation comme base de l'égalité des citoyens.*

> (It is fair to suggest that the universalism which characterizes French teaching arises out of the republican heritage and out of a certain conception of education as foundational for the equality of citizens.)

While the French system is geared up in every respect to respond to what is universal about children, English primary schooling aims to respond to everything that is particular, local and different: a particular school 'ethos' with rituals, badges and uniforms, classes named after particular teachers, and differentiated work to meet the individual needs of particular children.

Collectivism (F) – Individualism (E)

The republican project has always been anxious to make committed French citizens of whoever attends its schools. Education in France is always 'l'Education Nationale' (National Education) and the categories used to mark progress through the ladder of schooling are always national – the *petits, moyens, grands* sections of the *école maternelle*, the *cours préparatoire*, the *cours élémentaire* and the *cours moyen* of the *école primaire* and the various numerical levels, *sixième, cinquième*, etc. of the secondary cycle. The child's success is measured by the capacity to master the prescribed knowledge and skills for each rung of the ladder. In this way French children succeed by embodying the national identikit for the stage they are at. By contrast, English preoccupation with the individual stresses 'developmental' approaches, with each child presumed to have a 'unique' nature to be brought out and 'nurtured', and so children are expected to develop 'at their own pace'. Differentiation, wide variations in achievement at the same age, and the lack of any clear sense of a national structure of progress among primary pupils continue to be characteristic features of the English system.

INTERACTIONAL STYLE

Specificity (F) – Diffuseness (E)

In France, teachers and pupils relate to one another in clearly defined and bounded ways. They relate as teacher and pupil with the roles of each being closely circumscribed: the teacher there to teach the prescribed curriculum and the pupil there to learn it. In English primary education, teachers' and pupils' roles are much more diffuse, with the teacher seeing him- or herself as responsible for all aspects of the child's development – social, moral, cultural, spiritual, physical, aesthetic as well as intellectual/cognitive.

Affective neutrality (F) – Affectivity (E)

Teachers in France tend to view their professional obligations in a contractual manner. They have a specific duty to discharge on behalf of the French state, and they deal with the objects of that duty in an affectively neutral manner. It is not expected that they will develop personal relationships with their pupils. As Cousin (1997: 1) points out, French education explicitly mediates

> a universalist culture which is humanistic in nature and characterized by a clear distinction between the private sphere, the world of passion and specificity, and the public sphere, the world of reason and the universal.

In England, by contrast, the rich diversity of teacher–pupil interaction is meant to facilitate deeper relationships through which social, moral, emotional and spiritual values can be developed in the context of personalized relationships.

PATTERNS OF DISCOURSE

Objectified (F) – Personalized (E)

Key features of French pedagogic discourse focus on objectifications which are part of a national system, e.g. '*l'Education Nationale*' (assumption – 'education' is 'national education'), '*l'Ecole*' (capital E – assumption – school is a singular noun; any school is the School of the Republic), '*l'élève*' (the pupil in his/her generality, not any particular child). By contrast, English educational discourse is more personalized and concerned with 'the whole child' (assumption – all children are unique and teachers are responsible for promoting progress in every aspect of the children's individuality), 'meeting individual needs' (assumption – teaching starts from 'the child'), 'development' (assumption – children develop – teaching is not so much transmission of knowledge as promoting growth and understanding which occur through processes such as 'emergence', etc.). Similarly 'schools' have their own 'ethos' and are encouraged to present themselves as distinct communities with their own uniforms, badges and rituals.

NATIONAL CONTEXT, EDUCATION SYSTEMS AND PUPIL EXPERIENCE

Findings from the QUEST project reported in other chapters of this book suggest that the fundamental value orientations of the national contexts of England and France are institutionalized in the two countries' systems of schooling and that these influence pupil experience both explicitly and implicitly within the school setting and outside it. Almost 100 per cent of French 3-year-olds are in formal schooling and the national policy is to extend this to all $2\frac{1}{2}$-year-olds. At the point of entry they become part of this huge national system which has been the common experience of their parents, and their parents' parents and for several generations back all over France. Progressing from the *cours préparatoire* to the *cours élémentaire*, reciting *leçons*, preparing for regular dictation tests: all are examples of shared national experience which are part and parcel of the taken-for-granted discourse of everyday life to which children are exposed at home, in the neighbourhood and through the media. Only in a country like this could two hours of prime-time television on a Saturday night be devoted each year to National and International Dictation championships.

Few $2\frac{1}{2}$-year-olds are in any kind of educational establishment in England and formal primary education starts years later. In the primary classroom children confront a smiling teacher who is interested in them as persons. Each child finds his or her own individuality celebrated and his or her own creations valued and displayed. He or she is encouraged to make choices and to reflect on what he or she has learnt. He or she is expected to do his or her best and to develop his or her potential. He or she is encouraged to identify with his or her class and with his or her teacher, and beyond this with the school as a local moral community based on respect for individuals. He or she learns that it is most important to be a nice person. As that most English of English Educationists, Sir Michael Sadler (1979), observed at the turn of the century:

> The German is apt to ask about a young man, 'What does he know?'
> The American to ask, 'What can he do?'
> The Frenchman to ask, 'What examination has he passed?'
> The Englishman's usual question is, *'What sort of fellow is he?'*

The kinds of pupil identity these two approaches to schooling engender are evident in the responses of the pupil samples reported throughout the chapters of this book.

Chapter 4

Pupils as Learners in England and France

INTRODUCTION

The politicians and policy-makers who are responsible for making educational policy and school reform, the teachers who are responsible for implementing it, and the researchers who study its effects rarely ask directly how the pupils themselves perceive their experience of schooling. As a consequence we know relatively little about how young people define their school situation or how they see the role of school and of teachers in their lives. Yet there are important questions to be asked of those who are at the receiving end of schooling. If we are to understand what kind of educational provision is most effective in promoting learning, it is surely this question that should lie at the heart of all educational research activity.

It was in the light of this need that the QUEST project sought to explore pupils' different perspectives in England and France. We wanted particularly to examine the impact of national context on learning by exploring the social reality of schooling for pupils in the two contrasting educational systems of these two countries. The chapter draws upon data from the questionnaires given to 800 children in the two countries (see Chapter 2), which included both fixed response and open-ended questions, and on a small number of interviews with children, whom we have called 'movers', who had experience of schooling in both England and France. The aim was to explore similarities and differences in the educational experience and attitudes to schooling, teaching and learning of primary school children in the two countries.

In particular we were concerned to explore the relative significance of national culture and national context when compared with differences in teacher professionalism and teaching approach in structuring pupil identities and perceptions of the social world of school. The findings which we report on here emphasize a socio-cultural perspective in which what is significant is not necessarily the 'objective' features of a learning situation, but the ways in which these are construed and understood by subjects within that culture and setting (Bronfenbrenner, 1979;

Bruner, 1990). While the focus here is on national context and culture, Chapter 10 considers the significance of intranational differences in socio-economic status, gender and, to a lesser extent, ethnic identity for pupil attitudes to learning and schooling.

In recent years, questions about learning goals and attempts to identify ways to promote more effective learning by examining educational practices in different countries have gained increasing prominence as a result of a growing international interest in comparing national standards of achievement. However, as we argued in Chapter 1, it is not sufficient simply to identify apparent success and the practices which go with it without also attempting to understand the cultural context in which these occur. Politicians have been enthusiastic about the notion of cultural policy-borrowing, yet the research evidence is beginning to suggest that such efforts to transplant educational ideas are misguided and inappropriate (Phillips, 1989; Alexander, 1996).

This chapter aims to contribute to the debate by emphasizing the significance of a more holistic understanding of the cultural context in which motivation and learning outcomes are situated. By giving a voice to primary pupils it also represents an attempt to highlight the differences between the intended and the experienced curriculum in both countries, between what policy-makers and teachers intend when planning curriculum tasks and what pupils actually experience in the classroom (Pollard *et al.*, 1997).

As we suggested in Chapter 2, there is a good deal of research evidence which documents the differences between teachers in England and France (Broadfoot and Osborn, 1993; Osborn and Broadfoot, 1992), but relatively little is known about the implication of these differences for pupils' learning. A small-scale qualitative study by Planel (1996) suggested that pupils' attitudes to school and their ability to manage their own learning were very different in England and France. In a previous ethnographic study of two French primary schools, Sharpe (1992a) demonstrated the surprisingly positive attitudes of pupils even in an inner-city school in a deprived area when faced by an apparently inaccessible and sometimes negative learning environment. Other inter-cultural studies which have included either England or France support these findings. For example, Elliott *et al.* (1999) compared the attitudes and motivation of pupils from Russia, the USA and Britain and found that British and American pupils were less positive towards school than their Russian peers and were more negatively influenced by an anti-work climate in many classrooms. Robinson (1989, 1990a, 1990b) compared samples of pupils in France, Japan, and England and suggested that English pupils' exhibited a lower self-esteem in relation to low achievement than their peers in France and Japan. They argued that this might be due to the relative lack of clarity and uniformity in the English educational system when compared to that of Japan and France.

This chapter aims to extend this previous work and to explore further the questions it raises. In both countries enormous effort and resources are currently being put into changing the nature of teachers' work. Consequently there is a pressing need to understand the significance of these changes for pupil learning. What are pupils' responses to the changes which are currently taking place in the classroom learning environment, and how are these responses likely to affect learning?

KEY DIFFERENCES BETWEEN PUPILS IN ENGLAND AND FRANCE

Our overall findings suggested that children in both countries shared many perceptions in common as a result of their shared structural position as pupils. In many respects the experience of schooling for the children in each nation of Europe may be becoming more like that in each other nation, as a result of Europeanization, the pressure of global economies, and international youth culture. However, there were nevertheless some highly significant differences in French and English children's views of schooling. On the whole children in both countries felt positively about their schools and their teachers but it was striking that French children were more strongly positive about school, more enthusiastic about teachers, and more likely to see teaching as helpful and useful to them. French children also presented themselves as more highly educationally-motivated and keen to do well in class. The following sections present some of these findings in more detail.

FEELINGS ABOUT SCHOOL

In the questionnaire children were asked to agree or disagree on a five-point scale with a series of statements about school and about their teacher. As Figure 4.1 indicates, French children were more strongly positive about school and about their

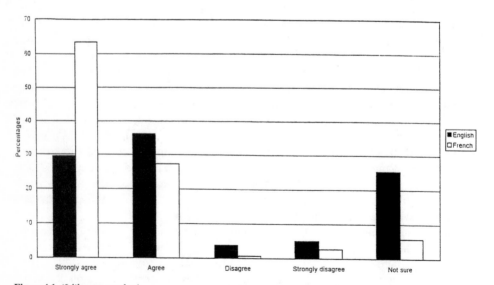

Figure 4.1 *'I like my teacher'*

teacher. They saw school as both useful and enjoyable as well as encouraging independence. For example, 64 per cent of French children strongly agreed with the statement 'I like my teacher' compared with 30 per cent of English children. They saw school as useful in helping them to get a job (77 per cent of French children strongly agreed that school helps you to get a job compared with 48 per cent of English children), and in helping you to learn how to use your spare time and to do things on your own. Significantly more French children agreed that 'the best part of my life is the time I spend in school' (Figure 4.2). On the whole French children also appeared to be more highly motivated to learn and to succeed than English children. Of French children, 86 per cent strongly agreed that they wanted to do well at school, in comparison with 66 per cent of English children; 43 per cent felt strongly that they really enjoyed most lessons, when compared with 20 per cent of English children. Although all children disagreed with statements such as 'I don't learn very much at school' and 'the work I do at school is a waste of time', French children refuted these more strongly.

However, English children were more likely to see the social uses of school. For example, 76 per cent of them, compared with 58 per cent of French children, felt that school helped you to get on with people. As we suggested earlier, English teachers felt responsible for children's social and personal development as well as academic objectives and these wider goals of schooling were reflected in the children's' responses. Like their teachers, English children had an 'extended' conception of the function of schooling, while French children had a more 'restricted' and more focused conception of what school is for. These striking differences were reflected in what children wrote in reply to an open-ended question which asked whether, in the children's eyes, their school was a good school and why. Children from the English

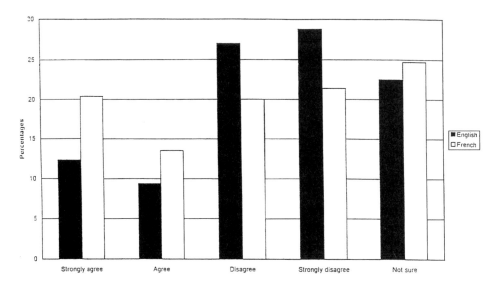

Figure 4.2 *'The best part of my life is the time I spend in school'*

inner-city schools wrote about the importance of their school being a caring school and having teachers who cared about you, while children in inner-city Marseilles and Calais wrote about the importance of having teachers who did not hit you and of obtaining a good academic level. The notion of a more active, caring school was almost absent from their replies. By contrast they had a much stronger notion of the school's role in producing good work and academic success.

C'est une bonne école. Il n'y a pas de voleurs et il y a un bon niveau.
(It is a good school. There are no thieves and there is a good academic level.)

Oui, parce que les maîtres sont gentils et ils ne nous frappent pas.
(Yes (it's a good school) because the teachers are kind and they don't hit us.)

C'est une bonne école parce que les maîtres et maîtresses nous font bien travailler.
(It's a good school because the teachers make us work hard.)

Oui, puisqu'il y a presque pas d'élèves qui redoublent.
(Yes (it's a good school) because there are hardly any children who repeat the year.)

Oui. C'est une école propre avec des poubelles pour jeter les papiers, les maîtres ne sont pas trop méchants et ils nous font travailler.
(Yes, it's a clean school with rubbish bins for throwing away the papers, the teachers are not too nasty and they make us work.)

C'est bon. On doit travailler et faire du calcul et faire des dessins et faire les devoirs.
(It's good. We have to work and do arithmetic and drawing and homework.)

On nous apprend à bien lire et à avoir de bons résultats.
(We are taught to read well and to get good results.)

In previous observation in French classrooms we had noticed that French teachers were far more likely to criticize children's work in an overt way in front of the class. However, this was reflected only partially in what the children themselves said. While to the eyes of English researchers, the French primary teachers were often surprisingly harsh with the children (it being not at all uncommon for a teacher to shout at a child and to threaten him (it was more often him) with 'redoublement' (repeating the year)), the children themselves were only slightly more likely to say that 'it quite often happens that the teacher says somebody's work is bad or wrong in front of the class'.

Although French children did perceive their teachers to be critical on some occasions, they were also far more likely to agree that their teacher often praised children for good work. In other words, assessment was perceived as more overt and public in French classrooms. It was also perceived as a normal part of classroom life which had continued in the same way since children entered the 'maternelle' at age 4 or 5 and was therefore not necessarily damaging to self-esteem in the way an English observer might assume. Other research in the early secondary years suggests that French pupils' self-esteem is, on the whole, higher than that of comparable English pupils despite an apparently harsher and more critical approach by the teacher (Robinson *et al.*, 1990a,b and 1992). This may well be a result of the 'distancing of the self' in French education and the separation of the personal and the cognitive. When the teacher criticizes it is only the child's academic performance that is being referred to, not other aspects of personality, and this is clearly understood by all pupils (Dubet *et al.*, 1996).

ATTITUDES TO SCHOOL WORK

The children were asked to rate the level of difficulty of the work they did at school on a five point scale. The results suggested that English children were more likely to find their school work difficult and to see it as taking a long time to complete. French children saw their work as a little easier and something which they could complete fairly quickly. They also found it relatively more interesting and more fun than English children did. English children more often saw work as a collaborative effort, sometimes done with others and when talking with friends. French children were more likely to see work as done individually in silence. This reflects the different pedagogical approaches observed in our previous research with more of an emphasis on either teaching the whole class together in France or on children working as individuals, while in England there was more of a balance between whole-class, group, and individual work. (See also Pollard *et al.*, 1994.)

All the children defined their school work as involving finding things out, but French children were more likely to see it as involving some rote learning as well. Again this reflects observations carried out in classrooms in both countries (Osborn and Broadfoot, 1992; Broadfoot *et al.*, 1996b). In both countries school work was seen as something which is useful and which is given a mark but the French children emphasized usefulness and the important role played by marks and formal assessment slightly more strongly. On the whole English children had a more holistic and broad perception of work and included social and physical skills in their descriptions of work while French children defined work in narrower terms as involving mainly cognitive skills.

MOTIVATION, LEARNING, AND SUCCESS AT SCHOOL

Clearly motivation and the reasons for wanting to do well educationally may have a strong influence on learning outcomes (McMeniman, 1989; Kozaki, 1985). The children were asked to choose from a set of possible reasons for wanting to do well and to complete the sentence 'When I want to do good work it's because ...' French children were more likely to fear being shouted at if they did not do their best work; but they were also far more strongly motivated by a desire for praise from the teacher (46 per cent compared to 18 per cent), by the urge to be the best in the class (Figure 4.3 shows that 46 per cent compared to 19 per cent were in strong agreement with this), and to get a good mark (71 per cent compared to 32 per cent). Overall, they appeared to feel much more strongly than English children about the importance of doing good work. Of the French sample, 86 per cent, compared to 60 per cent of the English sample, emphasized this. The results suggested that many English children actually did not want to be best in class, and felt only lukewarm

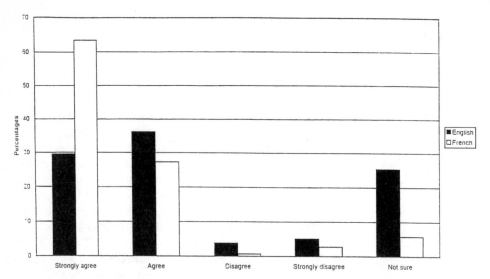

Figure 4.3 '*I would like to be the best in the class*'

about getting a good mark, or even about getting praise from the teacher. Only one-third were made happy by feeling that they had done good work compared with two-thirds of French children.

From the children's other comments it was clear that this lower motivation was a result of peer group pressure in the class. Pollard's (1985) ethnographic study of the social world of an English primary school identified sub-groups of 'goodies', 'jokers' and 'gangs' among pupils and documented pupil disapproval and avoidance of being a 'goodie', someone who got on with their work and took school seriously. The English children in our study similarly disliked the idea of being a 'goodie'. They often had friends who liked to fool around in class and even teased them if they did some really good work in class. French children very seldom suffered from this. English children were also less likely to see themselves as similar to their teacher's ideal pupil. It is possible that this finding is a sign of English children's lower self-esteem in relation to school success, but, in the light of the other findings mentioned above, it also reinforces the notion of children's adherence to an alternative set of values to those of the teacher, and the difficulties it would create with peers to be classed as a 'goodie'. Some English children actually said that they did not want to be seen as too good by the teacher, whereas no French children said this. When asked whether they thought that they were at all like their teacher's ideal pupil, some English children misunderstood the question and answered 'No, I wouldn't like him at all!' Another child said:

> She would like him to work a lot, not get in trouble at all, be a teacher's pet, and he will be a goody-goody. I work a lot but I am not a goody-goody. I am not a teacher's pet and I don't stay out of trouble at all.

Some other English responses to the question emphasized that their teacher would like a new pupil to have good behaviour and a desire to learn rather than high achievement:

> If I were a teacher I would want a well-behaved child that gets on well and likes to learn.
>
> I think our teacher would like a new child in our class to work hard and to enjoy it.
>
> Hardly ever being late, obedient, especially on his first day. And to try hard in lessons and not to talk in lessons.
>
> Clever, good, not bad and to fit in with everybody else.

Some felt a little like their teacher's ideal child but only in a qualified way:

> I think I am a well-behaved child and I get on with work but that's about it.
>
> I think I'm only a little bit like that child.
>
> I think I'm a bit like that child but not all the time. I try quite hard with my work and writing.
>
> Well I do fit in with everybody else but I am a bit dim so I am not clever.

The importance of caring and personal qualities was emphasized particularly by the children in one of the English inner-city schools:

> I think the teacher would like the person to be trustworthy, honest, caring, and the new person would share and work hard and not be a chatterbox and would be kind to others.
>
> I think a teacher would like the child to be kind, start off well at work and then get better and make a lot of progress, be polite and share with their ideas.

For French inner-city children a salient issue was that of some children's behaviour interfering with the learning process to the extent that fighting sometimes broke out. Many children in inner-city schools mentioned this and described their teachers' ideal pupil as someone who behaved well and worked hard.

In answer to the question 'If a new pupil arrived in your class what kind of pupil do you think your teacher would like?' children said:

> *Un gentil, un sage, qui ne parle pas, qui ne se bat pas, qui a de bons résultats et qui écrit bien.*
> (A nice sensible child who doesn't talk, doesn't fight, who has good results and who writes well.)
>
> *Un élève sérieux qui travaille bien.*
> (A conscientious pupil who works well.)
>
> *Une élève intelligente, gentille, pas copieuse et qu'elle travaille bien.*
> (A nice intelligent pupil who doesn't copy and who works well.)

It was often suggested by French pupils that personal characteristics did not matter. It was good work and results that mattered to the teacher.

> *Il n'y a pas d'importance, le principal c'est qu'il travaille bien.*
> (It's not important, the main thing is that he works well.)
>
> *Elle aimerait que ça soit une fille qui est forte en classe.*
> (She would like a girl who is clever in class.)

Occasionally, however, a hint of distancing oneself from the 'ideal' pupil emerged. For one child in a rural school, the teacher's ideal child was:

> *un petit Marseillais gentil qui ne cherche pas la bagarre et il porte des lunettes. Non, je ne ressemble pas à lui parce qu'il porte des lunettes.*
> (A nice little Marseillais who doesn't chat and who wears glasses. I am not like him because he wears glasses.)

Many more French children, however, did feel themselves to be similar to their teacher's ideal and appeared to feel no discredit in admitting to this.

> *Oui, parce que je ne copie pas, je suis gentille.*
> (Yes, because I don't copy and I am nice.)

> *Je suis gentille, je ne me bat pas et j'ai de bons résultats.*
> (I am nice, I don't fight and I have good results.)

> *Je suis sérieux, intelligent, actif et soigneux quand il le faut.*
> (I am conscientious, intelligent, active, and careful when I should be.)

All the children were motivated by wanting their teacher to be happy as a result of their good work, and by wanting to please their parents. French parents were perceived as slightly more likely to give a treat or money as a result, but less than half of the children in each country claimed to be motivated by this! Most children also felt that doing good work would eventually help them to get a job, although in each case French children felt more strongly motivated by these reasons.

It appears then that educational success is more important to French children than to English children, but, given this difference, how did the children think such success might be achieved? In their eyes why did some children do better at school than others?

The children were asked to choose the three most important reasons why some children might do better (Table 4.1). All the children attributed success to hard work and effort, although this was a more important factor for English children than for French. Most children thought that listening to the teacher was an important factor in educational success but French children thought this was more important. They also appeared to believe more strongly in innate ability, saying that success was due to being clever or to having better brains. However it appeared from other responses that French children saw cleverness or intelligence as something you could get better at in time rather than as a fixed quality. English children emphasized cleverness less

Table 4.1 *The three most important reasons given by pupils for educational success*

I think some children do better at school than others because

England	%	France	%
1. they work harder	77.1	1. they listen to the teacher more	68.5
2. they listen to the teacher more	59.4	2. they work harder	55.2
3. they don't mess about so much	58.2	3. they're clever	45.9

and attributed some children's success to 'not messing about so much'. The difference in meaning attributed by pupils in the two countries to the notion of being 'clever' underlines the need for extreme care in establishing the precise nuance of key terms.

CHILDREN'S PERCEPTIONS OF THEIR TEACHER

It was noticeable that when the children wrote about their ideal teacher, English children had wider terms of reference for discussing both what a good pupil and a good teacher should be. French children seemed to have a narrower, more school-focused vocabulary for discussing these issues, describing their teacher or fellow pupils as 'sympa', 'gentil' or not, 'aimable'. English children, by comparison, produced much more varied descriptions of both teachers and pupils and used more conceptual language, reflecting the more 'extended' functions of English education and the English school's greater emphasis on the whole child, rather than the 'child as pupil' which is the dominant emphasis in France (Osborn and Broadfoot, 1992). For English children there seemed to be no one acceptable way of talking about school. The vocabulary they used was drawn from language they would use in many other contexts and seemed to reflect the more active encouragement given to them to use their imagination and creativity in their writing, which we discuss in detail in Chapter 8.

The children were asked to say, by ranking a list in order (see Table 4.2), what are the most important things a teacher should do. There was a high level of agreement among all children that 'explaining things well' was the most important, and 'paying attention to children who find things difficult' was third in importance for children in both countries. However, 'making children work hard' was second from top on the list for French children and near the bottom (sixth) of the English children's list. In contrast it was highly important to English children that teachers always be fair, whereas French children did not regard this as a prime concern (fourth).

Table 4.2 *What are the most important things that a teacher should do?*

England	France
1. Explain things well.	1. Explain things well.
2. Always be fair.	2. Make children work hard.
3. Pay attention to children who find things difficult.	3. Pay attention to children who find things difficult.
4. Give children work which will be useful when they are adults.	4. Always be fair.
5. Make the work interesting.	5. Give children work which will be useful when they are adults.
6. Make children work hard.	6. Make the work interesting.
7. Be strict.	7. Let children choose what they want to do.
8. Let children choose what they want to do.	8. Be strict.

Somewhat surprisingly in view of the supposedly greater emphasis on pupil choice in English primary education, the importance of letting children choose what they want to do came at the bottom of the list for English children and almost at the bottom for French children. However, other recent research conducted by the ESRC-funded Primary Assessment Curriculum and Experience (PACE) study, which conducted a detailed examination of the impact of the National Curriculum and National Assessment on English primary schools between 1989 and 1996, has also suggested that being able to choose becomes less important for children as they progress through primary school and that this parallels a tightening of structure and increasing teacher direction as a result of the introduction of a National Curriculum and national assessment (Pollard *et al.*, 1994). It may simply be that English children forget what having choice is like by the time they reach the upper stages of primary education. They may also be feeling the pressure, filtered through the concerns of their teacher, of the national assessments at age eleven. Child choice has never been an important part of French pedagogy and the recent Jospin reforms (Jospin, 1989) aimed at 'centring education on the child' do not seem to have greatly affected the dominance of the teacher in the French classroom. Not surprisingly, few children in either country saw 'being strict' as an important function of the teacher.

The data above suggest that the importance of hard work and the work ethic is more firmly entrenched in French schools and accepted as necessary by children. This was confirmed when the children were asked to write in an open-ended way about their teacher. French children consistently wrote that they wanted teachers who made them work hard while English children wanted teachers who did not give too much work and consistently mentioned a concern with fairness. English children also emphasized the teacher's strong concerns with responding to individual differences while French children's responses demonstrated the shared nature of both pupils' and teachers' objectives, in particular those of completing the syllabus and moving up to the next class. These differences are illustrated in the following exemplar responses to the prompt: To my mind a good teacher should:

England

not always keep us in if it was someone else's fault and not really give us hard, hard work.

be helpful, caring, not too soft, determined that all her pupils will go far and most of all like children, very understanding.

Nice teachers are not always doing hard hard work, giving us a bit of play, not being strict all the time, not like if you get one question wrong and you get told off.

be able to understand the child and know their abilities and help the child learn.

always teach you properly by telling you what to do before starting a piece of work.

let us play outside all day.

be fit, 'varietible' (give lots of variety) and do lots of enjoyable stuff like cartoon art, lots of creative writing and lots of computers.

France

> *Elle devrait se consacrer à tous les élèves même aux meilleurs élèves. Elle doit au moins finir le programme de classe.*
> (She should devote herself to all the pupils even to the best pupils. She should at least finish the syllabus by the end of the year.)

> *nous faire bien travailler pour passer dans une autre classe. Nous aide.*
> (She should make us work hard to go up to the next class. Help us.)

> *Une bonne maîtresse devrait être un peu sévère, un peu gentille et surtout elle doit bien expliquer les leçons pour que toute la classe comprenne.*
> (A good teacher should be a bit strict, a bit nice and above all she must explain the lessons well so that the whole class understands.)

> *nous faire travailler au maximum et d'être gentille avec nous.*
> (make us work as hard as possible and be nice to us.)

> *Avant si on fait une exercice il doit faire une exemple.*
> (If we are doing an exercise he should give us an example.)

> *bien élever ses élèves en leur disant de ne pas bavarder, de leurs expliquer leur travail, comment ils doivent le disposer et de ne pas copier le voisin.*
> (Bring the pupils up well, telling them not to chat, explain their work to them, how they should do it and not to copy their neighbour.)

> *bien apprendre les leçons qu'il faut au enfant.*
> (teach well all the lessons that children should learn.)

For English children the personality and moods of the teacher were more significant and they often wrote that they wanted teachers who 'don't get cross', 'aren't grumpy', whereas French children seldom mentioned the teacher's personality and moods. In general they wrote about their good teachers in a more impersonal way.

English children often mentioned that they wanted a teacher who spoke clearly, while French children wanted one who wrote clearly, perhaps reflecting the preponderance of blackboard work in French teaching.

The emphasis on teachers who give hard work in France may be related to the stronger perception held by French children that work is something which is useful both to their time in school and in their adult lives. They also had a clearer perception of the school's main function as a learning one and the teachers' role being one of helping them. They were willing to accept the dominance of the teacher as it was for their own benefit. As Planel (1996) points out, the French system has less time for non-conformity in primary education. In order for children to succeed at school they need to be more passive and to accept the system. On the other hand, they receive more consistent encouragement both from within schools and from the wider society in return for that conformity.

THE MOVERS STUDY

As part of the QUEST research we also carried out a small exploratory study with ten children in each country who had experienced both English and French education. These interviews, conducted with children outside the main sample, most of whom had attended school in the other country as part of a six-month exchange programme, were intended to generate illuminative insights and to provide a form of triangulation with other pupil data, rather than to lead in themselves to generalizations. The children were interviewed in groups for approximately one hour and were very articulate; they seemed keen to recall their experiences and to recount anecdotes. Possibly there was a sense in which the group discussions were therapeutic for them since the experience of living away from home and family and attending school in a different country might well be seen as a stressful experience for such young children (aged 9–11 years). The sample of schools which children had experienced were geographically dispersed, in areas of different socio-economic status and of different sizes. The children were recalling their experiences of anything from two months to two years ago. Their responses are organized under three sections: what the children liked best and least about school in the other country, their perceptions of teachers, and how hard they felt children in the other country worked compared with themselves.

What did you like best about your school in the other country?

The English children who had spent time in France liked the fact that there were more breaks in French schools and that they had Wednesdays off. (French primary schools are closed on Wednesdays, theoretically so that the children can have religious instruction outside school since, in accordance with the republican ethic, there is a strong emphasis on the lay nature of education (OECD 1996, etc.) They also mentioned the lack of uniform and the good school dinners as a positive aspect, together with the lack of bullying.

In general, the French children particularly mentioned sport and gymnastics as positive aspects of English schools and the easiness of some of the lessons such as maths. They also commented positively about the school hours, the fact that the English school day was less long and that school finished at 3.15 p.m.

What did you like least about your school in the other country?

The English children complained about the length of the school day in France, the amount of homework they were given and its content. They particularly disliked doing 'recitation' and having to learn things by heart. They also mentioned issues such as the way subjects were taught, the teachers, and the restrictions on movement around the class.

As Mary recounted of her experiences in a CM1 class:

In England you sit round tables and you talk to each other and you do your work and you have fun. In France you get like a set amount of time to do your work. You sit in rows, you don't talk to each other ever and it's very strict, very formal. The French way teaches you more but in the English way we get taught near enough the same thing in the end … we'll get it taught further on in secondary school whereas they'll get it taught in primary school but I think like because you're kids … you're meant to have fun and I think it's too hard to make kids sit in silence and to expect so much of just like children.

Imogen commented on her French classroom:

It was set out like a Victorian classroom. All the tables and chairs were in rows behind each other. It was a bit too stiff for me. I much prefer a warm casual environment ... you get on better I think.

Some of the children commented on differentiation in the English learning situation and contrasted it with the emphasis in France on bringing all children to a common level.

David said:

In England they teach you to your own level ... in France they expect you to do the same thing.

Mary pointed out:

There we got taught like just altogether, you got kind of separate but in the same classroom – all the clever ones went into this class and the not so clever ones in this class and the slow ones in that class (where there were two or three parallel year groups in the same school).

The English children referred frequently to the amount of homework they were given in French schools:

Mary: You get just the same amount as you do in English secondary school, quite a lot if not more.

Oliver: The other children got lots.

Rachel: You had loads, you had like to learn poems.

Emily: You had to learn poems off by heart ... say it out loud to the class ... then we did lots of maths for homework and learning verbs.

The French children, talking about their schools in England, complained particularly about the lack of systematic emphasis on learning for homework and wondered how it could be justified for the teacher then to be angry about the children not having learned what she had taught.

Jeanne argued:

Ce qui me plaisait le moins c'est qu'on apprenait pas les leçons ... pour aller à la maison ... quand on était à l'école et on nous citait quelque chose ... ben on connaît pas. Moi j'avais pas de devoirs pour aller à la maison, mais en tout cas les autres ils n'apprenaient jamais des leçons quand ils allaient chez eux. C'est un peu stupide parce qu'après la maîtresse se fâchait parce qu'ils ne savaient pas la leçon. Elle disait, 'mais pourtant tu le sais ça', puis elle faisait pas des exercices de suite ... des leçons ... pour aller à la maison.
(What I liked least was that we didn't learn the work ... the homework ... when we were at school and we were told something ... well something we didn't know. I didn't have homework to take home (because she was a French visitor), but the others they never learned the work when they went home. It's a bit stupid because afterwards the teacher got angry because they didn't learn the work. She said 'but you know that', then she didn't follow it up with other exercises, with work to take home.

Like Jeanne, Gilles too was struck with not having 'leçons':

On n'avait pas des leçons à apprendre ... on avait des devoirs sur feuilles, mais pas de livres comme 'La Balle aux Mots' ... c'est complètement différent. Il y avait des livres de maths ... c'était facile.
(We didn't have 'leçons' to learn ... we had homework on pieces of paper, but not books like 'La Balle aux Mots' ... it's completely different. There were maths books ... it was easy.

All the children were in agreement that there was either less homework than in French schools or in some cases none at all.

Julie complained about the size of the class and the noise:

> *On était plus nombreux et un peu plus bruyant en classe. On était 34 ... J'ai jamais vu tant d'enfants dans une salle.*
> (There were too many in the class and it was a bit noisy. There were 34 ... I have never seen so many children in a classroom.)

Perceptions of teachers

The English children commented on the strictness, the discipline of the French teachers and how they shouted and sometimes manhandled children. They also alluded to French children's fear of teachers:

Emily said:

> In French school they were a lot more strict ... you had to be terribly silent.

Ashley argued:

> The teacher? Wicked when you got things wrong, when you got things right and you were good she was quite nice ... like most teachers. She was different (from English teachers), strict ... because she was allowed to hit you, but teachers here are not allowed. My English teacher: most of the time he's nice, funny too.

Edward described the two teachers he had in France:

> We had a maths teacher, she was very strict ... she was the strictest ... she just gave us some sheets, we just got to work, then at the end she got people, picked people out the class to go do it on the board. The English teacher was a bit better, but she still didn't ... well we had conversations with her ... we sometimes had whole-class discussions and stuff.

He recounted how:

> You couldn't get out of your chair, you couldn't talk, you couldn't look at anyone else's work or anything. We had separate desks ... we didn't do anything like to disturb it (the work), like make a noise or something.

When the children were asked 'why did everyone do as they were told?' Edward said:

> If we didn't (behave) we could get sent out the classroom or shouted at. I think they were kind of frightened of the teachers, in case they got told off, at the same time I think they kind of respected them.

Emily commented:

> I can't honestly remember anyone not doing what they were meant to do. In English school at that age it's just fine if you don't do it you don't get told off for it, you just kind of ... it just doesn't really matter.

Mary added:

> In England it's more kind of school's like a fun thing ... you go and you get to mess about with your friends ... you do a bit of work but you're now expected to do a lot ... whereas in France you don't have fun ... you sit like in lines and you can't look at each other ... you just work all the time.

In contrast the French children talked mainly about the niceness and the 'sympathique' nature of their teachers in England although this sometimes caused them difficulties in getting on with their work, because of the level of noise and movement that was allowed in the class.

Several children described their teachers as *'super-gentille'* and *'sympa'* (super-kind and understanding). Gilles said:

> *Elle était très bien, elle était sympa. En Angleterre on a pas eu de punitions ... elle n'a jamais crié ... c'est vrai ... on a eu de la chance. Dans la famille en Angleterre aussi ça ne criait pas.*
> (She was really nice, very 'sympa'. In England they didn't have punishments ... she never shouted ... it's true ... we were lucky. In our family in England they also never shouted.)

Yaunes saw the teacher as *'gentille ... moins sérieuse ... c'était le directeur qui a donné les punitions'* (nice, less serious and conscientious ... it was the head who gave out the punishments).

However, Jeanne reflected on how this niceness might sometimes be a constraint on the children's work:

> *Elle était tres gentille. Elle corrigeait ... en même temps qu'elle corrigeait elle ne regardait pas les autres enfants ... Il y en avait qui chantaient, qui se levaient, c'était vraiment désagréable à travailler ... la maîtresse des fois elle voyait rien.*
> (She was very nice. She corrected your work ... while she was correcting she did not watch the other children ... Some were calling out or getting up, it was really unpleasant trying to work ... there were times when the teacher didn't see anything.)

One of the English pupils also reflected a similar point saying that the teacher in France was much stricter but that:

> Now (in England) the teacher is much nicer even if we don't get on with our work.

How hard did pupils in the other country work compared with pupils in your own country?

The English children talked of how hard they had to work in French classrooms, of the punishments that were meted out to those who did not work, and of children sometimes being manhandled and reduced to tears.

Mary said:

> They worked harder because they were expected to ... they were humiliated if they didn't ... kind of almost punished if they didn't do as well as various people wanted them to. The humiliation by the teacher made them work.

Imogen added:

> The only reason we worked harder was because the teacher would get us into trouble again if we didn't ... for no other reason.

And Edward backed this up:

> Yes, because they were scared of the teacher. You could kind of feel it. They kept their heads down ... I never saw a single head go up ... In France all there is is work, work, work, have some dinner, go home and more work. You just came in, sat down and did work. They got straight into the lesson ... no chat or anything.

Emily commented on the greater orderliness of the French classroom:

> They were more organized ... when they walked in (into the classroom) they sat down and they got their work out and they did it. At our school (in England) like we had to be

told to sit down, told to stop talking. It was really orderly ... if they didn't do it they'd get really told off.

Several of the children reported seeing children being pulled by the hair or the back of the neck, being pinched on the upper arm and even kicked ('not hard, just as a warning sort of thing').

Duncan thought that the parents were aware of the physical punishments their children were receiving, but that they 'knew that it was good for their children'.

Several of the children talked of the French teacher's use of humiliation to control pupils, but in spite of this they also sensed that there appeared to be a shared understanding between teacher and pupils about the aims of education which mitigated the effect of such treatment.

Mary commented:

It was really weird because even when she was telling them off and bringing them to tears and stuff, they got like upset, but they just kind of took it as her, because they really, I don't know, they had this strong bond with her, they *liked* her which is strange, because she wasn't a nice lady. They just kind of thought ... she's doing it for my best ... like it's fine what she's doing.

Some of the children reported hearing French teachers say 'tu es nul' (you are stupid) to a pupil. In a brief discussion of why it seemed possible for French teachers to say this to a pupil, while it would not be permissible for an English teacher to say 'you are stupid' to a child, Mary said that she thought that because French teachers expect to treat all children the same, they cannot treat special categories of children differently or make allowances. If a child had learning difficulties this implied that the teachers and parents had failed. She thought that everyone was expected to succeed in the French system, so that the teacher saying 'tu es nul' to a pupil was done to frighten and humiliate the child into doing better.

Significantly, most of the English children thought that in France, children were further ahead with their work, particularly with maths.

The French children who had spent time in England were unanimous in their view that English pupils worked less hard than French pupils. As Jeanne put it:

Dans la classe ils étaient vraiment dissipés ... ils chantaient dans la classe ... Mais je crois qu'ils apprenaient beaucoup de choses ... alors nous on apprend les fractions ... eux ils les apprenaient beaucoup plus vite que nous.
(In class they were really distracted ... (they really frittered away their time) ... they called out ... but I think they learned a lot ... we learn fractions, but they learned them a lot quicker than we do.)

Jeanne agreed with the interviewer that perhaps in France children learned more through small successive stages whereas in England they were taught in larger single segments and learning came more all at once.

Yaunes also argued that:

Ils travaillaient beaucoup moins ... le matin ils ne faisaient que des Maths et de l'Anglais ... en France on fait des dictées.
(They work much less hard ... in the morning they only did maths and English ... in France you do dictation too.)

This lack of hard work was perceived to be connected with the lack of emphasis in England on rote learning.

Gilles said:

> *Ils travaillent moins ... premièrement ils ont rien à apprendre (par coeur) ... C'est moins travaille ... Ils doivent pas écrire ... euh, si ... il y a pas de poésie là-haut ... il y a pas de livres ... c'est tout. Les leçons de géographie ... histoire ... on les apprend pas.*
> (They work much less ... first they don't have anything to learn by heart ... It's less work. They don't have to write ... there is no poetry over there ... there are no books ... that's all. Geography and history lessons ... they don't have to learn them (by heart).)

Julie commented on the wider range of activities and curriculum coverage and saw this as meaning less work.

> *Ils travaillent beaucoup moins ... il y a moins d'activités ... d'avantage de gym ... ils se servent des ordinateurs ... ils font l'art plastique, ils passent tout l'après-midi à le faire.*
> (They work far less ... there are fewer activities ... more gymnastics ... they use the computers ... they do art and they spend an entire afternoon doing it.)

Several of the French children found the level of movement and noise in the class rather disruptive.

Gilles said:

> *En classe ils travaillaient mais au lieu de rester assis ils faisaient toujours le tour de la classe, ils discutaient ... des fois ils allaient à la poubelle mais ils y allaient par un côté ou par un autre. La maîtresse voyait ... une fois elle dit comme ça, mais elle ne s'énerve pas, elle dit, 'Scott, reste assis'...*
> (In class they worked but instead of staying seated they kept walking about the classroom, they talked together ... sometimes they went to the wastepaper basket, but they went by a roundabout way. The teacher saw ... sometimes she said like this, without getting upset: 'Scott stay in your seat' ... There was more noise ... they talked more ... I couldn't concentrate. I prefer to work in silence.)

There was some disagreement over whether English children were further ahead or behind in their work. Some of the French children thought that English children were behind, particularly in maths and language, whereas others thought that the wider curriculum meant that English children were ahead because they did things which were not covered in France.

SUMMARY OF MOVERS' COMMENTS

The comments of these children who had experienced both systems highlight the enduring influence of national context on school goals, on teacher expectations and, consequently, on pupils' school experience. Pupils in both countries contrasted the relative severity of the regime in French classrooms, the concentration on hard work and the expectation of prolonged and concentrated effort with the relative freedom and ease, the greater emphasis on work as 'fun', and the more relaxed attitude of the teacher in England (even to the point of his or her ignoring disruptions from other pupils). Both talked of the emphasis on bringing all children to a common level in France compared with the greater emphasis on differentiation and individualization in England. What these pupils said confirms the findings from other parts of the study including the questionnaires, the group interviews, and the observation.

DISCUSSION, SUMMARY AND CONCLUSIONS

The findings presented here suggest strongly that while children in both countries shared the role of pupil in common and developed many common strategies and responses to schooling as a result, there were nevertheless striking differences in their perceptions of what it meant to be a pupil. Overall, the French primary school children in the sample appeared to be more positive and enthusiastic about their school and their teacher. They saw their teacher as helpful and useful to them and were less concerned about the personal characteristics of the teacher, and more concerned that he or she should make them work hard. Compared with English children they appeared more strongly motivated towards educational success and academic goals. The interviews with the 'movers' reinforced these overall findings with illustrations from the contrasts drawn by the children themselves between the two school regimes.

To what extent are these differences a result of differences at the level of the individual teacher and teaching methods, or alternatively differences at the level of the school, or even in the organization of the national education system and the national context? Although, in England, primary teachers and teaching methods are currently being blamed for many of the social ills that exist, it seems highly unlikely that these differences in pupil motivation are a result of pedagogy, or of the personality and motivation of teachers. Our findings suggest that the personality of the teacher is less important to French children and that the teacher's role as an imparter of understanding and as an educator is more important. From our previous research we also know that English teachers feel responsible for a wider range of educational objectives concerning their pupils. It is English teachers who emphasize learner-centred objectives more. They try harder to make work interesting and relevant and to engage the motivation of children. Paradoxically, in England, where teachers apparently work hardest to develop positive relationships with pupils, a negative sub-culture opposed to the teacher's values emerged. In France, where teachers' relationships with their pupils are more formal rather than personal and based on greater inequality in authority, children expressed the greater liking for teachers and for school, and also the greater degree of consensus with teachers' values, and were more strongly motivated towards educational success.

It is more plausible that the educational values of the children derive from other sources related both to the school climate and ethos, the influence of peer group culture and wider familial and cultural values. As Woods (1990) points out, pupils' liking and disliking of school may relate to their own personal agenda rather than the official one. Their attitude to school may relate to different criteria such as obtaining social approval and popularity with peers. Measor and Woods (1984) and Pollard (1985) describe an 'informal' pupil culture in England which differs from the formal one and where the teacher's positive values of hard work and effort are translated by pupils into a negative one of being a 'boff', a 'goodie-goodie' or a 'keener'. In France, however, the peer culture seems more positive towards school, at least at primary level, and from our observations it would seem that the pupil culture largely shares official school values. In part this may be a result of the separation of the person and the system, of personal and academic competences in French education (Dubet *et al.*, 1996).

However, pupils' motivation and attitude to school is also likely to be a result of differences in the values and culture of the wider society as reflected in familial and inter-generational values. In France as we discuss in the next chapter, there exists a clearly visible 'ladder of progress' through school. Educational values are shared by children, teachers, parents, the media, and politicians. Educational success and intellectual endeavour are more highly valued, prized, and understood in the wider society. French pupils are motivated by the long-standing existence of a clear and publicly understood learning pathway in the French education system and consequently have a clearer perception of the school's main function as a learning one (Sharpe, 1992a; Planel, 1996). There is no doubt however, that the clear separation in pupils' minds of 'work' and 'play', and the explicit and immediate feedback which they receive, also emphasizes the school's educational function. So too does the teacher's clear focus on learning goals, without the many and sometimes conflicting obligations which primary teachers in England are expected to meet.

The lesson for English education seems to be that changing teaching methods will not necessarily produce the desired result of higher standards; that there is a need to work on peer-group values and on attitudes in the wider society by harnessing the media to encourage the nationwide developing of a culture that is more positive and supportive of learning and of educational success. School ethos may also make a considerable difference (Rutter *et al.*, 1979). The creation of a school climate in which there are high and consistent expectations of all pupils and a clear and continuing focus on learning, may also be vital. Success needs to be positively valued and rewarded and a sense of pride in the school inculcated (National Commission on Education, 1993 and 1996). It may also be important that teachers are released from some of their many other obligations and enabled to focus more single-mindedly on the task of teaching.

It seems clear from the findings presented here that, in spite of the many contemporary pressures towards greater homogenization of educational systems, the national culture and educational traditions of England and France currently continue to lead to significant differences in the way in which pupils define their relationship to school. Our research emphasizes the extent to which pupils' attitudes to learning and schooling are situated in a wider cultural context. It suggests that policy-borrowing by simply importing one limited aspect of other countries' educational systems (for example, methods of whole-class teaching, as is being advocated currently in England) without taking into account this wider cultural context is unlikely to resolve the problems of any one educational system.

Chapter 5

Pupils as Citizens in England and France

Over the past fifteen years in England there has been a progressive focusing of the interest shown by policy-makers in the relationship between the quality of school education and the well-being of society and the economy. In the mid-1980s the concern was expressed largely in terms of curriculum and the perceived failure of schooling to equip pupils with the requisite knowledge, understanding and skills to meet the needs of commerce and industry in an era of growing competition within an increasingly global market. It was this concern which led to the landmark 1988 Education Act and the introduction of a National Curriculum through which what was to be taught during compulsory schooling could be closely prescribed centrally to ensure that all children were prepared for their future adult lives and employment.

By the early 1990s attention had begun to turn to pedagogy and to worries that widely used teaching methods, especially in primary schools, were failing to produce the required standards of achievement in pupils, despite the introduction of a National Curriculum. This precipitated unprecedented intervention by government and its agencies in the specifics of strategies teachers were using to deliver the National Curriculum programmes of study. The report of the 'Three Wise Men' (Alexander, Rose and Woodhead, 1992) was heavily critical of prevailing orthodoxies in primary teaching styles, and heralded a number of initiatives intended to change the way teachers approached the task of teaching. The establishment of OFSTED and its framework of inspection had far-reaching effects on teacher behaviour at all levels and in all phases of schooling. Central pedagogic prescription reached new heights with the introduction of the literacy and numeracy hours (DfEE, 1997, 1998).

In the late 1990s anxiety was being expressed about the pupils themselves, their apparent lack in many cases of moral and civic values and consequent indiscipline inside and outside school. The specific teaching of 'citizenship' was widely advocated (Crick, 1998; Tate, 1997). This threefold shift in focus might be characterized thus:

Time period	Focus of concern	Locus of concern
Mid-1980s onwards	Knowledge	School curriculum
Early 1990s	Pedagogy	Teacher–pupil relations
Late 1990s	Values	The pupil as citizen

Policy-making attention has arguably thus moved from a preoccupation with the form and content of what is presumed to be *external to the pupil* (i.e., what is to be taught) through a debate about the nature of the interactional process by which learning is *mediated to the pupil* (i.e., the organization of teaching) to something approaching a moral panic about what is actually *internal to the pupil* him- or herself in terms of his or her developing identity as a citizen. The QUEST study of primary pupils in England and France has endeavoured to address the three areas of pupil experience which relate to these policy concerns: pupils' curricular achievements in language and mathematics; pupils' perceptions of teaching, learning and schooling; and pupils conceptions' of themselves as citizens of England or France, the last-named being the focus of this chapter.

Earlier work by QUEST team members (for example, Broadfoot and Osborn, 1992) had revealed the extent to which teacher behaviour and attitudes in the two countries differed systematically. Qualitative and quantitative research had revealed how important were teachers' beliefs about themselves and their role in determining how they act in the classroom, and these beliefs were found to be strongly determined by the national context:

> the national context within which teachers work deeply influences their professional ideology, their perceptions of their professional responsibility, and the way in which they carry out their day-to-day work ...
> ... it is the ideology, or to put it another way, the conception of their professional role, which plays the most fundamental part in determining what teachers do (Broadfoot *et al.*, 1988: 265).

Broadfoot *et al.* (1988) argue that teachers' ideology and the discourse they use to express their professional values and understanding are shaped by the particular national context in which they work. Thus, the responses that the primary teachers they studied in England and France made to both closed and open-ended questions followed clear national patterns. These patterns appeared to override other variables such as socio-economic differences in the catchment area of the schools: French teachers working in difficult inner-city areas were more like other French teachers situated in more affluent areas than they were like English teachers teaching in similarly challenging English schools. In other chapters a parallel pattern to this is reported in relation to pupils' attitudes to schooling. In this chapter, though, the influence of the national context on pupils' attitudes to national identity, pride and citizenship is examined.

NATIONAL PRIDE, IDENTIFICATION AND CITIZENSHIP

As part of the questionnaire survey (described in Chapter 2) concerned with their life in class and at school pupils in each country were asked six multiple-choice questions about their conception of themselves as being English or French. They were asked to agree or disagree with statements intended to assess their feelings of national pride; the extent to which they identified themselves with their country and had a sense of 'belonging' to it; the importance they attached to having a particular nationality; how well they felt their primary schooling was preparing them for future citizenship in their society; the degree to which they had been explicitly taught about the multicultural character of the country; and how far they believed they were part of a country in which everybody is equal. Analysis of the answers given by the two national pupil cohorts to these survey questions revealed clear differences in their attitudes to national identity.

ISSUE 1: NATIONAL PRIDE

The QUEST survey findings indicate overall that French pupils are significantly more proud of their nationality than are English pupils.

Two features stand out from the figures in Table 5.1. The French pupils appear to have a high level of pride in their nationality and to be very definite about this, with more than half of the positive responses felt 'strongly'. The English profile of figures suggests an altogether more diffident attitude, with a more even spread across the four categories of response and a notably higher number who elected to express no view. Further breakdowns of the results revealed no major differences between the attitudes of girls and boys in each of the national samples, nor between pupils in advantaged and disadvantaged areas. The figures for English boys are slightly higher than for English girls (66 per cent total positive as against 59 per cent) but overall the pattern of responses corresponds to those of the whole cohort shown above. There is here therefore prima facie evidence that nationality appears to be the main determinant of the strength of feeling of national pride in the two pupil samples, overriding both gender and social class.

ISSUE 2: IDEAS OF BEING ENGLISH/FRENCH

Given this powerful influence of nationality on the extent to which pupils express feelings of pride in their country, it is interesting to ask the slightly different question

Table 5.1 *Sense of national pride*

'I feel very proud of being French/English'

	Strongly agree %	Agree %	Disagree %	Strongly disagree %	Not sure %	No answer %
England	35	27	10	7	20	1
France	57	21	5	7	8	2

Table 5.2 *Self-identification and sense of belonging*

'I consider myself to be very French/English'

	Strongly agree %	Agree %	Disagree %	Strongly disagree %	Not sure %	No answer %
England	38	27	12	5	16	2
France	70	15	4	5	5	1

of how far pupils believe themselves to be 'English' or 'French'. Here too the results are unambiguous, providing an even starker contrast.

From the percentages in Table 5.2, French pupils seem unequivocal in their identification of themselves with France, whereas again the English response is much more restrained and more evenly spread across the response categories, and also again with a relatively high number of 'not sure' choices. The contrast in the 'strongly agree' results is striking, with the French figure being almost double the English figure. There is the same phenomenon with English boys and girls as in the national pride question, 71 per cent total positive boys against 61 per cent girls, but in both cases there is a much higher 'agree' response and much lower 'strongly agree' response than in the French sample. There is this time a more marked effect of social class, as shown in Table 5.2a.

The sense of being French appears to be somewhat less strong in the disadvantaged areas than in the advantaged areas, although the total positive figures in both cases remain significantly higher than for their English counterparts. This slight diminution in enthusiasm for being French in less favoured areas may reflect the greater proportion of children from ethnic minority backgrounds in Calais, and even more in Marseilles – in the schools in this socio-economic category included in the study – some of whom actively distanced themselves from French nationality, as reported below in the analysis of the open-ended answers to a question about national pride. Quite why there is a corresponding opposite result in England, with rather more enthusiasm for being English apparent among the pupils in disadvantaged areas is difficult to explain with any certainty. If the theory developed in the next section that French pupils typically adopt an 'unproblematic' approach to

Table 5.2a *Self-identification and sense of belonging: socio-economic areas*

	Strongly agree %	Agree %	Disagree %	Strongly disagree %	Not sure %
England					
advantaged	28	30	21	4	17
disadvantaged	46	25	7	6	16
France					
advantaged	75	13	2	2	8
disadvantaged	60	17	6	9	8

national identity while English pupils in general appear to have a more 'consumerist' attitude, it may be that the extent of this is greater among more affluent pupils, and that in less-favoured areas pupils still have a more 'taken for granted' feeling of loyalty. Evidence presented in the next section suggests that in both countries sport, especially football, plays an important part in providing icons through which feelings of national identification are mediated, but that this may be more exclusively the case in England. To the extent that this argument is valid, it may be that such feelings are more keenly felt in less privileged areas.

Equally, it is arguable that because of the broad difference in the multicultural policies of the two education systems, ethnic-minority children may be more likely to feel 'comfortable' in England than in France, with the result that there is less overt distancing of themselves from the host country. This is, though, a complex argument. In essence French education policy is geared toward an assimilationist model which is firmly rooted in republican principles of equality and equal entitlement. The fundamental aim of the system is to provide a uniform educational entitlement grounded in the values of French civilization to all children living on French soil, whoever they are, wherever they live, and, to a significant degree, whatever their particular character, dispositions or abilities. Interestingly, of course, the French have always treated their colonies as French soil and imposed the same pedagogic regime everywhere, thereby creating the apocryphal absurdity of African native children chanting 'nos ancêtres les gaulois', a nonsensical injunction to these children to identify with an ethnic history totally removed from their home culture. The basic intention of the national education system in France has always been to make good French citizens. This is an uncompromising version of the universalist conception of equality of opportunity. By contrast the English education system has traditionally adopted a much more 'particularist' approach, with emphasis placed on the value of difference at all levels: differences in regions, differences between schools, and individual differences between pupils. Consonant with this cultural tradition there has been much stress laid on the importance of multicultural education as a crucial element in the provision of equal opportunities. The argument here is that unless the child's home culture, and language, is valued in the school context, the child in reality will not be able to access the curriculum through which the possibility of equal opportunity is created.

The point at issue is not which of these approaches has the most to recommend it educationally, or whether one or the other is morally superior. It is, rather, to contrast the two situations in which ethnic minority children have to make some sense of what a question about how English or French they feel might actually mean. In the English classroom children with an ethnic-minority background encounter a context which is intended by policy-makers to be sympathetic to their cultural differences and which is required to provide preparation for their future lives in a multicultural society. In the French classroom they encounter a context which is intended by policy-makers to induct them into French culture. Prima facie, then, it might be argued that ethnic-minority children might feel more 'at home' in English education.

However, it could be argued that precisely because of the policy of teaching all pupils that England is a multicultural society made up of diverse socio-cultural groups, all of whom are to be valued and cherished, encouragement is actually being given to ethnic-minority children to reinforce their sense of attachment to their inherited ethnic origin. And possibly, therefore, some 'disagree' or weaker 'agree' responses to the above question actually reflect a stronger sense of being Asian, Afro-Caribbean or whatever, within English society. Furthermore, it is arguable that because of the English cultural tradition of emphasizing difference, and because of the stress on cultural diversity in English education, what it means to be English at all, for any pupil of whatever origin, is altogether vaguer and more elusive than what it means to be French. It may well be that all pupils in France have a much more sharply defined idea of what it is that they are associating themselves with, or dissociating themselves from, than pupils in England.

The QUEST data do not allow for separate analysis of the responses of ethnic-minority children. However, while the above analysis is therefore necessarily speculative, the QUEST findings do clearly show that the two different national contexts nevertheless produce different degrees of overtly-stated loyalty in pupils as a whole. What is interesting, though, is that in response to questioning about whether all pupils felt they were being prepared by their schooling for life in a multicultural society through learning about the life of children who are not of French/English origin, their responses suggested that the intentions of policy-makers were not carried through to the lived experience of the classroom.

On the surface the results shown in Table 5.3 would tend to suggest that English pupils as a whole do not have a strong sense of the multicultural dimension to their schooling that prevailing policy formally requires. The French pupils appear to recognize that this is not a strong feature of their schooling but seem reluctant to give high negative responses. Could this be some sort of 'halo' effect, as if they wish to be constantly positive about their experience of schooling? An endemic difficulty with any use of questionnaire strategies is of course the impossibility of being sure what sense respondents make of the question, and this is perhaps an even more acute problem when the respondents are 10- and 11-year-old children. It may be that children on both sides of the Channel felt less certain what was being asked of them in question 3 than in the two previous questions. It is interesting nevertheless that once again the same pattern of response emerges, the higher French agree response, the greater English diffidence and uncertainty. Analysis by gender reveals almost no divergence at all from the figures for the whole cohort, but there is some difference

Table 5.3 *Perception of education for a multicultural society*

'In class I learn about the life of children who are not of French/English origin'

	Strongly agree %	Agree %	Disagree %	Strongly disagree %	Not sure %	No answer %
England	16	25	19	7	29	4
France	27	28	14	16	13	2

Table 5.3a *Perception of education for a multicultural society – socio-economic areas*

'In class I learn about the life of children who are not of French/English origin'

	Strongly agree %	Agree %	Disagree %	Strongly disagree %	Not sure %
English advantaged	11	17	31	9	32
English disadvantaged	21	33	13	6	27
French advantaged	23	28	16	19	14
French disadvantaged	31	29	13	13	14

between the responses of children in advantaged and disadvantaged areas. These are shown in Table 5.3a.

The surprising finding is that pupils in the disadvantaged areas in both countries felt more definite about having the experience of learning about other cultures. As already indicated, the QUEST data did not include specific study of ethnic-minority children in the two countries, and the extent to which their possibly greater numbers in the schools in the less-favoured areas included in the samples affected these results cannot be assessed with any certainty. Nevertheless it remains the case that in each category the French figure is higher than the corresponding English figure.

This pattern continues in the responses to the final question asked about national identity, concerning whether it was felt to matter which country one belongs to. Answers to this question confirm the general finding that being English is of less significance to the English pupils questioned than being French is to the French pupils questioned, as demonstrated in Table 5.4.

Almost three-quarters of the French sample agreed that their nationality matters,

Table 5.4 *Commitment to societal membership*

'I think it matters what country I belong to'

	Strongly agree %	Agree %	Disagree %	Strongly disagree %	Not sure %
England					
Whole cohort	**25**	**17**	**26**	**14**	**16**
Boys	28	21	22	14	15
Girls	22	14	31	15	17
Disadvantaged	29	17	22	14	18
Advantaged	19	19	32	17	13
France					
Whole cohort	**48**	**26**	**7**	**4**	**15**
Boys	48	26	4	4	18
Girls	50	28	6	4	12
Disadvantaged	57	23	3	3	14
Advantaged	43	30	7	4	16

while less than half of the English sample thought this. Only 9 per cent of French pupils but 40 per cent of English pupils rejected the idea. There is a repeat of the phenomenon of English pupils in less-favoured areas appearing slightly more patriotic, but this intranational difference pales before the clear re-emergence of the same pattern of international contrast evident in the other tables of results. What stands out from the findings presented above in Tables 5.2, 5.3, and 5.4 is therefore a clear picture of different levels of identification with the nation on each side of the Channel. The high level of consistency of the results for boys and girls, and for advantaged and disadvantaged schools in each country, is marked.

ISSUE 3: IDEAS ABOUT CITIZENSHIP

In connection with the general enquiry about attitudes to national identity and national pride, the QUEST questionnaire survey included two further questions about the different approach to citizenship characteristic of the two countries. In France the notion of the citizen is a central part of everyday lived experience and discourse. The fundamental principles of liberty, equality and fraternity proclaimed at the time of the Revolution over two hundred years ago continue to act as powerful underpinning value orientations for French social life at all levels from major national institutions down to mundane interaction in routine encounters. The idea that every 'citoyen' of the French state should be treated equally, simply by virtue of his or her citizenship in the Republic, and irrespective of who he or she happens to be, is deeply embedded in the French psyche.

It is consequently viewed as important that new citizens should be educated in citizenship in order that they should properly understand their rights and duties and be able to meet their civic responsibilities in an informed manner, and French state education has always included civic education as a compulsory element in the national programmes of study.

English nationals remain technically 'subjects' of the monarch, and although parliamentary sovereignty is of course long established, English society continues to display a remarkable preoccupation with class-based cultures where distinctions of language, manners and self-presentational style retain considerable importance. While there may be similar concerns in both countries about the social attitudes and behaviour of young people, the cultural and historical references cited by policy-makers in each are different. Both may use the term 'citizenship', and 'citizenship education', but the nuances surrounding each expression are not the same. There has never been specific compulsory education for citizenship in England, but the idea has been very much at the forefront of educational policy discussion in the late 1990s. Nevertheless, there is a sense in which – through the broader medium of moral education, delivered through such practices as assemblies and religious education (both of which are unknown and actually forbidden by law in France) – English education delivers to children some forms of social learning which correspond to aspects of *l'education civique*. As Table 5.5 shows, however, the responses of pupil cohorts in both countries to these efforts are relatively lukewarm.

Table 5.5 *Perception of education for citizenship*

'In class I learn about what is expected of me as a future French/English citizen'

	Strongly agree %	Agree %	Disagree %	Strongly disagree %	Not sure %	No answer %
England	9	21	24	13	30	3
France	32	27	10	10	15	6

Only just over a half of French children think that they are being taught something which the French national curriculum treats as central to national educational provision. Nevertheless, this is almost twice as many who think they are being prepared for citizenship by English primary education, in a cohort where one-third were not sure whether they should agree or disagree. However, there is yet again the same general pattern of English 'spread' and a greater French 'definiteness'. The results of analysis by gender and social class follow the same format as for the whole cohort.

As with 'citizenship', so 'equality' is also a much-favoured term in current political and educational discourse in both England and France, but with somewhat different historical antecedents and cultural implications in each country. Formally at least, the equality of citizens has been the cornerstone of French political life for the past two centuries. Equality, especially as it applies to education, has really only been a major value in England in the post-war era following the 1944 Education Act and the concern to provide 'equality of opportunity'. As shown in Table 5.6, answers to the question of whether all citizens are equal in England/France displayed considerable uncertainty on both sides of the Channel.

There was little divergence from their respective national norms between the responses given by boys and girls, or by children in different socio-economic areas, in each sample. Whether the higher French figure actually reflects the higher profile of 'equality' in everyday discourse in France as described above is impossible to ascertain from a single statistic. The discussion below in the next section of pupils' open-ended responses does furnish clear evidence of a greater recourse by French pupils to standardized notions of the equality and liberty of the citizen. At the same time, though, this outcome could possibly be the same 'halo' phenomenon referred to earlier.

Table 5.6 *Perception of social equality as a cultural value*

'In France/England all citizens are equal'

	Strongly agree %	Agree %	Disagree %	Strongly disagree %	Not sure %	No answer %
England	12	20	25	16	25	2
France	27	14	14	20	22	3

SUMMARY DISCUSSION

Throughout the analysis of pupils' questionnaire responses to questions covering the three issues of national pride, identification and citizenship, one clear finding stands out which is of great significance: the influence of nationality takes precedence over other key social variables in determining patterns of responses. In all of the above findings, French girls were more like French boys in their answers than they were like English girls. Similarly pupils in disadvantaged areas in one country resembled more closely their advantaged compatriots than they did their socio-economic counterparts in the other country. With all the emphasis being given in the late twentieth century to internationalization and globalization, these findings present a salutary reminder that the nation state, at least in these two cases, continues to exert a powerful influence over hearts and minds, values and attitudes.

WHAT IS THERE TO BE PROUD OF?

Of course multiple-choice answers do not, as noted previously, reveal the thinking which lies behind the response given. For this reason, in addition to the multiple-choice questions detailed above, children were asked to write a response to the open-ended question:

A good reason for being proud of being English is ...
Cite une raison pour laquelle on peut être fier d'être français ...

Explaining quite why one feels pride in anything is not always easy, least of all for children, and during the process of questionnaire-design there was some apprehension on the part of the QUEST team that this question might not generate any particularly valuable or informative responses. However, despite all the difficulties that were apparent in asking children to write open-ended responses, even the sheer practical task of handwriting, let alone conceptualizing ideas about national pride, what this question produced unveiled fascinating insights into distinctly different ways of thinking about national identity in each of the two countries.

REASONS TO BE PROUD OF BEING FRENCH

In attempting to account for why they felt proud of being French, the majority of French children in the sample referred to one or more of four types of explanation:

- emotional attachment
- birthright
- French civilization
- historical glory.

Emotional attachment

By far the most common response written simply described loving the country. It was as if it were enough just to say that one loves one's country because one does. Love, as it were, has no reason beyond itself. It just is. One feels pride because one has this emotional attachment, and one has this emotional attachment because one feels pride. It is unproblematic, unconditional, obvious and taken for granted. Its very taken-for-grantedness makes it difficult to say anything more. Actual responses took the following forms:

> *parce que j'aime ce pays. Il y a tout*
> (because I love this country. There is everything)
>
> *parce que j'aime la France*
> (because I love France)
>
> *il y a beaucoup d'ambience et qu'il y a de beau paysage*
> (there's lots of atmosphere and there's beautiful countryside)
>
> *car on fait des chose intéressantes et c'est un beau pays*
> (because you do interesting things and it's a beautiful country)
>
> *pour notre beau pays*
> (for our beautiful country)
>
> *parce que c'est un beau pays*
> (because it's a beautiful country)
>
> *parce que c'est bien*
> (because it's great)
>
> *parce que les Français sont bien*
> (because the French are great)

Even where, in the above examples, writers have sought to add justification by supplying further information, this tended only to reinforce the basic sense of strong affection. The use of ideas of beauty ('*un beau pays*') to give further justification for loving the country actually already carries intrinsic connotations of emotional attachment. The notion of '*la belle France*' does not mean simply that geographically there are some beautiful views to be seen; rather this is beauty in the sense of 'inner radiance' conjuring up images of warmth, gentleness, loveliness, almost treating the country somehow anthropomorphically as a living being. There is a famous French popular song dating back to the 1940s whose popularity has reverberated down across the decades, '*Douce France, cher pays de mon enfance*', and which translates literally as 'Gentle France, dearest country of my childhood', but which in fact evokes a whole nostalgic world of 'Frenchness', a sort of constantly reminisced and reawakened dreamworld of happy memories, feelings and associations. It is to this sense of being at ease and comforted in the warm glow of reassuring familiarities that these sorts of response are keying in.

Birthright

These responses are equally unconditional, and implicitly assert the basic proposition that if one is born in a country one will naturally love it.

parce que je suis français(e)
(because I am French)

parce que je suis né(e) en France
(because I was born in France)

parce qu'on est né en France
(because you are born in France)

The position is analogous with children and their parents, who are loved because they are givens in the child's life as a result of the accident of birth. For these writers it just seems axiomatic that you love the country you were born in. Given, however, that so few of the English children assumed this to be so, it follows that the proposition cannot simply be taken at face value. Moreover, one does not necessarily just love one's parents because they are there. Usually the sense of love grows in response to the cherishing and nurturing that the child receives. Thus behind this second type of response probably lurks the same kind of sentimental attachment which underpinned the 'I love this country' first type of response. Some children also applied this principle to their town as a part of France,

parce que je suis Marseillais et que je suis né à Marseille
(because I am Marseillais and I was born in Marseilles)

which expresses exactly the same kind of a priori conviction.

French civilization

There was much evidence that French pupils had assimilated the language of liberty, equality and fraternity, although the emphasis was on the first two. The most striking response of this type was the following proud declaration:

car la France est un pays magnifique et démocratique et accueillant
(because France is a magnificent, democratic and welcoming country)

but this 'party manifesto'-style parading of key civic values was rare, and most responses were much less elaborate, although nonetheless still clearly imbued with the same ideological and textual style.

parce qu'ils sont tous égaux
(because they are all equal)

pour la liberté et l'égalité
(for freedom and equality)

parce qu'on est libre
(because we are free)

car la France est un pays libre, donc nous sommes libres
(because France is a free country, so we are free)

nous sommes tous égaux
(we are all equal)

In the survey questionnaire this open-ended question followed directly on from the multiple-choice questions which, as reported above, included the statement, 'In England/France all citizens are equal'. It could be said therefore that pupils who wrote the above responses were simply taking their cue from the research instrument. However, what is significant is that not a single English pupil sought to account for his or her national pride in terms of the equality of citizens, even though the prompt was just as much there on the paper in front of his or her eyes. This was a purely French conception. Here then is strong evidence of the phenomenon described by the Bristaix team (Broadfoot and Osborn, 1992), a distinctive ideology associated with a national context, the lexicon and discourse of which has been absorbed by individuals living within it. By 'absorbed' is meant not that these children understood fully what is involved in the liberty and equality of citizenship, but rather that they knew that these are the terms through which French adults express the special value of being French and living in France, and had at least begun the process of identifying themselves with them.

Historical glory

Some French pupils pointed to what might be called 'past glories', the idea that one can take pride in one's country because it has had a glorious history. Such responses included:

pour son histoire
(for its history)

pour savoir tout ce qui s'est passé en France
(to know everything which has happened in France)

pour les monuments crées en France comme la Tour Eiffel, l'Arc de Triomphe
(for the monuments created in France like the Eiffel Tower, the Arc de Triomphe)

These ideas can again at root be seen to be expressions of affection and attachment. As with the other three principal types of response, the fundamental idea is that the nation is an attractive collective being which one would want to be part of, and in this case the statement is extended back in time to imply that it has always been so.

Thus in one way or another, all the main forms of response written by French pupils create an image of France as something worthy of affection in and for itself, and the tone in which they are written is overwhelmingly expressive.

REASONS TO BE PROUD OF BEING ENGLISH

If the predominant tone of French responses can be characterized as expressive, the majority of English written responses adopted a decidedly instrumental tone. What obviously preoccupied the English children most were the practical benefits and advantages associated with the country. The principal kinds of explanation for a sense of national pride offered by English pupils could be characterized as:

- sporting prowess
- the English language
- pragmatic advantages
- evidence of superiority.

Sporting prowess

This was the most common approach taken by English pupils. What seemed to spring immediately to most minds, and this appeared to be so for both boys and girls, was English standing in sport, especially football. The reasoning seemed to be that the question required the identification of something which made England best in international comparision, and the obvious area would be internationally famous football teams. Examples included the following.

> because we have good football teams
> they are a very good football country
> what they have done at most sports
> we won the world cup in 1966

This appeal to international standing was sometimes linked with other areas too:

> Man Utd come from England, so do Eternal
> good music, good sports teams

What is particularly noteworthy here is the immediate appeal to things rather than feelings, and things which can be seen to make England great, rather than any assertion that greatness in whatever form naturally inheres in the country or the nation.

The English language

After football teams, the second most cited 'thing' which might be seen to justify English pride was the English language:

> English is a very well known language and it is known worldwide
> I can talk to people and they understand
> I know one language and no others
> you can talk to people in Great Britain easily

Here too, though, the emphasis is on practicalities rather than intrinsic value, beauty or wonder in the language itself. What impresses these writers is how useful it is that English is major world language.

Pragmatic advantages

It is in responses in this category that English pupils' predisposition to calculate the advantages and disadvantages of being English becomes particularly explicit and overt. Once again the bottom line seems to be responding to the question in terms of comparing England with other countries in an effort to show that it is 'better', and in this instance pointing up some conditions of life which are unequivocally better than in other countries:

> we are very lucky because we don't live in a poor country
> I don't live in slums like in Africa and we don't have a hard life
> you have pork, turkey, beef, chicken and lamb (a child who had lived in the Philippines where meat was expensive)
> we don't tolerate wars or fighting and you need a licence for a gun
> it's not too hot or cold
> we can have clean water and food to live on
> we have good computers
> English people are good and healthy

There is a sort of *Which?* magazine strategy being adopted here. These writers are essentially trying to justify their 'choice' of nationality in the way that any consumer might seek to defend his or her choice of car, television or personal computer. One informs oneself of the options and then plumps for the best deal offering the best value for money. Thus, looking around the world it seems fairly evident to these pupils that most other countries fail to provide the same material standard of living as is found in England, and it makes sense therefore to be English. This really appears to be more about being glad that one lives in England and grateful that one has not got to live elsewhere than being proud of being English, certainly than being proud of being English for its own sake. If a 1940s popular French song captured the continuing spirit of French *amour propre* in the minds of the QUEST pupils in Marseilles and Calais, it could be contended that for the English cohort the basis of national belonging is conjured up in nineteenth-century Gilbert and Sullivan where it is said of the hero of *HMS Pinafore* that 'resisting all temptations to belong to other nations he remains an Englishman'.

Evidence of superiority

Another 'thing' to which English pupils appealed in thinking about national pride was a motley catalogue of 'superior' facts about England. The burden of the argument here is much the same: compared with what's in other countries there are some remarkable things associated with England, and by associating myself with England I am associating myself with the kudos attaching to these things.

that we join in with most major worldwide matters
we have the hardest language
we haven't been invaded since 1066
Lots of special people come from England
We are a strong country for how small we are

At work in the reasoning behind these responses is still the weighing up of advantages and disadvantages, with the implication that these 'facts' warrant the imputation of superiority to England, by comparison with other countries.

SUMMARY DISCUSSION

The fundamental difference then between the English and the French responses to this question is that while in France the whole emphasis was on the intrinsic value which is assumed naturally to inhere in being French, in England there was an automatic assumption that national pride had to be justified by reference to something specific against which the English might be seen to be better than others. The idea that love of country might be some kind of natural response to being born there was scarcely in evidence among the English responses. Where any kind of reference of this sort was made, the terms in which it was expressed tended to be much less imbued with emotional engagement; for example:

because you belong to the country
being an independent country
I've been told about the country and that's where I come from
to be with your people

The mental set evoked in these statements still has more in common with the 'consumerist' approach outlined above than with the expressions of patriotic feeling found in the French responses. It essentially revolves around the notion of 'feeling comfortable' in England, feeling 'at ease' among your own kind, rather than being inspired to feelings of pride by the idea of being English. There was actually little reference made to the national 'icons' of England, and again where this *was* done, the tone was distinctly dispassionate.

because we have a good queen
we have pubs and good football teams

By contrast, where French responses pointed to 'external' references, such as sport, this would often be expressly linked with the writer's feelings:

d'aller au stade vélodrome pour voir l'OM (Olympique Marseille)
(to go to the stadium to see l'OM)

quand Marseille gagne
(when Marseilles wins)

quand un Français ou une Française gagne aux Jeux olympiques
(when a Frenchman or Frenchwoman wins in the Olympic Games)

This kind of comment draws attention to the 'collective sentiment' aspect of sport, the sensations felt when celebrating the achievement of the regional or national team. This basic difference of approach was further emphasized by the English pupils who specifically refused to acknowledge that there was any reason to be proud of being English:

> I don't want to do this question because there is no point. Being English makes no difference to me. If I was born French I wouldn't want to do this one either.

Some went further:

> I don't agree there is any good reason to be proud of being English
> I am not proud of being English because we have a bad reputation
> I am not proud of being English
> There is nothing to be proud of

The consumer can be seen here too, objectively detached, weighing up the available information, and deciding in this case that the 'product' is not good and not worth buying into. For particular reasons discussed earlier in the chapter some of the children from ethnic-minority backgrounds in both samples expressed negative views of the nation within which they were living:

> *Je ne suis pas fier parce que je suis Musulman*
> I am not proud (of being English) because I am a Muslim

> *Je ne suis pas fier parce que je suis Italien/Tunisien*
> (I am not proud because I am Italian/Tunisian)

> *Je ne suis pas très d'accord avec les Français* (child with Arabic name)
> (I am not very much in agreement with the French)

It is important to stress that these were minority views in both samples, even among children who were probably of ethnic-minority origin. The only indication of ethnic status available to the QUEST team was each child's name. Future comparative research focusing specifically on the attitudes towards national identity of ethnic-minority children living in England and France would certainly be very useful.

The fundamental contrasts in the experience of national pride articulated in the responses of the English and the French pupil samples in the QUEST survey, to both the multiple-choice questions subject to quantitative analysis and the open-ended question analysed qualitatively above can be considered in relation to a number of different orientational dimensions, as indicated in Table 5.7.

Table 5.7 *English and French pupils' attitudes to national pride*

	England	France
basic conception	location	collective identity
main orientation	objects/things/facts	emotions/feelings/ideas
attitude	problematic	unproblematic
commitment	conditional	unconditional
attachment	instrumental/extrinsic	expressive/intrinsic
engagement	dispassionate	fervent

For pupils in England, being English appears to be at root a matter of living in that country. England is a place, and if that is where you live then you are English. French pupils seem to be much more metaphysical, wrapped up in the idea of France as a collective identity and being French as incorporation within this overarching supra-individual entity. Asked to account for their feelings, English pupils typically refer to objects and facts, while French pupils talk about feelings and ideas, which of course is a much more difficult thing to do, and this may account for the higher rate of non-response to the open-ended question in the French sample. For the French children in the sample, being proud of being French is obvious and unproblematic, whereas the English children seemed to need to think about it, rationalize it and take nothing for granted. As a consequence, it is arguable that the English children's commitment is conditional, and the French children's commitment is unconditional. The English responses suggest an instrumental attachment, dependent upon the continuing flow of the good things which make living in England better than living anywhere else, these good things being extrinsic motivators to attachment in the sense that they are mainly material conditions rather than anything specifically 'English'. By contrast French children's attachment is expressive in the sense that it is based on emotion, and motivated by factors which are intrinsic to being French. While the French pupil sample's predominant style of engagement with being French might be characterized as 'fervent', the English pupils remain throughout typically 'dispassionate'.

The really interesting question, of course, is why such clear differences should exist. There is a great deal of evidence, both from the QUEST study reported in this book and in earlier work by QUEST team-members and other researchers, that the 'national contexts' of France and England are characterized by fundamentally different underlying value orientations, and that it is these which guide thought, action and all manner of taken-for-granted assumptions about the social world in which English and French adults and children live out their daily lives. The basic finding is inescapable: like the teachers in the Bristaix study (Broadfoot and Osborn, 1992), the pupils in the QUEST study responded for the most part according to whether they were English or French. This chapter has presented findings about systematically structured differences in attitudes to national identity. Other chapters in this book report similarly systematically-structured difference in attitudes to schooling and education. The results of this research strongly suggest that such attitudes are social phenomena, and not a matter of mere individual variation. Data analysed above indicate that even something as apparently 'personal' as feelings of pride in belonging to a nation actually varies not so much with the vagaries of personality and temperament as with which nationality an individual has been inducted into. National context appears thus in this arena also to exert a determining influence.

This is not to imply that circumstances do not change. It may well be that the inherent individualism of much English culture has been reinforced or sharpened by policy decisions taken over the past two decades, and that this has brought to the fore a more evident 'consumerist' approach in what may seem unlikely areas. The lesson though for policy-makers, in this area as in others, is that they disregard the implications of the national context at their peril. If the analysis presented above is correct, English children's sense of national pride will not metamorphose into something corresponding to the unconditional love of country apparent among the French pupils just by the introduction of lessons in citizenship, any more than their attitude to school will be made more positive by importing characteristic French teaching methods into English primary classrooms. To be effective, educational policies need to take account of the social realities which affect pupils' (and teachers') daily lived experience. This point will be developed further in the final chapter.

Chapter 6

Classroom Processes and Pupil Outcomes in English and French Primary Schools

One aim of the study was to examine the links between classroom processes and pedagogy, pupil motivation and attitudes to learning, and pupil achievement. In this chapter we first give an overall picture of the observed classroom processes, through systematic observation and field notes, and consider the relationship between these and pupil outcomes in relation to achievement and identity formation. Secondly we try to analyse some of the key differences we found with reference to Tonnies (1955) concepts of *Gesellschaft* and *Gemeinschaft*.

Although it would be unwise to generalize too much from a relatively small amount of classroom observation data, the research revealed some potentially important differences and similarities between the two countries. During the time they were observed, French children were more likely to be apparently 'task-engaged' in the classrooms studied (68 per cent compared with 57 per cent in England) with English children more likely to be apparently distracted (24 per cent compared with 13 per cent in France), as shown in Table 6.1. Children in both countries spent roughly the same amount of time 'managing tasks' such as collecting materials and resources and organizing their paper and books.

These significant differences in task engagement are likely to be associated to some extent with French pupils' typically higher levels of motivation across all types of schools (see Chapter 4). However, they are more strongly associated with the dominance of the teacher in the classroom setting. Teachers were actually 'instructing' (i.e. engaged with children directly on an area of the curriculum) for 33 per cent of the observed time, whereas teachers 'instructed' for only 20 per cent of the observed time in England, as shown in Table 6.3. Overall in England children spent 60 per cent of their time without directly interacting with the teacher, while children in France spent only 40 per cent of their time without some form of interaction with the teacher, a finding that reflects the ubiquitous use of the traditional French '*leçon*' which involves teacher-exposition followed by individual practice and a final whole-class evaluation and feedback session.

Table 6.1 *Child activity*

		Task-engagement	*Task-management*	*Distracted*	*Distracted and TM*	*Assessment (explicit)*	*Waiting for teacher*	*Waiting for other*	*Out of room/ sight*	*Reading to teacher*	*TOTAL*	*%*
England	N	3,078	772	1,282	21	0	47	131	31	38	5,400	53.6
	%	57.0	14.3	23.7	0.4	0.0	0.9	2.4	0.6	0.7	100.0	
France	N	3,184	631	628	47	0	86	83	21	0	4,680	46.4
	%	68.0	13.5	13.4	1.0	0.0	1.8	1.8	0.4	0	100.0	
Total	N	6,262	1,403	1,910	68	0	133	214	52	38	10,080	100.0
	%	62.1	13.9	18.9	0.7	0.0	1.3	2.1	0.5	0.4	100.0	

Table 6.2 *Child interaction*

		Alone	*With teacher whole-class*	*With teacher one-to-one*	*With teacher in group*	*Other adult one-to-one*	*With indiv: girl*	*With indiv: boy*	*With group of boys*	*With group of girls*	*With mixed group*	*TOTAL*	*%*
England	N	0	1,450	176	201	71	476	329	61	109	95	2,968	49.3
	%	0.0	48.9	5.9	6.8	2.4	18.6	11.1	2.1	3.7	3.2	100.0	
France	N	0	2,325	71	161	1	86	168	34	30	176	3,052	50.7
	%	0.0	76.2	2.3	5.3	0.0	2.8	5.5	1.1	1.0	5.8	100.0	
Total	N	0	3,775	247	362	72	562	497	95	139	271	6,020	100.0
	%	0.0	62.7	4.1	6.0	1.2	9.3	8.3	1.6	2.3	4.5	100.0	

Conversely there was more child-to-child interaction in England (39 per cent of observed time compared with 16 per cent in France) and more of this child-to-child interaction was gender-based in England, as shown in Table 6.2. Pupils were likely to be task-engaged more in France because the teacher was in direct interaction with them more often. This was relatively easy for teachers in France to maintain because of the prevalence of whole-class teaching methods, as Table 6.4 shows (62 per cent of observed time in France compared with 39 per cent in England), whereas English children spent a greater proportion of their time working individually (51 per cent against 34 per cent in France) and on group work (8 per cent compared with 0.8 per cent in France, which helps to explain some of the higher child-to-child interaction). Typically in France, children were not encouraged to interact with their peers while working, whereas in England such interaction was tolerated and sometimes encouraged, depending on the nature of the task.

However, task-engagement was not directly associated statistically for individual pupils with whole-class teaching. We tested the hypothesis that for the same individual pupils there would be differences in pupil activity according to pedagogic context (i.e. differences in the proportion of time they appeared task-engaged compared with the amount of time they were distracted or managing tasks, according to whether whole-class teaching, group work or individual work was taking place). In England there were no significant differences in pupil activity according to pedagogic context (Kruskal-Wallis ANOVA). In France also, most of the differences were non-significant, but when pupils were working individually, significantly higher levels of apparent distractedness were observed, compared with those levels of distractedness observed in whole-class and group-work contexts. This appears to suggest that it is the typical dominance of the teacher in the French classroom setting rather than a high level of intrinsic motivation, which keeps pupils apparently on task. It also suggests that more whole-class teaching in England would not necessarily result in a higher level of apparent pupil task-engagement.

Pupil perceptions from the questionnaire data confirmed the classroom observation data. English pupils were more likely to say that they felt free to move around the classroom (61 per cent compared to 34 per cent of French pupils) and 43 per cent of them said that they spent much of their time sitting quietly, compared to 73 per cent of French pupils. More French pupils also thought that they spent their time listening and watching the teacher (French pupils 89 per cent, English pupils 67 per cent) and answering teachers' questions (French pupils 89 per cent, English pupils 67 per cent). English pupils thought it was important to have a teacher who spoke clearly, while French pupils thought it was particularly important to have a teacher who wrote clearly, possibly reflecting the preponderance of blackboard work in French teaching.

Perhaps more important than these bare figures, however, is the nature and content of the interaction between teacher and pupil, as illustrated by the following example on p. 95.

These brief extracts from two lessons, one English and one French, illustrate the profound ideological and culturally-rooted differences of pedagogical approach

Table 6.3 *Teacher activity*

		Instruction (curriculum)	Control (behaviour)	Direction (TM)	Assessment (explicit)	Encouragement (support, facil.)	Negative (discour, crit)	Hearing children read	Other	No recorded observation	TOTAL	%
England	N	1,090	128	467	120	191	17	124	21	3,242	5,400	53.6
	%	20.2	2.4	8.6	2.2	3.5	0.3	2.3	0.4	60.0	100.0	
France	N	1,559	152	413	164	83	45	98	287	1,879	4,680	46.4
	%	33.3	3.2	8.8	3.4	1.8	1.0	2.1	6.1	40.1	100.0	
Total	N	2,649	280	880	284	274	62	222	308	5,121	10,080	100.0
	%	26.3	2.8	8.7	2.8	2.7	0.6	2.2	3.1	50.8	100.0	

Table 6.4 *Main pedagogic context*

		Class teaching	Individual work	Cooperative group	Group with teacher	Other	TOTAL	%
England	N	58	76	10	2	4	150	53.6
	%	38.7	50.7	6.7	1.3	2.7	100.0	
France	N	80	44	1	5	0	130	46.4
	%	61.5	33.8	0.8	3.8	0.0	100.0	
Total	N	138	120	11	7	4	280	100.0
	%	49.3	42.9	3.9	1.4	1.4	100.0	

between the two countries. The French teacher's goal is that pupils should master the material being taught; the English teacher's emphasis is on encouraging the children to think for themselves and on the promotion of understanding and knowledge through problem solving.

English maths lesson on area of polygons:

This is not so much a lesson as a direction of tasks for the children to do. The children work on their own. The teacher tells them 'you can talk to each other to help each other'. The children swap books to mark the first bit – so some ensuing discussion. The teacher moves around helping individuals. She gives encouragement and practice feedback. The children are doing maths work on area and angles. Children measure different angles then move to the teacher's instruction on angles. There is a switch from individual work, with the teacher helping and working with individuals, to whole-class teacher instruction; some children are not listening but continuing with own work. The class lesson follows on. The teacher brings a boy to the front and makes him stretch his arms out. She moves him round 90°/180°, etc. Children volunteer to move him. Then other children put up their hands if they agree/disagree with the moves made.

French maths lesson:

Without explanation or contextualization the teacher launches into the process of multiplying decimals by 1000. The usual procedure is employed (Procédé La Martinière) – they have to listen (raising their arms) to the question, e.g. 3.3 × 1000, then the teacher thumps the table. The pupils write the answer privately in silence on their little slates and wait. The teacher thumps again and they have to hold up their answers. After all slates have been checked by the teacher walking up and down the rows the order is given to wipe the slates clean and another thump is given to the teacher's desk. Next question and so on. Wrong answers treated as an outrage to be harshly criticized. A little later, one child is sent to the board to write '*le titre de la leçon*' – proportionality. The teacher refers to four situations involving proportionality in earlier lessons. The teacher questions pupils on how much they remember; a lot of this is inviting pupils to join in orally, e.g. '*on multiplie par le même nombre*' ('we multiply by the same number'). This all refers to p. 158 of the CM2 manual. All attention is directed to p. 159. One child reads aloud and the rest follow. The teacher questions in order to ensure that the pupils understand what is required at the CM2 level. '*Allez, on se met au travail*' ('Let's get on with the work'). Class descends into silent concentration.

This example illustrates the clear link found in the research between national attitudes to the role of education, teachers' pedagogic approaches and pupils' learning outcomes. In the French case we found that for the majority of the time the majority of the teachers observed continued to organize their lessons around the concept of *la leçon*. Although this word looks like a direct equivalent of its English counterpart, it does in fact have a quite precise connotation, describing a sequence of events which characterize a teaching episode in French schooling. It is possible to identify eight stages in the process as shown below.

La leçon
Stage 1: introduction and presentation of principles/formulae
Stage 2: work on practice of principles/formulae
Stage 3: collective correction of work

Stage 4: the *leçon* – writing of rules and 'points de repère' (key points to be remembered)

Stage 5: learning/memorizing the *leçon* (often as homework)

Stage 6: *contrôles* – formal written tests of knowledge

Stage 7: collective correction of *contrôles*

Stage 8: recording and reporting of pupils' results

Our observations, both quantitative and qualitative, point to a possible association between the French teacher's dominance in the traditional *leçon*, with its emphasis on repetition until each principle is thoroughly learned, and the success of French pupils in computational skills where thorough rehearsal and practice may be important and the aim is that all pupils are brought to a common level of understanding. Conversely, the observation and achievement data together suggest that English pupils who are expected to work more on their own and are given more differentiated work may, as a result, be in a better position to develop problem-solving strategies in maths and creativity in writing – where these pupils are likely to be encouraged and less likely to be shouted at or told off if they get things wrong. However, they may be in a worse position when tackling such tasks as computation if they have not been as thoroughly grounded in skills for tackling these as French children are.

For example, Tall (1993/1996, cited in Harries and Sutherland, 1998) argued that children who fail in mathematics are often actually carrying out a more difficult maths than those who succeed. Lower-attaining pupils in both Tall's study and in our analysis of English pupils were more likely to use primitive mathematical objects and primary processes, for example counting to solve addition problems, or repeated addition to solve problems which could be more effectively solved using multiplication. In Tall's view those pupils who work in this way are consistently carrying out more time-consuming work than other pupils and may be more likely to struggle as a result. The crucial argument for this analysis seems to be that some of this approach may be taught to pupils through classroom teaching or through textbooks, but that, failing this, pupils left to work alone may struggle unnecessarily to work through procedurally as described above. Harries and Sutherland suggest that textbooks in England and possibly also maths teaching does not pay enough attention to the use of all forms of external representation as discussed by Tall. They conclude that:

> English pupils are often introduced to a wide variety of mathematical ideas and ways of solving problems without being presented with any support to make links between these ideas. We conjecture that when this approach is used it must be very difficult for all but the most exceptional pupils to make sense of and thus learn mathematics (Harries and Sutherland, 1998).

Overall our research suggested that in English classrooms the teacher typically made much more effort than was observed in France to motivate children through arousing their interest in the topic being taught and avoiding negative feedback. Teachers were concerned that pupils should feel psychologically comfortable at school and saw this as a precondition of effective learning. Several teachers observed use friendship as the basis of grouping within the class. In the course of interview discussions one commented that:

> the main priority is to provide a warm environment which the children feel safe to learn in, to encourage respect for themselves and for others, to provide the means for education basically.

Another observed:

> I let them choose who they sit with. I would rather they were happy than anything else. I do tell them they stay there as long as they are working; if their work starts to suffer one has to move. This tends to work.

The English teachers tended to spend most time having the pupils work in groups. French teachers tended to spend most of the time teaching the whole class. The very different kinds of pedagogic regime, class and school environment typical of each country were, as indicated in previous chapters, associated with contrasting typical pupil outcomes in terms of attitude, identity and achievement. Some of the key issues to emerge from this are discussed below in the context of specific pupils whom we profiled. A sample of detailed profiles is given in Chapter 9.

FEELINGS ABOUT SCHOOLS, CLASSES AND TEACHERS

As indicated in Chapter 4, despite experiencing classrooms which were typically more formal and authoritarian, French primary children appeared to be much more positive and enthusiastic about their schooling and their teachers. They saw their teachers as helpful and useful to them and wanted the teacher to make them work to achieve known learning goals. The French children emphasized the role of school as a place where you worked or should work hard (Ahmed, Ludovic: his ideal school '*c'est des maîtresses qui font travailler*'). They stressed the role of the teacher as an educator (Jean: '*le maître veut que ... je travaille bien*'; Ludovic: a good teacher '*devrait travailler un peu plus*'; Corinne: a good teacher should '*apprendre aux enfants des choses bien come lire, écrire*').

English pupils, on the other hand, tended to advocate the social role of school. School was a place of learning but also provided a setting for relationships with other children and with adults (Tina and Sandra: 'the teacher wants us all to ... get on with each other'). The teacher was seen not only as transmitting knowledge but also as someone who should help children in a more general way (Timothy: 'a good teacher should be nice as well as teaching something'; Ronald: teachers should be 'kind and loving, help you in any way ...'; Tim: teachers should 'teach children ... They have to be also kind'; John: teachers should be 'nice, kind ... and make sure the children are doing their work'; Richard: a good school should provide 'lots of things that make us happy').

POSITION IN SCHOOL

When children were asked how well they thought they were doing in school, most English pupils were not able to give their position, as they are not normally told this information. However, this did not mean that they were not aware of their general level of achievement in individual subjects, in particular English and maths (Richard: 'I'm not too good in maths. I'm doing all right in my English'; John: 'I'm doing well in my maths'; Sandra thinks that she is hopeless at maths and English; Tim: 'I'm good at some maths and not so good at English sometimes'). This might not always have been an accurate reflection of their standard, and their view of their overall achievement was generally impressionistic (Christine: 'I think I'm in the middle'; Eloise: 'I think I'm doing quite well'). This can be explained in the way their work is marked, with ticks, levels, comments. Most children also mentioned parents' evenings and reports as a way of knowing what their level was.

In contrast, most French children knew precisely what their position was. Even if it was not officially stated on their report, they had a more accurate measure of their achievement through marks and averages (Marcel: *'je suis dans les cinq derniers, à peu près 24ème'*, his last average was 3.22 out of 10; Odile: 9th out of 28 and her average was 7.35 out of 10; Jean: *'moi, j'ai eu 6,4* (out of 10) *et je suis dans les bons'*).

But all children, regardless of nationality, were aware of who the best and the worst pupils were in their class. They could work it out by asking their friends what their marks were or how they had been doing in their tests.

ROLE OF SCHOOL IN THE PUPILS' FUTURE

A larger proportion of French pupils had a more definite idea of the role that school might play in their future. They were more aware of progression through school and of the need to achieve a certain standard in order to move on to the next class. *'Redoublement'*, repeating a year, was known to be the sanction if you failed to reach a given level (Corinne: *'ce que je veux c'est … ne plus redoubler'*; Marcel: *'je voudrais passer toutes mes classes'*).

French girls, in particular, stressed the importance of a good education leading to a better job (Corinne: *'si je veux rentrer à la fac il faut que je m'accroche'*; Anais: *'j'espère pouvoir continuer mes études et faire un travail dans la médecine'*: Jeanne: *'je voudrais avant tout passer mon bac pour être pharmacien'*).

English pupils were also conscious of the part that school would play in their future, but in a more diffuse, less specific way (John: 'I can see myself doing lots of tests and exams'; Sandra: 'I want good marks in my SATS so I can get to a good college'; Tina: 'I will go to college and I will get a job').

IMPORTANT SUBJECTS

Nearly all English and French pupils recognized the importance of language, English or French, and maths in the curriculum (Corinne: '*le français ... pour s'exprimer ... pour bien savoir parler*'; Jeanne: '*le calcul ... il faut savoir compter*'; Ludovic: '*le français, pour pas faire des fautes, pour mieux parler, pour mieux écrire, pour savoir mieux lire*'; Francesca: '*les mathématiques ... pour plus tard*'; Tim: 'you learn to count in maths ... and ... because you learn to read and write (in English)'; John: 'because you use words a lot ... and ... maths helps you with your numbers'; Sandra: 'because when you get older ... you (have to) add up ... and people (have to) understand what you're writing'; Eloise: 'English, so if you're writing to someone important they understand it ... and maths, because it could help you in the future').

LANGUAGE

As the analysis of pupil strategies in language has already revealed, English pupils showed better inferential skills in the reading comprehensions. This was particularly true of pupils from areas of higher socio-economic status such as Eloise and Tim. By contrast, French pupils even from higher socio-economic zones showed poor levels of inferential skills.

French pupils were also outperformed by English pupils in the set grammar test. English pupils, from areas of low socio-economic status in particular, did consistently better than their equivalent counterparts in France – Timothy, Sandra, John and Richard in England in comparison to Francesca, Ahmed, Marcel and Jean in France.

English pupils tended to think more independently and to produce more imaginative stories, not necessarily better spelt or structured. French children conformed more to a given pattern, often modelling their writing on the traditional European folk tale or fairy tale. These findings are explored in greater depth in Chapter 7.

MATHEMATICS

In mathematics, French pupils demonstrated higher levels of competence in computation, in particular for subtraction, multiplication and division.

The analysis of problem-solving skills showed that English pupils were more willing to take risks and to think independently and that they were more likely to use non-standard methods of calculation such as tallies or repeated addition, although these were not always efficient. These findings are discussed at greater length in Chapter 8.

LOW ACHIEVERS

There were striking differences between the lower-achieving case study pupils in the two countries. It was noticeable that, like all the French children, the lower-achieving pupils in France had a clear notion of school as providing them with a ladder of progress through the educational system and into future careers. Even Anais, one of the lowest achievers, stated this clearly as did Marcel: *'mais maintenant c'est pas facile la vie ... pour avoir tout ce que je veux il faut que je me mette au travail'*. (But life is not easy nowadays ... to have all I want I need to get to work now.) All the low-achieving children had a clear idea that it was important for them to study for and pass the baccalauréat (equivalent of A Levels). In contrast, most of the low-achieving children in England did not see school as playing much of a part in their future lives. For many of the English lower-achieving pupils, one of the main purposes of school was to provide an environment where pupils could be happy. In France, by contrast, even the lower-achieving children, like most of the rest of the sample, had a strong awareness of school as a place where pupils had to work hard and make an effort. These findings demonstrate the significant and different impact of the national context on pupils' attitudes to school and to their learning.

CLASSROOM PROCESSES AND THE EXPERIENCE OF SCHOOLING

The pupil achievement and academic learning outcomes referred to above are analysed in greater detail in the chapters which follow. The remainder of this chapter is concerned with attempting to locate the defining differences between the two systems in terms of characteristic social processes in contrasting classroom environments which seem to us to match quite closely Tonnies' well known distinction between 'Gemeinschaft' and 'Gesellschaft', often rendered in English as 'Community' and 'Association'. Tonnies was attempting at the turn of the twentieth century to articulate the essential qualitative difference in social relationships between forms of interaction based on 'given' networks, such as families and small communities, and those based on more formal structures such as commercial organizations and bureaucracies.

At the level of the school and its constituent classroom social processes it is possible to see in England something akin to Gemeinschaft with a focus on social cohesion and integration, and in France something approaching Gesellschaft where the predominant focus is on goal achievement. While it is undeniable that schools in both systems have elements of both types of social organization, our findings indicate that there is a clear difference in the balance between the two: while English primary schools do clearly have orientations towards goal achievement, much of the discourse and activity is actually directed toward establishing an integrated community of persons; similarly, while in France teachers and pupils do develop enduring social relationships, these are overtly organized around, and largely instrumental to, the pursuit of public, defined specific goals. We would wish to argue on the basis of the evidence presented in this book that the predominance of Gemeinschaft in English primary education and of Gesellschaft in French primary education is related to the institutionalized value orientations embedded in the two national contexts discussed in Chapter 3.

GEMEINSCHAFT: ENGLISH PRIMARY SCHOOLS AND THE FOCUS ON
SOCIAL INTEGRATION

Holistic conception of school

School is perceived as a community in itself where children live and work as full
persons 'in the round'. The personalities, characters and temperaments of everyone in
the school (including secretarial, technical and administrative personnel) are
acknowledged, discussed openly, and woven into the fabric of daily life. Their
family and other relationships outside school are considered important matters which
can be legitimately discussed inside the school. As a community the school is
expected to care about and care for the people whose daily lives are lived out within
it. One English pupil told us clearly 'a good teacher should look after people'.

Concern with individuality

Individual differences are celebrated and responded to. There is less easy recourse to
assigning individuals to categoric types than was apparent in French primary
schools. English teachers seemed to be constantly interested in the behaviour of
children as individuals. One English teacher, in the course of an interview, noted:

> We were talking about the Hebrides and the island of Eriskay, and two boys today
> borrowed the atlas on this desk and found the Inner and Outer Hebrides on the map and
> were very excited about it. They were so interested.

Expectation that teachers should 'understand' pupils

Pupils expect teachers to know what they are like as 'people' and to take account of
this in their interaction with them. Teachers believe that they need to know their
pupils thoroughly in order to teach them effectively. In describing her relationship
with the children in her class, one English teacher commented:

> We go through phases where I think they are wonderful and other times I feel I really
> have to moan a lot. They go through phases too, when their attitude seems better than at
> other times. They seem to be affected by the weather badly and this affects us all. I like to
> think I have a good relationship with them but I don't want to be too presumptuous. I
> do try [to] treat them as human beings. I am not sure if some parents do that. Some
> children need so much attention, they don't know how to relate in a non-violent way. I
> think some of them are happier at school than they are at home. I like to try [to] meet
> them halfway.

Pupils more readily develop positive self-concept with regard to teacher's perceived ideal

Because the English primary teachers' typical view of an ideal pupil is embedded in
the Gemeinschaft spirit of 'wholeness' and incorporates wide personal and social

behavioural characteristics as well as achievement criteria, pupils have more opportunity to develop a positive sense of their school self. Thus, even where they have a view of themselves as not doing very well, they may still feel that their teacher values them as a 'person' who has a place within the classroom and school community. One English teacher having described a 'below-average' pupil who 'wanders around the classroom wasting time often' commented that 'I feel he gets compared unfavourably to his brother a lot, and I feel that is why there are problems ... he can be kind, considerate and sensitive.'

Perception that teachers judge pupils by personal and social characteristics

English teachers expect, and are expected by the pupils themselves, to assess pupils as moral agents within a local social setting, as whole people rather than just as pupils engaged in academic learning. Much of the evidence of pupil attitudes presented in this chapter and elsewhere in the book testifies to this concern for a broad basis of personal judgement. However, one part of our evidence is particularly illuminating. Within the pupil interviews we showed the pupil groups a picture of a teacher apparently remonstrating with a pupil and asked them to tell us what they thought was going on. The picture is shown below.

Characteristic French responses to this situation were concerned with failure in academic classroom learning, whereas English responses tended to focus on behavioural issues. The following French response is typical of many.

L'élève sait pas ses leçons. Il a mal écrit ou il a fait des fautes. Il a écrit des bêtises.
(The pupil has not learnt his lessons. He has written something badly or made mistakes.
He has written something stupid.)

The dialogue below between two English pupils and the interviewer illustrates typical
English approaches.

P1: I think that he's misbehaved. And she's just about to punish him.
P2: He's being told off.
P1: He could have flung pencils across the room, been fighting, bullying, not doing his
work properly.
P2: Writing on books.
Interviewer: Not his books – other people's books – right?
P1: Painting on the walls. Eating in class.
Interviewer: What do you think the teacher is saying?
P1: Things like, 'don't ever do it again and your punishment is ...'
P2: And if he'd been painting on the wall or drawing on books, 'you have to rub it all off
or buy them a new one'. Or if he's been eating other people's packed lunches, 'give them
yours'.

Throughout the French responses there were many references to concepts such as
faults, mistakes, errors, all of which are directed towards the idea that teachers get
cross when a mistake is made in class. In the English responses the predominant idea
is that teachers get cross when children misbehave knowing that this is something
they should not do. This emphasis on behaviour was apparent also in answer to the
questionnaire question about what a good teacher expects of a new pupil. English
responses stressed personal characteristics.

'the teacher would like a new pupil to be good, well-behaved, well-mannered, who is
always helpful and polite'
'the teacher would like a new pupil to be a nice and kind person who would get on with
the other children'
'the teacher would like a new pupil to be generous, quiet, obedient, hardworking and get
most of the tasks done on time'.

Expectation that teacher control strategies should be humanistic and personalized and directed to all aspects of school life

It follows from the 'holistic' conception of school and the emphasis on individual
personality that teacher control strategies should be predominantly focused on
humanistic and personalized forms of behaviour management. English primary
teachers considered themselves responsible for behaviour in all aspects of school life
throughout the school day, in class time and during periods of recreation. English
pupils shared this expectation and similarly based on personal characteristics their
assessments of what makes a good teacher.

'a good teacher should be nice and kind to you and doesn't shout'
'a good teacher should be nice, kind and friendly ... he would like a new child to be
good, polite and well-mannered'

'a good teacher should be kind, make you giggle, give you work you like, does not shout a lot and is never upset'.

Expectation that learning should be fun

Given the preoccupation with personality and relationships to be found in English primary schools it is unsurprising that both teachers and pupils expect that learning should be framed within a context which engenders motivation, interest and a commitment of the self. English pupils declared that,

'Children learn better if the teacher is interesting and makes it fun. If a teacher is really really strict it makes the child hate school, so they won't learn anything'
'a good teacher should be amusing and fun to have as a teacher'
'a good teacher should do interesting and fun work with us'.

Greater breadth in the 'content' of schooling

While the heyday of thematic teaching based on 'topics' in English primary schools is long gone, and the pantheon of the National Curriculum forms the inescapable reference point for both teachers and pupils in thinking about the 'content' of schooling, there remains nevertheless a broader approach in England than in France. This greater breadth operates at two levels. In relation to the curriculum as a whole there is a greater scope of coverage, and it is arguable that – since the Dearing reforms which reduced the amount of prescribed content and also made available time to be used as schools deemed fit in their particular local circumstances – the possibility exists for schools to return to something more or less similar to the pre-1988 consensus on a 'broad and balanced' primary curriculum. Even in the era of the prescribed literacy and numeracy hours which absorb ten hours per week there is considerable time available after statutory requirements have been met. At another level a broad view is also implied in the way that overarching terms are used in an undifferentiated way. It is interesting that in our review of pupils' written and oral responses it was clear that while English pupils almost universally did 'English', French pupils did not do 'French'. Almost universally though, what they did do was *conjugaison, grammaire, vocabulaire, expression écrite, orthographe* (conjugations, grammar, vocabulary, written expression, spelling), each of which had quite specific and uniform meanings in all the sample schools.

Acceptance of differences in ability as the explanation for differential achievement

Differential achievement was in both countries perceived to be due to varying levels of ability and varying degrees of effort. However the balance between these two was typically seen to be different in our two sample national populations. In England, because of the greater focus on individual differences, there was more recourse to notions of limitations on natural ability. For example, in discussing the different groups within her class one English pupil observed, 'Yellow group's the lowest, and some of them don't do very well. They try as hard as they can but ...' In France, however, the most common approach taken by pupils in addressing the question of why children don't learn was to refer to lack of effort. Typical observations were, '*il n'écoute pas la maitresse ...*', '*il fait des bêtises*', '*il ne fait pas ses devoirs ...*' (he doesn't listen to the teacher, he plays the fool, he doesn't do his homework).

Judgements of schooling focus more on community, environmental, social and behavioural aspects

English pupils seemed orientated towards the 'community' aspect of education in assessing whether theirs was a good school. Characteristic observations included:

'I think my school is good because it is jolly and bright'
'our school is a good school because there are kind teachers and a good headmaster'
'... because it has a swimming pool'
'... because we have got grounds and another playground with a monkey frame and tunnels'
'a good school is having lots of things to do, everybody happy and everybody being nice to each other'
'it is not a good school, it is full of bullying'
'I don't like this school a lot because it is noisy and people get beaten up'

This kind of comment contrasted sharply with the French pupils' much greater emphasis on a good school as one where learning is successful. '*Les maîtresses nous expliquent ...*', '*les maîtresses sont sérieuses ...*', '*on arrive à comprendre*', '*nous on fait plus de devoirs*'. ('The teachers explain things to us ...', 'the teachers take their work seriously ...', 'we manage to understand', 'we do more homework'.)

GESELLSCHAFT: FRENCH PRIMARY SCHOOLS AND THE FOCUS ON DEFINED GOAL ACHIEVEMENT

Utilitarian conception of school

School is conceived of as an agency through which pupils receive an entitlement accorded to all as of right. Its prime purpose and its *raison d'être* are focused on the delivery of this defined uniform service. Teachers, pupils and parents have a common expectation that school will equip children with basic skills and knowledge. In writing about good schools and good teachers French pupils in our sample made clear their view that they expected to be taught. A good teacher for example should 'explain things so that we learn the things we don't know', '*un bon maître explique pour qu'on apprenne des choses que nous ne connaissons pas*'.

Little expectation that learning will be intrinsically interesting, enjoyable or relevant

French children in our samples expected that lessons would involve effort and hard work. They typically did not expect lessons to be 'fun' or to be of immediate relevance to their lives outside school. Pupils thought that teachers would expect them to leave their own immediate concerns and interests in order to follow the teacher's instructions whether they thought this would be enjoyable or not. In answering the question about what a teacher would be looking for in a new pupil the following response represented many, *que j'écoute ce qu'il a dit et que je répond aux questions qu'il a posé* ('that I listen to what he says and that I answer the questions he has asked').

Strong orientation to the future, later stages of schooling, and occupational success

It was clear that French children had a much greater consciousness of their place in the national system of schooling and understood more acutely how their performance at any stage of primary schooling would affect their progress through the various stages of secondary schooling. In the face of the evidence we collected, we developed the concept of 'the ladder of progress' to denote the taken-for-granted background to so much pupil thinking about education among our French sample. This concept is discussed in detail elsewhere in this book, but it is important here to note that by comparison with the English sample who seemed much more to inhabit a primary school world focused on the themes of childhood, French pupils were much more orientated towards the future, and were more aware of the link between the acquisition of basic skills and knowledge and future occupational success.

In talking, for example, about why certain subjects were more important than others, one French pupil commented, '*conjugaison ... pour plus tard ... quand on veut copier ... quand on veut faire une lettre. Orthographe ... pour pas faire de fautes. Calcul ... pour savoir compter ... quand on fait du travail ... si on est docteur ... quand on fait des billets ... des trucs ...*' ('Conjugations ... for later ... when you want to copy ... when you want to do a letter ... Spelling, so you don't make any mistakes. Arithmetic ... to know how to count ... when you do some work, if you are a doctor, when you make out notes and things ...').

Teachers expected to exert authority and to teach what it is necessary to learn

French pupils did not expect teachers to be personally nice or friendly. They expected them to be in authority and to make them learn. They did not expect teachers to form personal relationships with them. French pupils wrote of a good teacher that '*un bon maître devrait être respecté*', '*un bon maître devrait faire de bons exercices*', '*un bon maître devrait être gentil quand il faut et méchant quand il faut*', '*un bon maître devrait faire travailler les élèves*' ('a good teacher should be respected', 'a good teacher should give good exercises for us to do', 'a good teacher should be kind when it's necessary and hard when it's necessary', 'a good teacher should make the pupils work hard').

Perception that teachers are concerned with academic work rather than personal, social or behavioural characteristics of pupils

French children rarely referred to personal characteristics in talking or writing about their conception of a teacher. They thought that what teachers wanted was *de bonnes notes … pas d'erreurs à l'expression écrite et dans les mathématiques … Ils cherchent les fautes d'orthographe, les fautes dans la dictée. Ils veulent qu'on explique bien … qu'on comprenne bien, qu'on soit attentif dans le travail, qu'on écrit les phrases avec soin … un élève qui ne se lève pas de sa chaise* (good marks … no mistakes in written expression and in mathematics. They look for spelling mistakes, mistakes in dictation. They want us to explain clearly, to understand well, to pay attention to our work, and to write sentences carefully, … a pupil who does not get up out of his chair). By contrast, one of the English pupils we interviewed told us in a typical response that teachers liked 'well-behaved children who are polite and hardworking. And also children that aren't forever working, who can have fun as well. Mrs S and Mrs X are like that as well'.

Pupils know precisely how they are doing without reference to self-esteem

English pupils tended to be much vaguer about how they were doing in school. There is no corresponding English equivalent to the French stages of schooling and English teachers seemed to be more anxious to protect children's sense of achievement and self-esteem. One English pupil told us, 'sometimes she puts a little H with a circle, and that means that you've done it really well, the H is for a house point … And she puts remarks in our books. If we've been good, we get these little small notes which go home to our parents saying that we've done well and if we've done really well, in assembly we can get a medal or a certificate.' During another interview with English pupils we were told,

> Pupil: I think I'm doing quite well.
> Interviewer: Have you got any idea whether you're top of the class, middle of the class ….
> Pupil: No, probably about the middle.

The French pupils in our sample, however, all knew that what mattered were the grades, *on sait avec les notes*, you know (where you are) by the marks.

> *Moi, je suis quatrième … quand on a reçu le contrôle.*
> *Si on a des mauvaises notes on voit qu'on travaille mal.*
> *Des fois le maître il écrit très bien, bien, travail propre, assez bien, vu, mal écrit, travail pas.*
> (I'm fourth … when we got the test back.
> If you get bad marks you know you're working badly.

Some times the teacher writes very good, good, neat work, fairly good, seen, badly written, work not done.)

Also very common in France was the practice of giving *classements*, a rank order of pupils based on an aggregated grade made up of all the marks gained during a given period. *Il y a un classement ... on en a déjà eu trois ... il y en aura à peu près six.* (There is a rank order ... we have already had three ... there will be six of them.) Even where teachers did not formally construct *un classement*, the pupils knew how to work it out for themselves: *Pour trouver la moyenne générale on additionne les contrôles puis on divise* (To find the overall average you add up all the test marks and then you divide).

Pupil satisfaction linked to evidence of achievement

While there was a stress on pupils being happy in English primary schools, in French primary schools 'having a good day' tended more often to be linked to getting good marks in tests. The following two contrasting responses symbolize the difference we found to be quite widespread between the two national pupil samples. Talking about a 'good' day at school, an English pupil told us,

Pupil: It was last week ... cos I was doing really well and I was allowed to do jobs for the teacher. I like to do art with another teacher and that was when I got a certificate.
Interviewer: For being helpful or for organizing it?
Pupil: For organization, good work and helpfulness and kindness to my friends.

For a French pupil, though, the best day was,

C'est quand j'ai eu un 20 en orthographe et puis quand on a un bon classement et quand on dit que je travaille bien ... quand j'arrive à faire un exercice.
(It's when I got a 20 in spelling and when you get a good position in class and when they say I am doing good work ... when I manage to get an exercise right.)

Greater readiness to attribute failure to lack of effort

French pupils in our sample tended to explain school failure in terms of poor application and effort. In trying to account for why some pupils do better than others, French pupils did not have an equivalent vocabulary of terms based on ability, and tended not to describe their peers as bright, clever, intelligent, thick, dim, etc. but refered instead to effort, determination, perseverence, distraction, inattention, etc.

Peut-être qu'ils apprennent mieux leurs leçons
Johnny travaille pas bien ... il dort toujours en classe ... Il est dans la lune. Il n'apprend pas ses leçons.
(Perhaps they learn their lessons better.
Johnny does not work very hard. He's always asleep in class. He's away with the fairies (literally 'in the moon'). He doesn't learn his lessons.)

Fear of failure motivates effort

As reported in Chapter 4 we found much higher levels of motivation generally among our French pupil sample. Our evidence suggests that this is grounded in a positive desire to progress through the stages of schooling but also in the fear of failure. The fear of failure appears to be strong because it is based on two key features of primary schooling in France:

- the belief that any child who works hard can achieve the appropriate level for his or her age
- learning is 'public' in the sense that it is known and understood by everyone inside and outside school, and in the sense that performance in the classroom is 'public' for everyone present to witness.

Thus many pupils in our French sample told us of how anxious they felt about making mistakes, especially at the blackboard in front of the whole class.

> *C'est quand je fais une opération sur le tableau. Une fois je ne savais pas mes tables et Monsieur X m'avait grondé.*
> *Avec les terminaisons ... dans les dictées ... les reconstitutions de texte ... on doit recopier deux fois le texte, cinq fois les mots, et quand c'est le vendredi, il efface des mots, et nous on doit recopier le texte.*
> (It's when I'm doing a sum on the blackboard. One time I didn't know my tables and Monsieur X told me off.
> With the terminations ... in the dictations ... the reconstructions of text ... you have to copy the text twice, and the words five times, and when it's Friday, he rubs off some words and we have to rewrite the text.)

More restricted range and greater uniformity in descriptors used to characterize teachers, pupils and schools

The basis of assessment which French pupils characteristically used in judging schools to be good was academic progress. For the most part they thought their school was a good school, and other schools were less good, but the judgements were clearly based on a narrower set of criteria than was apparent among the English responses.

> *C'est une bonne école puisqu'il n y a presque pas d'élèves qui redoublent*
> *Je pense que c'est une bonne école parce que les maîtres nous expliquent très bien les exercices et sont trés gentils*
> *C'est une bonne école parce qu'il y a de bonnes maîtresses*
> *C'est une mauvaise école parce qu'il y a des maîtres qui ne sont pas assez sérieux.*
> (It's a good school because there are hardly any pupils who have to repeat the year.
> I think that it's a good school because the teachers explain all the exercises clearly to us and they are kind.
> It's a good school because there are good teachers.
> It's a bad school because there are some teachers there who aren't serious about their work.)

SUMMARY DISCUSSION: THE COUNTRY CLUB AND THE POST OFFICE

Underlying all of the national contrasts in classroom processes we have reported in this chapter and elsewhere in this book is a fundamental difference between the English concept of a school and the French concept of a school. Arguably it could be said that in England there are schools, and in France there is *the* School, *l'Ecole*. England has schools which are local communities in their own right with distinctive collective identities providing for local children in their particular circumstances. France has one school, *l'Ecole Unique*, and which like a secular version of the Church Universal (Sharpe, 1997), provides education and instruction indiscriminately for all children living on French territory. In some senses the contrast is like that between a country club and a post office. A country club is a Gemeinschaft based on strong social relationships which one feels part of and through which one develops and expresses part of one's personal identity and character. It is a place where one is known as a person and where one feels comfortable and cared for. The post office, however, is a Gesellschaft, serving a specific function. It does not matter which post office one goes to; the service is essentially impersonal and the same everywhere. One's personal life is centred elsewhere: one is only there for the service provided. The country club is concerned with social cohesion and integration; the post office is concerned with efficient performance of a service: goal achievement. The position outlined above in the chapter is thus summarized in the diagram below.

	French schools	*English schools*
Focus:	Goal achievement	Social integration
Relationships:	Gesellschaft	Gemeinschaft

This, however, is to look at things at the level of the school. If one looks at the level of the nation it is possible to see the converse. France's educational history has, as outlined in Chapter 3, always been focused on social integration at the level of the whole society, for three important reasons:

- to overcome the divisiveness of historic religious rivalries;
- to assimilate newcomers and new generations of children into French culture;
- to build a strongly patriotic population in the face of hostile nations across multiple land borders.

At the national level, England's educational history, by contrast, has been concerned with a form of pragmatism that is not so far removed from an orientation to goal achievement. The national system, such as it was and such as it is, developed as it became necessary to respond to changing circumstances. Workers needed to be taught to read, girls needed to be taught science, everybody now needs to be taught to use information and communications technology. In other words the national system has been tweaked whenever it was felt necessary to do something to achieve a particular goal. There has never been anything like the strong French concern with nation-building. Thus at the level of the nation it could be argued that the positions are the other way round.

	France	*England*
Focus:	Social integration	Goal achievement
Relationships:	Gemeinschaft	Gesellschaft

As Broadfoot contends, it is important to consider the actual operation of different education systems at different levels of functioning if one is to avoid being misled by the mere appearance of formal administrative arrangements. In this case it would be a crude and unhelpful oversimplification to assert that in the matter of education France has a centralized system and England a decentralized system. Only in this way can we begin to understand 'the increasing convergence in the form of control between societies at the present time, a convergence which ... cannot be explained simply in terms of movements along the continuum between centralization and decentralization' (Broadfoot, 1997: 121).

Gemeinschaft is essentially to do with shared understandings, background expectancies, taken-for-granted assumptions about the social world. What is being suggested here is that such shared cultural understandings in the field of education operate at the level of the nation in France, and at the level of the local school in England. Gesellschaft is essentially about deliberately entering into social relationships for a specifically defined purpose, and this requires much more limited investment of personal identity and the self. Here the focus is on understanding a narrow complementarity of role expectations in order to achieve a given outcome. What is being suggested here is that such narrow concerns with goal achievement operate in France at the level of the school and in England at the level of the nation.

Both countries, however, have to provide for both social integration and goal achievement and the issue is one of balance between the two. Furthermore both countries are facing similar challenges in both areas: social integration in the face of increasing mobility, globalization, electronic communications, economic threats, etc.; and goal achievement in the face of unprecedented rates of social change and technological development. There is therefore some apparent 'convergence', but Broadfoot's caution is warranted. This does not mean there will be a meeting in some putative 'middle': the cultural differences we and others have found are real and deep-rooted. It is nevertheless interesting, though, to try to conceptualize this movement in conceptions of schooling in the two countries.

On the basis of our evidence we would argue that French schools are high on goal achievement but low on social integration. There has been some movement toward social integration at the level of the school such as the '*projet d'école*' initiative, but this does not yet appear fundamentally to have changed the ethos of schooling. The French system, however, has been high on national social integration and also fairly high on goal achievement. The English system has by contrast been low on social integration and, until recently, fairly low on goal achievement. English schools have always been high on social integration and are becoming more focused on goal achievement.

It is important to emphasize the limitations of this sort of conceptualizing. It is useful in terms of presenting an overall analysis which is grounded in data presented in the above text. It is however an analytic tool and not itself a description of reality.

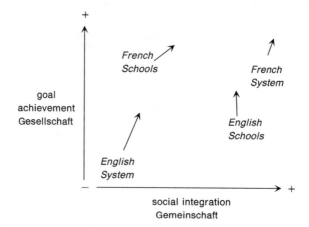

Figure 6.1 *Gemeinschaft and Gesellschaft in French and English primary schooling*

It is also only part of the whole range of evidence which we wish to put forward about the importance of considering the national context in any discussion of comparative education and pupil outcomes. It should be read in conjunction with evidence put forward in other chapters of this book.

Chapter 7

National Differences in Performance in Language

INTRODUCTION

This is the first of three chapters in which we explore how French and English pupils differed in their performance on a test constructed from elements of both French and English National Assessments in Language and Maths. The design of this test, its administration and marking is described in detail in Chapter 2, together with details of the efforts that were made to ensure that the test was as representative as possible of the different curriculum content and approach of the two countries. In this chapter we first briefly recap the nature of the assessments that were undertaken in Language – French in France and English in England – and then present some of the most salient results. The emphasis in both this chapter and the next is on a detailed comparison of the features that distinguished the performance of children in each of the two countries. These features provide powerful evidence of the different strengths and weaknesses of the two national groups, and hence of the significant role played by culture in influencing both what is taught and what is learned.

WHAT DID THE LANGUAGE TEST INVOLVE?

The performance of the socio-economically matched sample of 295 English children and 313 French children in national language skills was tested in 2 complementary test papers (see Appendices). In both 1996 and 1997 these tests were administered by two trained bilingual researchers following national test written instructions which had also been informed by pilot tests in both England and France. Language 1, which lasted 25 minutes, consisted of items drawn from both the English and the French 1995 national tests as well as a purpose-designed QUEST test item. Language 1 comprised two reading comprehensions. The first, Reading Comprehension A, was taken from the French test item and assessed the fairly basic language skill of retrieval from a text. The second, Reading Comprehension B, which was selected and reduced from the English national tests, was at a higher level and involved inferential reading skills. The third test item in Language 1 consisted of an assessment of children's underlying grammatical skills by their correct identification of the spellings of three homonyms which are a frequent cause of confusion in the two respective languages. In the English test they were:

'they're', 'there' and 'their'
'where', 'were', and we're'
'to', 'too', and 'two'

In French they were:

'peux', 'peu', 'peut'
'a', 'as', 'à'
'habiter', 'habitait', 'habité'

The fourth test item in Language 1 assessed children's use of punctuation, using an item from the French national test. This item also contained an assessment of children's handwriting using criteria taken from the English national test. The final test item in Language 1 was taken from the French national tests and assessed children's knowledge and application of the alphabet. Test items were marked following the national marking instructions of the original source.

The second language test, Language 2, was taken from the English national tests and consisted of a story-writing task. The test, which lasted 40 minutes, was administered and marked following English national assessment guidelines. Not wishing to overburden the children or the schools we were working with, children were not also tested in the French version of 'Expression Ecrite', which requires a more formalized type of 'creative' writing.

WHAT WERE THE RELATIVE LEVELS OF CHILDREN'S OVERALL LANGUAGE ACHIEVEMENTS IN THE TWO COUNTRIES?

The performance of English children relative to French children was strong in both language tests (see Table 7.1). The average score for English children in Language 1

Table 7.1 *Assessment scores for England and France (averages expressed as percentages)*

Country		Maths a	Maths b	Lang.1	Lang.2
England	1996	43.0	39.9	65.1	46.1
England	1997	42.1	36.8	67.8	47.5
	All	42.7	38.8	66.0	46.6
France	1996	58.8	32.4	61.8	44.2
France	1997	61.6	33.2	56.0	42.1
	All	59.7	32.6	59.9	43.5
Overall Average		**51.4**	**35.7**	**62.9**	**45.0**

Table 7.2 *QUEST assessment results*

LANGUAGE ONE 1996 and 1997 - ITEM BY ITEM

READING COMPREHENSION A (FRENCH ITEM)

| | 1996 | | 1995 | 1997 | |
	English % correct	French % correct	French National %	English % correct	French % correct
Q1	86	86	91.5	83	82
Q2	66	65	79.9	66	54
Q3a	51	51	65.5	59	45
Q3b	60	61	73.1	65	53
Q4a	74	77	83.7	78	67
Q4b	77	84	87.6	81	78

READING COMPREHENSION B (ENGLISH ITEM)

| | 1996 | | 1995 | 1997 | |
	English % correct	French % correct	French National %	English % correct	French % correct
Q5.1	43	47	34	32	35
Q5.2	44	51	38	33	32
Q5.3	54	32	57	65	33

GRAMMAR ITEMS (QUEST ITEM)
Q6

| | 1996 | | 1997 | |
	English % correct	French % correct	English % correct	French % correct
Pupils getting 1–3 out of 9 correct	8	13	5	17
Pupils getting 4–6 out of 9 correct	21	36	24	34
Pupils getting 7–9 out of 9 correct	68	48	69	47

PUNCTUATION (FRENCH ITEM)

| | 1996 | | 1995 | 1997 | |
	English % correct	French % correct	French National % for 4 full stops/capital letters	English % correct	French % correct
Q7a - capital letters	42	29	20.3	46	22
Q7b - full stops	40	24	22.6	43	18

Table 7.2 *QUEST assessment results (continued)*

HANDWRITING (ENGLISH ITEM)

| | 1996 | | 1995 | 1997 | |
	English %	French %	English National %	English %	French %
Level 1	10	0	3	0	0
Level 2	27	16	75	20	22
Level 3	62	83	22	75	74

| | 1996 | |
	English %	French %
High SES Level 3	87	87
Low SES Level 3	48	78
Boys Level 3	56	75
Girls Level 3	67	91

ALPHABET (FRENCH ITEM)

| | 1996 | | 1995 | 1997 | |
	English % correct	French % correct	French National %	English % correct	French % correct
Q10	58	65	61.9	61	65

was 65 per cent in 1996 and 68 per cent in 1997 compared to an average score for French children of 62 per cent in 1996 and 56 per cent in 1997. Similarly the Language 2 results show English children slightly outperforming French children with English children achieving an average score of 46 per cent in 1996 and 47.5 per cent in 1997 compared to an average score for French children of 44 per cent in 1996 and 42 per cent in 1997.

The quantitative results are also useful as they indicate the relative performance of English and French children in the separate areas of language skills that made up the language tests (Tables 7.2 and 7.3). Overall English children performed better than French children at inferential reading comprehension items, use of homonyms, punctuation, handwriting, spelling and purpose and organization in story-writing. French children performed better than English children in their use of the alphabet.

As might be anticipated, the quantitative results revealed a relationship between gender and children's performance levels and also between the socio-economic zone of the school and children's performance levels. Perhaps the most important aspect of these quantitative findings is that English children performed relatively well compared to French children at language skills. Secondly, and equally important, they indicate that in language skills, social-class differences affected the performance of English children more strongly than that of French children. However, what these

Table 7.3 *QUEST assessment results*

LANGUAGE TWO 1996 and 1997

AVERAGE SCORES

	1996		1997	
	English %	French %	English %	French %
Overall	46	44	47	42
Average purpose score	47	42	49	42
Average grammar score	42	44	41	38
Average style score	47	48	49	49
Average spelling score	63	46	61	44

PURPOSE AND ORGANIZATION

Marks	1996		1995	1997	
	English %	French %	English National %	English %	French %
2	6	7	1	2	7
4	32	39	20	28	43
6	38	39	37	45	37
8	16	10	33	17	8
10	5	1	8	4	0
12	1	0	1	0	0

GRAMMAR

Marks	1996		1995	1997	
	English %	French %	English National %	English %	French %
1	28	21	7	29	29
2	21	22	21	28	16
3	26	35	38	14	49
4	14	10	27	20	0
5	7	9	7	4	3
6	1	0	1	1	0

STYLE

Marks	1996		1995	1997	
	English %	French %	English National %	English %	French %
1	1	1	1	0	0
2	35	29	21	23	38
3	40	48	46	53	49
4	17	17	25	19	8
5	4	2	6	2	0
6	0	0	1	0	0

Table 7.3 *QUEST assessment results (continued)*

SPELLING (QUEST ITEM – SATS HAD A SEPARATE SPELLING TEST)

	1996		1997	
	English %	French %	English %	French %
Level 1	37	68	40	77
Level 2	35	22	30	11
Level 3	25	9	27	10

findings cannot tell us is *in what ways* and *why* English and French children performed differently.

We do know that the performance results of English and French children did not seem to be related to overall curriculum time in the classroom, as our classroom observations showed that curriculum time coverage in the subjects of English and French was similar in both countries (Table 7.4). English took up 43 per cent of classroom curriculum time in the English classrooms compared to French taking up 44 per cent of French classroom curriculum time. We also suspected that a developmental constant in children's reading comprehension must be the explanation for the startlingly similar scores for correct answers to Reading Comprehension A Question 2 'What is the name of the main character in the story?':

	1996		1997	
	English %	French %	English %	French %
Q1 correct	86	86	83	82

Table 7.4 *Percentage of total observed classroom time spent on different aspects of the language curriculum in England and France*

	England %	France %
Percentage of total observed time spend on national language	48.6	41.2
Time spent on QUEST items	2.1	5.8
Reading comprehension	3.5	4.3
Vocabulary	1.4	1.5
Spelling	6.9	–
Dictation	–	0.7
Punctuation	–	1.4
Reading (silent, aloud to class, aloud to teacher)	10.4	2.9
Grammar	–	15.9
Verb conjugations	–	5.8
Writing (diaries, poems, stories, plays, self-evaluations)	18.7	1.5
Oral skills (debates, discussions)	3.5	–
Drama (play-reading in French context, imaginative group-work in English context)	2.1	1.4

Data based on descriptive notes taken during 24 hours in four English schools and 23 hours in four French schools. The descriptive notes were taken together with systematic observation which was conducted randomly in 36 ten-minute sessions in each school.

With the exception of these two inferences, the quantitative findings can only document *what* each national sample was able to do. Not only are such results incapable of yielding answers to the 'how' and 'why' questions, they also cannot, even more significantly, suggest what remedies might be applied to redress any perceived weaknesses in either system because these figures give us so little real understanding of children's performance in language skills. In order to gain more insight and arrive at a more meaningful understanding of children's performance we have to turn to the qualitative assessment of English and French children's performance which were a particular feature of the QUEST study. (Gender and social-class differences were not assessed qualitatively as this was beyond the scope of the project.)

WHAT DIFFERENCES OF APPROACH CHARACTERIZED THE TWO NATIONAL GROUPS?

The quantitative results and the process of script marking indicated that there were three key language areas which would be fruitful in terms of cross-national findings. These were the more open-ended tasks concerned with inferential reading (Reading Comprehension B), story-writing (Language 2), and the more structured tasks of punctuation and the use of homonyms in Language 1. Thus, a representative sub-sample of children's scripts was chosen as the basis for a more descriptive and in-depth assessment of children's performance. Since the data on children's performance in Reading Comprehension B was based on only three test items, the sample taken for the analysis of inferential reading was the total 1997 scripts of 103 English scripts and 100 French scripts. The analysis of children's performance in the use of homonyms and punctuation in Language 1 and story-writing in Language 2 was based on a random sample of 50 English and 50 French children's scripts (the same children for both language tests in order to compare performance across difference tasks) drawn from the total of eight schools that took part in both the 1996 and 1997 tests.

How did English and French pupils' performance in inferential reading differ?

The qualitative analysis, which was based on all the 1997 scripts, indicated first that the construction and assessment design of this English test item was poor. Secondly it showed that English children were performing even better than the quantitative results had shown as it could be seen from English children's errors that they were using inference more than the mark scheme could actually show. Their responses to Q5.1 'What was Gita's opinion on first hearing about the family outing to Bokenham?' were not always directly in answer to the question: e.g. Girl – 'It was different because you could get dressed up': a response which used inference but did not give her a correct mark as it did not answer the question.

There were other instances of English children inferring associations in Q5.1 but not achieving a correct answer: e.g. 'She felt it would be a long journey' or e.g. 'He didn't feel like having a long journey in the car because it was hot', whereas the typical French response to Q5.1 was a variation on a quotation from the text about '*se mettre à tomber des cordes*' (the skies would open).

Surprisingly too, there were many examples of English children who correctly answered Q5.3 'How had Gita's opinion changed by the end of the report?' but failed to answer Q5.1 'What was Gita's opinion on first hearing about the family outing to Bokenham?' and Q5.2 'Which words tell you this?', although in order to respond correctly to Q5.3 it was necessary to have first understood the answer to Q5.1 and infer that the girl in the text had not enjoyed her day out. The indication again was that English children were stronger at inferential skills than the quantitative results had originally shown, as some English children were using inference even though their responses were incorrect. The mark scheme was masking the English children's more developed use of inference.

The error analysis of French children's scripts showed that they were not making their answers explicit enough to achieve a correct mark in Q5.3. This may be the consequence of lack of training in answering questions of this type, as many of the French responses used a 'Why?'/'Because' structure rather than a response to a 'How?' question. The French children's responses indicated that they had received training in a more mechanistic 'Why? ... Because ...' structure:

> e.g. Girl – '*Parce qu'elle a dit que c'était bien.*' (Because she said it was good.)
> e.g. Girl – '*Parce qu'il y avait le spectacle.*' (Because there was a fair.)
> e.g. Girl – '*Elle a changé d'avis parce qu'il y avait des foires aux livres.*' (She changed her mind because there was a bookfair.)
> e.g. Boy – '*Parce que la foire aux livres lui a plu.*' (Because she enjoyed the bookfair.)

Further evidence that French children's responses were functioning in a different and more mechanistic model was that there were more instances of French children quoting (appropriately or inappropriately) from the text. The main strategy of French children appeared to be to quote from the part of the text that they hoped contained the answer. There were also more French responses which tried to quote evidence from the text that the girl in the story had changed her mind, without explicitly stating that she had done so:

> e.g. Girl – '*Elle a vu des animations.*' (She saw some events.)
> e.g. Boy – '*En voyant le château il n'était pas comme les autres.*' (When she saw the manor which wasn't like other ones.)
> e.g. Boy – '*Pierreclos est un endroit plein d'animations.*' (Bokenham Manor is a place with lots of activities.)

Other errors in Q5c were answers which did not respond to the 'How ...' type of question:

> '*Elle ne regrette pas.*' (She doesn't regret it.)
> '*Il a passé une excellente journée.*' (He had an excellent day.)
> '*Elle dit qu'elle va recommander cette visite à tout le monde.*' (She says she will recommend it to everyone.)

There were also more French answers that could be categorized as 'nonsense'. Furthermore, English 'wrong' answers were often nearer the mark than French 'wrong' answers.

This detailed analysis showed that English children were performing even better at inferential skills than their overall scores had suggested and that the weaker scores of French children related perhaps to different procedures in, and to different ideas about, reading comprehension in France. This detailed analysis helped to explain why French children seemed to perform relatively poorly in inferential reading skills in that the structure of the test items (which were of English national test origin), and the type of reading skills that they required, belonged to a model that was unfamiliar to French children. The analysis suggested that the French children were working in the more mechanistic way that they had been taught which values the skills of accuracy, retrieval directly from the text and structured sequences. English children performed better because the more open-ended nature of this language task required the application of skills and attitudes in which they had been trained. The analysis suggested that the English pedagogic approach values the skills of empathy and understanding and places more emphasis on pupil co-textual experience. Pupil achievement is directly related to the model of learning that pupils encounter in the classroom and the opportunity that pupils are given in practising it. Assessment must be contextualized in order to be valid.

What are the implications of this analysis of children's performance at reading for teaching and learning?

Overall the analysis showed that there was a band of low attainers in both countries, though probably more in France, who could do very little with reading comprehensions of this kind. It showed also that English teachers were doing quite well in developing inferential comprehension skills in their children but that some English children were still experiencing difficulty in precisely and explicitly articulating their understanding in order to fit an assessment schedule which required a clearly defined answer to gain a mark.

Other data from our research indicated that there are fundamental differences in the approaches of the two countries to reading. Reading is primarily regarded as an enjoyable activity in English classrooms and some English children's comments reflected this enjoyment. One English girl, in writing about what she envisaged herself doing in the next ten years, commented on the importance of reading in her life. She thought she would be 'using reading to help me learn more, instead of just reading for pleasure', and 'finding books that I can enjoy for a while, rather than reading lovely books that don't last for long … when I'm 18, 19, 20 or 21 I think I'll probably still like reading'.

Reading, as opposed to reading comprehension, was observed to take up more time in English classrooms than in the French ones – 10 per cent of English classroom time was spent on reading compared to 3 per cent of French classroom time (although slightly more classroom time was observed to be given over to reading comprehension in French than in English classrooms, as shown in Table 7.4. An English 10-year-old who had returned recently from 6 months of schooling in a French CM1 class (one of the QUEST 'movers') remarked that in France, 'we did dictées and stuff and we sometimes did reading but I think we do more reading here in England'.

In France, reading, '*la lecture*', is taught as a subject. In their interview responses to naming subjects studied in French classrooms, French children identified it, along with '*la grammaire*', '*les conjugaisons*', '*le vocabulaire*', '*l'expression écrite*'. By contrast, English children were more likely to name the undifferentiated subject 'English'. The comparison of pupil performance in reading tends to suggest that the English approach to reading as an enjoyable and less compartmentalized activity is more successful than the more mechanistic French approach in inculcating a desire to read.

How did English and French children's performance at spelling differ?

This is a difficult area for comparison as the English and French languages make different syntactic demands on children's learning. Greater priority is given to grammar work in French classrooms compared to that in English classrooms – classroom observation indicated that 16 per cent of French classroom time was taken up by grammar and 6 per cent was taken up by verb conjugations, yet no time was spent on grammar and verbs in the English classrooms, as Table 7.5 makes clear.

Nevertheless the tests' results revealed that English children had performed better in their spelling of homonyms in a structured test item. Similarly, in the open-ended task of story-writing, English children out-performed French children in spelling: and more English children than French achieved a level 3 (between 0 and 5 mistakes on the first page) in spelling in their story-writing. (Only 9 per cent of French children achieved this level in 1997, in comparison to 25 per cent of English children.) The analysis of 50 randomly chosen English and French story-writing scripts confirmed this finding, with only 16 per cent of French children reaching a level 2 (between 5 and 10 mistakes on the first page) or a level 3, and the majority of 84 per cent only reaching a level 1 (over 10 mistakes on the first page). This compares with only 36 per cent of English children at level 1, in this small sample, and 64 per cent reaching a level 2 or a level 3.

The analysis also revealed both similarities and differences in the types of error made by English and French children. Both English and French children were often inconsistent in their spellings from one sentence to another. For example 'their' might be correctly used in several sentences only to have 'there' substituted further down the page. Both English and French children made spelling errors that involved confusion over word boundaries – for example, '*t'elle m'en*' for '*tellement*' and 'not think' for 'nothing'. Both also had problems with homonyms, for example, '*c'est, s'est, ses, ces*' and '*are, our*', and '*whole, hole*'. Both also used oral language forms

Table 7.5 *Main curriculum context*

		RE	English/ French	Mathe- matics	Science	History	Geography	Art	Music/ Dance	PE	Tech- nology	Personal & Social	Non- curricular	Education civique	TOTAL	%
England	N	1	64	42	9	0	6	12	4	0	1	6	4	1	150	53.6
	%	0.7	42.7	28.0	6.0	0.0	4.0	8.0	2.7	0.0	0.7	4.0	2.7	0.7	100.0	
France	N	0	57	42	1	5	7	0	6	7	2	0	2	1	130	46.4
	%	0.0	43.8	32.3	0.8	3.8	5.4	0.0	4.6	5.4	1.5	0.0	1.5	0.8	100.0	
Total	N	1	121	84	10	5	13	12	10	7	3	6	6	2	280	100.0
	%	0.4	43.2	30.0	3.6	1.8	4.6	4.3	3.6	2.5	1.1	2.1	2.1	0.7	100.0	

inappropriately instead of written language forms. One example of this was a tendency to miss out the first part of the French negative as in '*on avait jamais vu*' instead of '*On n'avait jamais vu*' and in English, to use 'we was' instead of 'we were', or to use a double negative 'without no one' instead of 'without anyone'. In addition to these problems that were common to both sets of children, French children were more likely than English children to make errors in their use of tense and in their spellings of verb-ending markers of tenses and person.

Error analysis was also carried out on English and French pupil performance in five of the grammar items ('à', 'a', imperfect endings, infinitives, and past participles in the French test, and 'to', 'there', 'were', 'where', and 'too' in the English test) compared to the *same* pupil's performance with the same items occurring randomly in the 50 English and 50 French story-writing scripts. It was found that English children were more consistent than French children in spelling the item correctly in the two different test formats.

In items which were comparable in terms of their occurrence, for example 'there' and the infinitive or the past participle in French, and the occurrence of 'to' and 'à' (see Table 7.6), English children were more consistent in their spellings than French children. In 70 per cent of English scripts the item was mostly correctly spelt in both formats compared to 20 per cent or 10 per cent of French scripts in the first case; and in 84 per cent of English scripts the item was mostly spelt correctly in both formats compared to 52 per cent of French scripts in the second case.

Table 7.6 *The consistency in performance in spelling of a sample of the same English and French pupils in both structured and non-structured writing tasks*

(a)

	Occurrence of items in 13 randomly chosen French story-writing scripts	% of French scripts with language item spelt correctly in grammar items and story-writing
a	26	28
Past participle	32	10
Infinitive	39	27
à	60	52
Imperfect	104	30

(b)

	Occurrence of items in 13 randomly chosen English story-writing scripts	% of English scripts with language item spelt correctly in grammar items and story-writing
Too	2	12
Where	3	16
Were	15	4
There	35	70
To	78	84

How did English and French pupils' performance differ in their use of tenses?

Analysis of the inferential reading comprehension questions and the story-writing scripts suggested that English children were more able to manipulate tenses accurately. The more detailed analysis of the random sub-sample of 50 English and 50 French Language 2 scripts showed that more French children were inconsistent in their use of tenses – for example, starting their piece of writing in the past and suddenly changing to the present – than were English children. Of French children, 42 per cent made at least one error compared to 24 per cent of English children. An even more detailed scrutiny of individual pupils' work revealed a similar lack of consistency and relatively poor performance among French pupils. These errors related particularly to the use of the appropriate tense for the desired time sequence.

What are the implications of this analysis of children's performance in spelling and in the use of tenses for teaching and learning?

How can we explain the superior performance of English children in both spelling and the use of tenses? It may be that the emphasis on oral work in the English classroom, where children are encouraged to recount experiences and exchange ideas, is not without effect since such activity necessarily involves practice in the use of tenses. When the relatively better performance by English children in spelling, use of tenses and story-writing is taken together in the light of the time spent on different areas of the language curriculum in English and French classrooms (see Table 7.5), it can be suggested that the key difference may be the English emphasis on the *use* of language as opposed to the French emphasis on the study of its *structure*, and that the former approach may be more effective at this age level.

The classroom observations we conducted showed that there was more classroom time in England (19 per cent compared to 1.5 per cent of French classroom time) spent on using language in different writing situations such as writing diaries, stories, poems, plays and self-evaluations. Oral work also took up more of the language curriculum time in England (3.5 per cent compared to just under 0% in France.). Use of tenses is an intrinsic part of these tasks. French language lessons were more likely to emphasize structure and syntax. Grammar and verb conjugations took up 16 per cent and 6 per cent respectively of French classroom time compared to 0 per cent of the observed time in English classrooms. The QUEST 'movers' perceptions echoed these findings: a 12-year-old English girl who had spent 6 months in a French CM1 2 years previously, said: 'They taught you like all the conjugations like all the time'. Similar sentiments were expressed by a 13-year-old English boy who had also spent 6 months in a French CM1 3 years previously, 'It was all verb tables and tenses ... the verbs had to be underlined in red.' By contrast, a 10-year-old French boy, one week after returning from 6 months in an English Y6 class said: '*Des dictées il y en avait là ... il y avait quelque chose d'autre ... des mots à préparer ... une dictée de mots. On en faisait pas de grammaire.*' (We had dictations ... we also had ... words to prepare ... a spelling test. We didn't do any grammar.')

The French approach may be too abstract and too removed from the context of language-use for primary-aged children. If it is a question of achieving a balance between a structural and a functional approach to the teaching of language, our results in spelling and use of tenses indicate that English primary classrooms may have achieved a better balance than French ones in this respect. However the effect of the different syntactic demands of the two languages in their written form also needs to be taken into account.

These findings also highlight the relative contributions of quantitative and qualitative analyses in comparative studies and the important methodological implications of this. The quantitative comparison of curriculum time which was undertaken in the QUEST study based on systematic observation data (Table 7.5) had shown great similarity between the amount of classroom time spent on language in English and French classrooms. However, the qualitative analysis (Table 7.4), which was based on classroom descriptive notes, showed that the classroom time spent on different aspects of language within the overall category of English or French revealed important differences of emphasis which are related to culturally-derived value differences between the two education systems.

What were the differences between English and French pupils' performance at punctuation?

English children performed slightly better than French pupils in their use of full stops and capital letters in both formal exercises and open-ended writing. English children were also more confident in their use of paragraphs – 32 per cent used paragraphs compared to 18 per cent of French children – although this may be partly attributable to the demands of the English stories which were longer. English children were also more likely to use speech marks – 60 per cent compared to only 26 per cent of French children using speech marks. Again this may be attributable to the type of stories that were written, with English children favouring dialogue as a literary method. However, French pupils' use of commas to separate clauses or lists of words was significantly better with 74 per cent of French children using most commas correctly, in comparison to only 28 per cent of English children. However the performance of both English and French children in using capital letters and full stops was relatively weak, with about 40 per cent of each sample not using punctuation accurately.

These findings document *how* the performance of English and French children differed. Using other data from the project it was also possible to suggest *why* there were differences in performance. Principle among the reasons were cultural factors, which were expressed not only in different classroom practices but also, and perhaps more importantly, in the fundamental underlying cultural thinking about teaching and learning which was characteristic of the two countries being studied. The French children appeared to be operating in a more mechanistic way, with English children by contrast employing an approach to learning that was broader and more open, with an emphasis on co-textual and empathetic skills. The importance of cultural factors in learning outcomes can also be seen in the performance of English and French children at story-writing.

How did English and French children's performance at story-writing differ?

Using the randomly selected sample of 50 English and 50 French 1996 and 1997 scripts, the children's performance was analysed for style. The most significant differences were found in the stronger scripts where language style was more developed. The stronger English scripts achieved high scores in style through their use of imaginative vocabulary and descriptive passages; for example:

> I walked off into the inky darkness of the room. Everything was bare except for large flaring torches nailed to the wall. (Boy, high SES school, Bristol.)

The stronger French scripts achieved high scores though their use of a more literary vocabulary , such as '*lorsque*' or '*lors*' instead of '*quand*', or phrases such as '*à longueur de journée*'. They also tended to use more developed syntactic structures such as '*une fois libérée*'. Moreover there were more examples of children employing expressions such as '*connaître ... comme sa poche*' or '*ni vu ni connu*'. The English national test marking scheme was unable to show these cultural stylistic differences in the children's stories, differences that relate to how story-writing is taught in the two contexts and what each culture values and defines as a 'good' written style for primary-aged children.

The difference in emphasis in cultural values can be seen in the curricula requirements of the two countries. In the English curriculum there is more stress laid on children using their imagination, writing for 'imagined audiences' and using 'imaginative writing' (DFEE, 1995: 15). This is unlike the French curriculum for writing which makes no mention of children's imagination (CNDP, 1995: 59).

What seems to be more valued in the children's written productions in the French context is organization and structure. As the French curriculum states:

> *Les productions sont nombreuses et de plus en plus conformes aux exigences d'organisation et de présentation: articulation des idées, organisation en paragraphes* (CNDP, 1995: 59).
> (Writing is to be a frequent and various activity which is more and more subject to the demands of organization and presentation: the cohesion of ideas, organization into paragraphs.)

The French curriculum is advocating an approach to writing which imposes more demands on children compared to those of the English curriculum which even suggests that writing might be 'enjoyable' when it states that:

> Pupils should be given opportunities to write for varied purposes, understanding that writing is essential to thinking and learning, and enjoyable in itself. They should be taught to use writing as a means of developing, organising and communicating ideas (DFEE, 1995: 15).

It would seem that two at least of the English teachers in our sample of schools had managed to convey this enjoyment to their classes. Asked what they saw themselves doing in ten years' time some of their pupils expressed their enthusiasm for writing by declaring that they hoped to become authors! No French children expressed such a desire.

The most commonly used French text book in 1996, *Langue Française, La Balle Aux Mots, CM2* (Dupré *et al.*, 1988), also exemplifies some of the different values which the two countries hold about children's writing and about their writing style in particular, especially when it is compared with excerpts from the English text book *Reasons For Writing* (which are presented on p. 131). *La Balle Aux Mots* covers the five years of French primary education. Each book is divided into three sections corresponding to the work over three terms of ten weeks each. Within the period of one week's work the language skills are broken down into Grammar, Vocabulary, 'Expression Ecrite' (writing composition), Spelling and Verb conjugations. The example in Figure 7.1 from an 'expression écrite' page includes work on correcting verbs, style improvements, studying a text as a model and two tasks for writing. The first task is to finish an excerpt from an incident in a Pagnol story, the second task involves putting together a story from a given story-line.

These examples from the curriculum and text books show the importance of form and quality of expression in French written composition and how much less emphasis is placed on the development of creativity and the imagination. This point was well illustrated by one of the QUEST 'movers', a 10-year-old French girl, who had returned one week previously from her 6-month stay in an English Year 5 class. She seemed to be aware of the different emphases in English and French schools' approach to story-writing, in indicating that she felt there were fewer constraints in English story-writing:

> *En expression écrite en France on finit une histoire ... en Angleterre on peut choisir ce qu'on veut écrire sur une feuille.* (In '*expression écrite*' in France you finish a story ... in England you can choose what you want to write on a piece of paper.)

Because 'imagination' and 'creativity' are difficult concepts to define and even more difficult to assess, the research team were unsuccessful in trying to devise a culturally value-free mark scheme which would highlight the underlying differences between English and French scripts. However, it was clear that the English scripts were more individualistic in terms of style and content than were the French scripts. Social class also appeared to influence the level of creativity. Children from high SES schools in England and in France tended to produce more creative stories. A good example of English creativity and individualism is the story from an English boy in a rural high SES-zone school shown as Figure 7.2. It has been typed out, as the original is extremely difficult to read.

The nearest equivalent in terms of level and creativity from the French sample was the example shown as Figure 7.3.

These two examples not only exemplify some of the differences between what is valued in terms of style and imagination in the English and French contexts but also

Corriger des phrases

1 *Il manque le verbe dans certaines phrases, corrige-les :*

1. Nous écoutons de la musique classique. Le disque que j'ai apporté en ce moment sur le tourne-disque. Mes amis l'aiment beaucoup.

2. Le bouchon s'est enfoncé. J'ai tiré fort et le fil s'est cassé. Le poisson qui était trop gros dans la rivière.

3. La bicyclette à la main, l'homme marchait au bord du chemin. Une valise sur le porte-bagages et un chapeau à larges bords.

4. Pendant les prochaines vacances, je ferai du ski. Le matin les leçons et l'après-midi les promenades à travers les sapins enneigés. Mes vêtements me tiendront chaud et le soleil sur les champs de neige.

Dire de deux façons

2 **Quelques concurrentes seront éliminées dès le premier tour.**
→ *Quelques-unes* **des concurrentes seront éliminées dès le premier tour.**
De la même façon, transforme les phrases suivantes :

Quelques danseuses de la troupe deviendront des étoiles. → . . .

Quelques joueurs seront sélectionnés pour former l'équipe de France. → . . .

Quelques vins présentés à l'Exposition ont obtenu une médaille d'or. → . . .

Quelques pièces présentaient un défaut de fabrication : elles ont été retirées de la vente. → . . .

Reconstitution de texte

3 LE SENTIER
C'était un beau sentier de nuit, un de ces sentiers qui vous accompagnent, avec lesquels on peu parler, et qui vous font, tout le long du chemin, ur tas de petites confidences. On y marche san: crainte, avec légèreté. Comme ils ont conserve une grande innocence, ils ne sauraient vou; fourvoyer. Sur eux, le temps ne compte plus e l'espace fond amicalement dans le plaisir noc turne de la marche.

HENRI BOSCO, *L'Enfant et la rivière*, Éd. Gallimard.

Imaginer une suite

4 UNE FILLE BIEN PEUREUSE
Je me retournai.
« C'est vous qui faites ce bruit ?
— Je vous appelle ! dit-elle, sur un ton assez vif.
— Vous n'avez pas trouvé le chemin ? »
Elle me répondit, indignée :
« Vous savez bien qu'il est barré par d'énormes toiles d'araignée ! Il y en a au moins quatre ou cinq, et la plus grosse a voulu me sauter à la figure !...
Quand un garçon est galant, il n'abandonne pas une demoiselle dans un endroit aussi dangereux. »
Je croquai les derniers grains, et je ne répondis rien. Je réfléchissais.

MARCEL PAGNOL, *Le Temps des secrets*, Éd. Pastorelly.

• *Imagine la suite. Rédige-la.*

Raconter un fait

5 *Raconte, puis rédige cette histoire.*
Que deviendra le petit agneau ? Imagine.

Figure 7.1 *Sample from* Expression écrite *in the French-language textbook* Langue Française, La Balle Aux Mots CM2 *(see p. 128)*

A door opens

One fine morning in Wallopville, the postman popped a packet of all-sport cards through Dr. P. Rana's letter box. P. Rana ran downstairs as he heard it fall onto the floor, he rushed over to the pack and ripped it open. 'Okay!' he said, 'Um ... bubble gum as recommended by Axel Mangohead of the Fantastic Fowl!' (at which point he stuffed the gum into his fanged mouth) '(chomp) Now then ... (chew) er ... got, got need, got, n-e-e-eed and need. And ... Hang on a mo! A note!' He unfolded the note and read it. This is what is said –

> Dear P.M.
> We need your help! Chicken-dude, our ex-mascot, seeks revenge on us! He says he will attack us by Tuesday the 4th. We don't know exactly where we are yet, but please search everywhere!
>   from -
>   Slimeball Mcgee, Axel Mangohead and Nick Nautious of the Fantastic Fowl rugby club

P. Rana quickly ran into his fridge and came out as Piranha-Man! 'You can come too, Mega-Woof!' he said. They jumped into the Piranha-van and flew off. P.M. Waved the note at Mega-woof's nose. 'Go gettim, boy!' said P.M. Mega-woof barked excitedly and ran towards a door with a padlock. P.M. had heard strange tales about this door. Tales of ghosts, gouls and zombies that bleed from their eyes! But I'm a hero, thought he. I'm not scared of anything! And so ... *BOOM* he opened the door with a well placed stick of dynamite. It was dark and cold the other side of the door. Mega-woof whined feebly. 'Hello?' called P.M. 'Is anybody here? I'm the ... Milkman, yeah, thassit, the Milkman.' 'No milk today thanks' called a mysterious voice. 'It's fresh!' called P.M. 'Listen punk! NO MILK, okay?' suddenly Chicken-dude jumped out. 'SO ... ' he said, 'it's Piranha-man!' 'Yes, evil doer!' cried P.M. 'and I'm here to save the players! Take that!' he then hit Chicken-dude with an extremely wet and heavy fish. 'Oh-yeah?' shouted Chicken-dude. He pulled a hen from his belt and threw it like a boomerang towards P.M. P.M. fell to the floor! Suddenly Mega-woof ran up to Chicken-dude and bit him on the ... 'Ouch!' cried C.D. and off he ran.

HOW IT ENDED

The players were saved and P.M. received a lifetime supply of gum.

THE END

Figure 7.2 *A story written by a high-achieving English boy, exemplifying English characteristics of style and content*

highlight typical differences of approach to the development of story-line and content, which is the next focus of analysis.

As the examples of English and French stories already presented may have indicated, there was a difference between the content and story-line of English and French scripts. English scripts could be characterized as 'real life' in that they tended to deal with 'ego' in familiar settings, for example the English story commencing 'Tosh my best friend ...' A common English theme was 'Me and my friends down the park.' French scripts tended more to be re-creations of a middle-European folk tale set in the countryside, or in the distant past where the main character was not 'ego'. Figure 7.4 shows the results of the analysis carried out on the sample of English and French story-lines and settings.

   Data from other QUEST research instruments show that it is not a coincidence that English stories tended to conform to a 'real life' model and French stories to a

Il était une fois derrière une porte de maison en ruine, un couple Béatrice: grande, jeune, douce, belle, intelligente et un peu maigre. Son fiancé Richard, jaloux et un peu grognon lui aussi jeune, grand, fort et courageux. Ils vivaient heureux, tranquillement sans soucis, sans problèmes d'argent.

Tout allé bien jusqu'au jour à il commençaient à se disputer à propos des enfants que la jeune femme rêvait d'avoir. Et derrière cette porte, l'inséparable amitié de ce jeune couple se cassa. En colère la femme partit et prit ses jembes à son cou. Le jeune Richard était triste, puis versa des larmes d'amour.

Il décida d'aller à sa recherche il cherchait et criait 'Béatrice' où tu es, 'Béatrice' Le jeune homme était désespéré. La jeune femme ratrappa le jeune homme, elle cria 'Richard', 'Richard' et l'homme l'entendit. Ils se cherchaient notre jeune couple, à force de se chercher, ils se sont trouvés. Un jour plus tard il se marièrent et eurent beaucoup d'enfants.

Fin.

(There was once upon a time, behind the door of a house in ruins, a couple: Beatrice, who was tall, young, kind, intelligent and a little thin. Her fiancé Richard, was jealous, a little grumpy. He too was young, tall, strong and fearless. They lived happily, without any worries and with no money problems.

Everything went well until the day came when they started to argue about the children which the young woman dreamed of having. And behind this door, the inseparable bond between the young couple was broken. The woman left in anger and took to her heels. Young Richard was upset and wept tears of love.

He decided to go and look for her. As he searched he cried out, 'Beatrice!', 'Where are you Beatrice?' The young man was in despair. The young woman caught up with the young man. She called out, 'Richard!', 'Richard!' and he heard her. This young couple searched for each other and by dint of searching they found each other. The following day they were married. They had lots of children.

The end.)

Figure 7.3 *A story written by a high-achieving French girl, exemplifying French characteristics of style and content*

more 'traditional' model. The difference between the scripts is related to the different emphasis in the learning cultures of the two countries. This can be revealed through an examination of an English text book which was used in some of the English schools in the study. The opening section 'Ideas for Stories' of the English book in question, *Reasons For Writing* (Course book 4, Ginn 1993: 4), clearly shows the open-ended and unstructured nature of writing tasks:

Authors get ideas for stories from a variety of different sources. Some begin by thinking of a character and they build their story around him or her. Others think of an unusual happening or title. Sometimes they begin with an interesting opening sentence and simply see where it takes them to. What sort of starting point do you find helpful?

The structure and content of the text book is significant too. The first unit centres on the child's own self. It is entitled 'The sort of person I am' (pp. 2–3), perhaps implying that everything emanates from *ego*. There is a unit on characters (p. 38), the importance of a title (p. 39), using drafts (p. 8), and again with significance for the findings of this paper, a unit given over to the self and others as a group of characters (pp. 52–3).

	English scripts 'real life'	French scripts 'traditional'
SETTINGS		
At home or near home	37/50	15/50
including moving house	7/50	0/50
Forest, countryside or historical setting	4/50	23/50
Other, including unclear setting, different worlds, different country or no setting	16/50	12/50
ELEMENTS		
Magic, witchcraft, monsters and ogres	3/50	16/50
CHARACTERS		
Involving self and others	26/50	19/50
Others, self not mentioned	24/50	31/50

Data: 50 English, 50 French, QUEST story-writing scripts randomly chosen from the 8 English and the 8 French schools

Figure 7.4 *Incidence of characteristics in story-writing relating to a more 'traditional' model in English children's work and a more 'real life' model in French children's work*

What are the implications of these differences in children's approach to story-writing?

Although the quantitative results had shown remarkable similarity between the performance of English and French children at story-writing (Table 7.1: Lang. 2), the qualitative analysis presented in the preceding pages has given a very different picture. Among the significant differences between English and French children's stories was the greater use of imagination and of themselves in English children's writing. They wrote about what they knew best, their experiences, their real lives. The French teaching approach, by contrast, was more formal and structured and therefore encouraged a more structured response from children. When presented with the unfamiliarity of an open-ended writing exercise, where structural supports were not provided, many French pupils responded by giving their stories the structure and settings in story-writing that they were familiar with – typically, as suggested above, the story-line of a traditional mid-European children's story.

These two approaches to story-writing were also shown to be represented in the two countries' national curricula and text books for language. The differences in English and French children's story-writing can thus be traced to different cultural values. Kaplan (1966) used the term 'contrastive rhetoric' to describe the cultural differences which he found in his assessment of written compositions by learners of English as a foreign language. The students' productions of written English showed patterned variation according to their language and cultural group. Kaplan quotes Oliver (Kaplan, 1966: 1): 'Rhetoric is a mode of thinking', and he recognizes that modes of thinking are cultural: 'Logic (in the popular, rather than the logician's sense of the word) which is the basis of rhetoric, is evolved out of culture; it is not universal' (Kaplan, 1966: 2).

Takala as well concluded that:

> We may assert that there exist cultural patterns of expression and thought, that these patterns may be found both in what is said or written and in the manner of presentation; that these patterns have some relation to the lexical and grammatical constraints of a language; but that more probably these patterns are learned either in formal or informal schooling. From the foregoing, we might infer the legitimacy of an entity which we will call 'national style'... National style is a set of culturally determined expectations of what good writing should be (Takala *et al.*, 1982: 324–5).

There have been a number of other comparative studies showing cultural influences in written compositions: in English, Semitic, Oriental and Romance language texts (Kaplan, 1966); in Hindi and American English (Kachan, 1988); in American English and Thai (Vahäpassi, 1988; Bickner and Peyasantiwong, 1988); and Purves (1988: 12) also emphasizes the underlying cultural nature of writing.

Clearly cultural differences between English and French children's productions would not be expected to be as different as those between American and Thai children. The differences between English and French children's performance are more ones of degree, but they do amount to two cultural models which define a 'good story'. In short, we may say that the English model prioritizes *content*, the French model prioritizes *form*.

The QUEST findings have significant implications for international assessment, since they indicate the extent to which like is not being compared with like in a cross-cultural assessment of language skills. The results of our more qualitative approach to international comparisons of achievement call into question the validity of many international studies in the assessment of language, since it was found that the QUEST quantitative results were not only lacking in explanatory power but also distorted the results of children's performance. Our study highlights the importance of recognizing the degree to which children's performance is related to familiarity with the implicit values and underlying structure and content of test items. It suggests that the search for culturally neutral assessment items is a chimera, as doomed to fruitlessness as the Arthurian-inspired search for the Holy Grail. However, cross-cultural qualitative assessment is revealed by the same token as an important tool. Not only does it demonstrate the limitations of international quantitative assessment, it also provides for international comparisons which are meaningful and which can therefore increase our knowledge of teaching and learning. Such understanding must ultimately be the basis for improving children's learning.

Chapter 8

National Differences and Strategies in Mathematics

The sample of English and French children were assessed in three maths tests (see Appendices, pp. 220–33). Maths A, which lasted 25 minutes, contained question items selected from the 1995 French national assessments. Maths B, which lasted 30 minutes, consisted of a selection of items from the 1995 English national tests. In order to gain more understanding of children's performance in maths a third QUEST test was added, Maths C (25 minutes), which assessed children's skills at problem-solving (skills which are included in the English maths curriculum but which were not assessed in the 1995 English national tests). The criteria used for the selection of maths items from the national tests were first that they represented the breadth, depth and levels of their respective national curriculum, and second that they reflected the 'typical' national approach to maths, in terms of presentation and content. As in the language tests, the maths tests were administered and marked following national test guidelines.

HOW DID ENGLISH AND FRENCH CHILDREN'S OVERALL PERFORMANCE IN MATHS DIFFER?

The overall QUEST results indicated first that the national samples of children achieved better scores in their own national tests. Tables 8.1a and 8.1b show that English children performed better at the English maths test (Maths B) than did French children. For example, in 1996 the average English score was 39.9 per cent for the English maths test compared to an average French score of 32.4 per cent. Similarly French children performed better at the French test (Maths A) than did English children. For example, in 1996 the average English score for the French maths test was 43 per cent compared to a French average score of 58.8 per cent.

Secondly, when the results are compared according to the maths areas (number; shape, space and measure; handling data; and using and applying) covered by the tests, it can be seen that over both years of testing, English and French children had consistent relative strengths and weaknesses in different areas of the maths curriculum.

Table 8.1a *Results for number items on Maths B test*

		Number English items				
		1996		1997		
Question	Q type	English % correct	French % correct	English % correct	French % correct	Strongest
Q2a	$\div 5 = 22$	71.0	68.0	56.0	57.0	French
Q2b	$28 + 29$	57.0	84.0	54.0	88.0	French
Q3a	323×7	31.0	49.0	18.0	55.0	French
Q3b	$\times = 42$	43.0	50.0	35.0	45.0	French
Q4	Problem	36.0	32.0	33.0	29.0	English
Q5Cc	Problem	38.0	54.0	26.0	50.0	French
Q10a	Decimals	17.0	23.0	18.0	17.0	French
Q10b	Fractions	11.0	3.0	7.0	0.0	English

Table 8.1b *Results for number items on Maths A test*

		Number French items				
		1996		1997		
Question	Q type	English % correct	French % correct	English % correct	French % correct	Strongest
Q1a	$168.75 + 42.50$	62.0	71.0	63.0	75.0	French
Q1b	$463 - 167$	55.0	83.0	61.0	84.0	French
Q1c	$26|2782$	19.0	63.0	15.0	65.0	French
Q1d	4.28×3.5	8.0	49.0	4.0	54.0	French
Q2a	7.14×100	28.0	73.0	26.0	70.0	French
Q2b	$325.6 \div 10$	26.0	49.0	24.0	65.0	French
Q7	Problem	48.0	61.0	46.0	61.0	French
Q8	Problem	39.0	56.0	31.0	68.0	French

The overall QUEST results (also presented item by item in Tables 8.1a and 8.1b, 8.2a and 8.2b, and 8.3 with national results for comparison) showed that French children outperformed English children at numbers. They gained higher scores than English children not only at all the French number test items but also on 6 out of 8 of the English number test items. In the use of the four operations – adding, subtracting, multiplying and dividing – French children only slightly outperformed English children in addition. The performance of English children however dipped considerably in subtraction and even more so in multiplication and division. English children only outperformed French children on the English test of number in fractions and a problem-solving item which required only simple computational skills. The results indicate that English children had more difficulty with place value and decimal points than did French children.

In the area of shape, space and measure the situation was reversed with English

Table 8.2a *Results for shape, space and measure on Maths B test*

| | | Shape, space and measure English items | | | | |
| | | 1996 | | 1997 | | |
Question	Q type	English % correct	French % correct	English % correct	French % correct	Strongest
Q6a	Shape from above	18.0	14.0	21.0	8.0	English
Q6b	Shape from above	14.0	10.0	12.0	1.0	English
Q9	Symmetry	64.0	33.0	59.0	41.0	English

Table 8.2b *Results for shape, space and measure on Maths A test*

| | | Shape, space and measure French items | | | | |
| | | 1996 | | 1997 | | |
Question	Q type	English % correct	French % correct	English % correct	French % correct	Strongest
Q3a	Drawing a rectangle	88.0	96.0	86.0	94.0	French
Q3b	above cont.	49.0	75.0	50.0	69.0	French
Q3c	above cont.	34.0	62.0	32.0	52.0	French
Q4a	Geometric terms	3.0	16.0	9.0	20.0	French
Q4b	Geometric convention	76.0	61.0	69.0	67.0	English
Q5Ca	Perimeter	32.0	29.0	40.0	28.0	English
Q5Cb	Area	67.0	47.0	66.0	56.0	English
Q7	Rectangles	49.9	41.0	45.0	53.0	English

Table 8.3 *Results on handling data from Maths B test*

| | | Handling data English items | | | | |
| | | 1996 | | 1997 | | |
Question	Q type	English % correct	French % correct	English % correct	French % correct	Strongest
Q1	Averages	32.0	14.0	28.0	15.0	English
Q5Ca	Reading a chart	88.0	84.0	83.0	81.0	English
Q5Cb	Filling in a chart	70.0	57.0	67.0	58.0	English
Q7a	Probability	72.0	30.0	65.0	43.0	English
Q7b	Probability	40.0	13.0	65.0	36.0	English
Q7c	Probability	23.0	1.0	21.0	4.0	English
Q8a	Reading a pie chart	30.0	9.0	28.0	13.0	English
Q8b	Reading, estimating	24.0	8.0	14.0	9.0	English
Q8c	Explaining estimation	19.0	2.0	17.0	4.0	English

children tending to outperform French children. English children performed better than French children on all the English items in these aspects.

Furthermore, English children performed better than French children at half of the French test items in shape, space and measure. These items tended to be more 'visual' items. French children outperformed English children at geometric drawing skills and understanding of geometric vocabulary.

English children also performed better than French children at all the English 'handling data' test items. The QUEST children were not tested on French items 'handling data' as this area is covered under reading in the French national tests. Thus it can only be conjectured from the quantitative results that the reasons for the superior performance of English children in this area were due to the fact that neither probability nor averages are part of the French primary maths curriculum, rather than the fact that the test items were of English origin *per se*. (The salience of 'opportunity to learn' as a predictor of performance is reinforced by the French government's own comparison of national maths performance over time which found that pupils today)

> are better at ... arithmetic, in addition, subtraction and division; on the other hand, they are doing less well in multiplication and worse in ... old-fashioned types of problem-solving than [pupils] of the 1920s. It must be stressed that the comparison is based on performance at questions given at the beginning of the [twentieth] century and that the national curriculum ... has changed considerably over the years; this may explain why today's pupils, while having a broader knowledge of sections of the curriculum which are more recent or which were little taught formerly – in geometry, for instance – are experiencing real difficulties in areas in which they are given less practice nowadays' (Les dossiers d'Éducation et Formations, n° 62, February 1996, Ministère de l'Éducation Nationale, Direction de l'évaluation et de la prospective).

English children also outperformed French children in the area of using and applying maths which was tested through a problem-solving investigation into odd and even numbers on the new QUEST test paper Maths paper 'C'. The mark scheme, derived from Burton (1984), assigned children's work into six cumulative bands, presented here for the sake of clarity in 3 levels (Table 8.4).

The quantitative performance findings were useful as they did give some indication of the relative performance of English and French children in four maths areas. More importantly, they suggested patterns of performance in children's maths achievement at cross-cultural tests, patterns which were connected to national curricular content, national curricular values and overall degree of familiarity with test items. Thus the main findings from the quantitative results were that:

- Children's performance reflected national curricular content. English children performed better at a wider range of maths areas including probability, averages

Table 8.4 *Average of English and French pupils' percentages achieving levels 1, 2 and 3 in 1996 and 1997 on Maths C test*

| | Using and Applying English item | |
	English pupils	French pupils
< level 3	14%	10%
= level 3	44%	58%
> level 3	42%	30%

and investigative maths. French children performed at a higher level but in a narrower range of maths areas, for example in computation and geometry.
- Children's performance reflected national curricular values. English children performed better at items which required a more 'hands-on' or experimental approach, for example the maths investigation. French children performed better at items which required more technical expertise, for example computation.
- Children's performance was negatively affected by the unfamiliarity of another country's national test items.

These findings mirror those reported in Chapter 7 in which we suggested implications for international assessment as they imply that children's performance at international maths tests will also be affected by national curriculum content and values, and their overall degree of familiarity with test items.

Furthermore there are important methodological implications for international assessment which, as we argued in Chapter 1, arise from the limitations of the use that can be made of quantitative results alone. These results give rise to more questions than they do answers. The finding that French children perform better at number is comparatively useless in terms of understanding the nature of the English children's weaknesses and of suggesting remedies to improve their performance. As in the area of language skills the quantitative analysis of children's performance was not able to answer the questions of *how* and *why* one sample of children performed relatively better or worse than another beyond the fact that French children were seen to spend slightly more curriculum time on maths than English children – 32.3 per cent compared to 28 per cent (see Table 7.5). A more qualitative analysis arguably provides a more meaningful and ultimately more useful diagnostic approach using cross-cultural assessment. In the next section, we illustrate this argument through an exploration of some of the different ways French and English children engaged with the maths problems we set them.

HOW DID ENGLISH AND FRENCH PUPILS DIFFER IN THEIR APPROACH TO MATHS PROBLEMS?

In order to provide for a more in-depth analysis of the pilot test scripts, The QUEST team built in analytic codes during the marking process which would provide more understanding about the differences in English and French children's maths strategies. One such code was for children's use of algorithms, or methods for carrying out calculations. It emerged from the analysis that English children were more likely to use written algorithms for addition than French children but that French children were more likely to use algorithms for subtraction, multiplication and division. Since the English children performed relatively poorly and decreasingly well through the four operations, this suggests that French children were functioning at a higher level in computation. More French children were using mental arithmetic for addition and they were more skilled at correctly carrying out written procedures in subtraction, multiplication and division.

Another strategy code used was repeated addition. This analysis showed that English children were more likely to use repeated addition than French children. In

Table 8.5 *Percentage of English responses using repeated addition by gender and socio-economic zone of school in Maths B*

	1996 %	1997 %
English girls	25	24
English boys	17	17
English low SES	28	26
English high SES	7	6

both the 1996 and 1997 tests 21 per cent of English children used repeated addition as a strategy in multiplication compared to 0 per cent of French children. Furthermore the analysis showed a correlation between use of repeated addition and gender, and repeated addition and socio-economic status. English girls were more likely to use repeated addition than English boys and it was used more frequently by children from schools in low socio-economic areas (Table 8.5).

The quantitative analysis also included a strategy code for trial-and-error which showed that English children were on the whole more likely to use trial-and-error as a problem-solving strategy than French children; for example, in Maths B in 1997 14 per cent of English children used trial-and-error as a method compared to 4 per cent of French children. When use of trial-and-error was looked at in terms of socio-economic zone of school there was a stronger correlation between its use in England in high economic zones than there was in France. This suggests that the performance of English children reflected the relative dominance given to the strategy of trial-and-error in English maths teaching whereas French children were using the strategy more by default (Table 8.6).

Finally, the quantitative analysis was used to confirm a hypothesis from the pilot tests that English children were more likely to 'have a go' at a question than were French children. By comparing the percentage of questions left unanswered, particularly when children were faced by the unfamiliar items from another country's national tests, it could be seen that English children were less likely to leave questions unanswered. The 'no response' rate for French children was 33 per cent in the English maths test, Maths B, whereas it was 12 per cent for English children in the French maths test). This indicated that English children were more willing to try than

Table 8.6 *Percentage of English children by socio-economic zone of school using trial and error*

	1996 %	1997 %
English low SES	7	12
English high SES	15	20
French low SES	10	6
French high SES	5	0

French children when faced by unfamiliar demands, even though the results indicated that they were performing less well. Perhaps it was the fear of failure that acted as a restraint on French children.

By building in codes – which had been based on a qualitative analysis of pilot scripts – to detect the different strategies that children might be using, the quantitative results gave more information about the relative strengths and weaknesses of English and French children. It seemed that English children were less expert in their use of mental arithmetic and written algorithms in computation, often falling back on the use of repeated addition in multiplication. English children were also more likely to use trial-and-error as a method. This kind of analysis was much more revealing of the relationship between national cultural tradition curriculum emphasis and pupil performance than the overall tally of correct and incorrect responses among the two cohorts. There were, however, still many unanswered questions about *how* and *why* English and French children were performing differently, to which only a more in-depth qualitative analysis could provide answers.

The perceptions of English and French children about the differences between maths in the two countries had given some insights. Most French children who had been to school in England found that English maths was less advanced; for example, an 11-year-old French boy who had spent 6 months in a Year 6 class said that '*En maths, c'était un peu différent . . . le niveau était plus bas . . . je dirais qu'il y avait un an de différence.*' (In maths it was a bit different . . . the level was lower . . . I'd say there was a year's difference.)

However this boy was also displaying an awareness of a qualitative difference – 'it was a bit different'. Another 11-year-old French boy currently in a Year 6 class who had been in England for a year said: 'In France I think in maths they learn more, in England they don't learn very well, they're still in the same level . . . sometimes you learn things in England but you don't learn in France and sometimes you learn things in France that you don't learn in England'.

In what way was maths different? What could an analysis of children's scripts tell us about these differences?

Two random samples of 36 Maths A and Maths B scripts (18 English and 18 French) were taken from the 1997 QUEST tests. The analysis was first carried out independently and then in tandem on the total of 72 scripts by a QUEST researcher and a QUEST maths consultant.

We selected test items for the qualitative study according to two criteria. First was the suitability of the test response; for example, the item had to require a written response. Second was the significance of the response as indicated by the quantitative results; for example, there may have been a substantial difference in English and French children's performance, or one sample may have outperformed the other sample at its own national test item.

We selected a total of 16 test items; the majority of these were from the area of number, as it was these items that proved to fit the criteria the most closely. Number operations, and using and applying maths, proved to be the most significant areas of discrimination in terms of a cross-cultural analysis, as we illustrate in what follows.

WHAT DIFFERENCES AND SIMILARITIES DID THE FRENCH AND ENGLISH CHILDREN DEMONSTRATE IN APPLYING THEIR SKILLS IN THE USE OF A NUMBER?

One of the strengths of the QUEST project was that children's performance in number could be compared in four different formats: arithmetic problem-solving computations, horizontally and vertically arranged algorithms, language problem-solving computations, and multiplication and division by 10 and 100. In the sample of 36 English and 36 French children, their performance in the four computations was compared across these four different formats as the following examples illustrate.

Arithmetic problem-solving computations

Maths B	Q2a	$\square \div 5 = 22$
Maths B	Q2b	$\begin{array}{r} 2\square 8 \\ +29\square \\ \hline 555 \end{array}$
Maths B	Q3a	$323 \times \square 7 = 1518$
Maths B	Q3b	$\square \times \square - \square = 42$

French children outperformed English children at these English items although there were more French children who were perhaps puzzled by the unfamiliar format and left questions unanswered, or who used inappropriate strategies, e.g. adding instead of dividing: $17 \div 5 = 22$.

The approach of English children was to develop individual strategies. These varied in efficiency from *tallies* (Figure 8.1) to *multiples* of 5 (Figure 8.2) to another English child in Q2a who first worked out that $10 \times 5 = 50$, then did $20 \times 5 = 100$, and then added a further 2 lots of 5 to make 110 (Figure 8.3).

^{2a.} Write in the missing number.

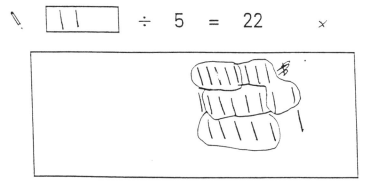

Figure 8.1

2a.   Write in the missing number.

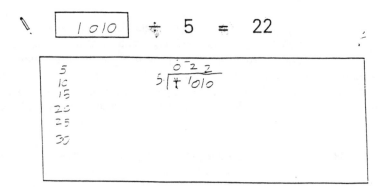

Figure 8.2

2a.   Write in the missing number.

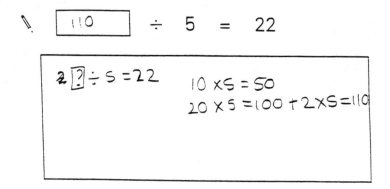

Figure 8.3

We found that English children were less likely than French children to use traditional algorithms, and that they made more errors where they did use them; for example, more English children made errors in carrying over one digit than did French children. Where English children made errors in their algorithms these were more serious ones than the French errors. For example, some English children had difficulty in correctly setting out:

Instead of   218   they wrote   218
             + 292   + 292

Some English children appeared to be disadvantaged by their lack of algorithmic skill, for example in Figure 8.4, where the child understood the computation required and used trial and error to try to multiply 323 by 27 or 57 but could not carry out the operation.

3a.   Write in the missing digits.

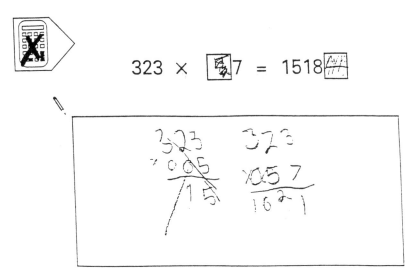

$$323 \times \boxed{\text{5}7} = 1518\boxed{}$$

Figure 8.4

There were also similarities between the strategies of English and French children. In the question in Figure 8.5, both English and French children were split between

2a.   Write in the missing number.

$$\boxed{} \div 5 = 22$$

Figure 8.5

those who carried out a direct multiplication of 5 × 22, or those who used trial and error of dividing a number by 5. Both samples were equally confused by taking the item to mean 22 ÷ 5 thus resulting in an answer of 4.4. Furthermore an equal number of English and French children were confused by decimal place value and arrived at the answer: 11 ÷ 5 = 22. There is some evidence that English children who fell into this trap did not understand decimal place value on the calculator. For example one English child wrote: 'I looked on the cogulator and 11 ÷ 5 = 22.'

Strengths and weaknesses

Addition

The overall results had shown that English children's performance at addition was not significantly different from that of French children but that their performance became progressively weaker when it came to subtraction, multiplication and division. Taking addition first, our more detailed analysis showed that one reason for the French children's slightly stronger performance was the incidence and the type of errors that they made. English children made more errors: 6 English children, out of the sample of 36, for example, made 'carrying over' errors compared to only 2 French children, and 4 English children made decimal point errors compared to 2 French children. English children made more serious errors, e.g. ignoring place value in 'carrying over', as in the following example:

> *168.75*
> *+ 42.50*
> *11010.125*

There is also some evidence to suggest that more French children were 'carrying' over mentally, particularly in the two high SES French schools, in that they gave less written evidence of 'carrying over'.

Subtraction

In subtraction, English children performed relatively poorly: 32/36 French answers were correct compared to 18/36 English answers. Again English children made more types of error and they made more serious errors: some English children had problems with the irreversibility of numbers in subtraction, for example:

> *463*
> *− 167*
> *304*

Where smaller numbers were systematically subtracted from larger numbers, some children added instead of subtracting; some gave the wrong answer with no written evidence as to working out; and some made errors in rewriting the computation. The errors made by French children, by contrast, were typically minor slips and careless errors such as $13 - 7 = 4$; these were also made by some English children.

Multiplication

In both the multiplication and the division items which had been set out in a familiar way for each country, the errors made by English children suggested that although they had had relatively little training in long multiplication with a decimal point and in long division, they were prepared to devise their own strategies. Whether these strategies were correct or incorrect, efficient or inefficient, in solving the problem, they illustrated English children's willingness to 'have a go' at the question. French children's errors in these two items represented errors made in their attempts to carry out a process which they had been trained to do. For example, in multiplication, some French children either omitted a decimal point or misplaced it; some made small errors in addition or multiplication:

$$\begin{array}{r} 4.28 \\ \times 3.5 \\ \hline 20\ 80 \\ 128\ 4. \end{array}$$

A very small number of French children forgot to write in a 0 or forgot to add on carried-over numbers. In division some French children seemed to have trouble carrying through the complete process of division right to the end; for example,

$$\begin{array}{r|l} 2782 & 26 \\ \hline 0182 & 1032 \\ \hline 14 & \end{array}$$

where the 1 of 182 was ignored and 26 was divided by 82 instead. There were also a few examples of computational errors. However, the errors made by English children in both multiplication and division suggested that they had not received the same amount of formal training and practice in the appropriate procedure. In multiplication, out of a sample of 36 English children 33 made incorrect answers. Of these answers, 24 revealed this lack of training and showed that children were having to devise their own strategies to attempt the test item; for example:

$$\begin{array}{r} 4.28 \\ 3.5 \\ \hline 13.40 \end{array}$$

where the tactic was to multiply decimal numbers by decimal numbers and whole numbers by whole numbers, so that $5 \times 8 = 40$, 0 and carry 4; $5 \times 2 = 10$, $10 + 4 = 14$, 4 and carry 1, then $3 \times 4 = 12$, $12 + 1 = 13$. Many of the English attempts were variations on this type of incorrect strategy. There were also six examples of English scripts where children were working out $4 \times 3 + 2 \times 5 = 13.00$ and five examples of English children trying $4 \times 3, 2 \times 5 + 8 = 13.08$. Another English child devised her own strategy of breaking down the operation into its smaller components:

$$
\begin{array}{r}
4.28 \\
\times 5 \\
\hline
2140
\end{array}
\qquad
\begin{array}{r}
4.28 \\
\times 3 \\
\hline
1200
\end{array}
$$

$$
\begin{array}{r}
21.40 \\
+12 \\
\hline
33.40
\end{array}
$$

only she forgot that it was .5 and not 5.

Division

Similarly in division, out of the sample of 36 children there were only 3 English children who arrived at the correct answer compared to 24 French children, and errors made by English children were more serious. Some English children's scripts demonstrated that they had little understanding of division as the resulting answer was often bigger than the sum that had been divided. Other written evidence showed lack of practice in carrying out long division; for example:

$$
\begin{array}{l}
1\ 2\ remainder\ 1 \\
26\overline{)2782}
\end{array}
$$

where $27 \div 26 = 1, 82 \div 26 =$ (about) 2, giving an answer of 12 remainder 1.

There was some variation between schools, with English children from some schools showing evidence of more training in the use of division; for example:

$$
\begin{array}{l}
1\ 7 \\
26\overline{)2782} \\
\ \ 26 \\
\ \ \ \ 182
\end{array}
$$

where the only error was that the zero of $18 \div 26$ had been forgotten.

It was interesting to note that French children used different methods to work out where to place the decimal point in their multiplication and division operations. In division they used the general strategy of $10 \times 10 < y < 100 \times 10$, for example in Figure 8.5a.

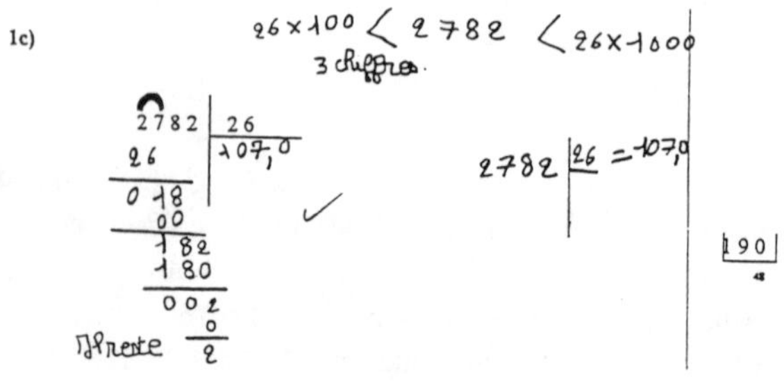

Figure 8.5a

However, in multiplication the decimal point was 'automatically' inserted. It was not clear in the latter case whether French children were estimating the product of the two whole numbers or counting the numbers of decimal numbers to position the decimal point.

Language problem-solving computations

Three items in this format were included in the QUEST tests. There were only minor differences in performance and errors made among both groups of children in the question in Figure 8.5b.

Both sets of scripts had examples of children calculating 36 + 36 but then forgetting to subtract 4; or children who apparently guessed at an incorrect answer (no evidence of any calculation), and examples of children using very varied incorrect techniques; for example, from a French child:

10	*12*	*14*	*16*	*+6*
−4	*−4*	*−4*	*−4*	*8*
				10
6	*8*	*10*	*12*	*12*
				32 cms

4. Here are some picture frame sizes.

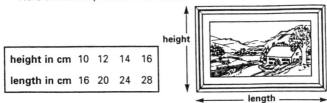

| **height in cm** | 10 | 12 | 14 | 16 |
| **length in cm** | 16 | 20 | 24 | 28 |

For each frame, the length is **twice** the height, **subtract 4.**

What is the **length** of a frame which has a **height of 36cm?**

72 cm ✗

Figure 8.5b

French children were, however, making errors that were more 'off the mark' in that 5 French children divided 36 by 2 before adding 4 to make an answer of 22 cms; no English children tried a division. French children were slightly more likely to use multiplication than addition and, interestingly, more French children used a horizontal calculation than a vertical one in this item:

$36 \times 2 = 72 - 4 = 68$

The following two examples provide a good illustration of the different strategies employed by English and French children. French children were more routinized in their approach to the question. They appeared to tackle the question with known techniques and a common structural approach. For example, all the French children in the sample who attempted the question in Figure 8.6 used a multiplication algorithm.

7.

During morning break 83 biscuits were sold by a group of 4 children. Each biscuit cost 3 pence.

What was the total price of all the biscuits sold?

Write your answer in the box:

Can you explain how you worked this out?

....

....

....

Figure 8.6

The following response from a French girl also illustrates the French technical and structural approach. The girl realized that what was required of her was multiplication. She wrote '*C'est une multiplication*' and then carried out the operation:

Il y a 83 petits pains qui coutent 3F chacun alors on fait 83 $\times$ 3   = 249
petits pains   3 F   le montant

Some French children had a problem with interpreting the language in the Maths A Q7

$83 \div 4 = 20, 75 \times 3 = 62.5$

or they realized the item required an algorithm but chose an incorrect one.

$83 \div 3 = 27$ *reste 2*
Le montant total de cette vente est de: 27,2 francs.

In the next example, taken from the English national test (Figure 8.7), French children's errors were to do with computation as a result of the use of incorrect information from the data of the item, for example using the age of the children:

9.50 × 11 = 109.5 F

5. (suite)

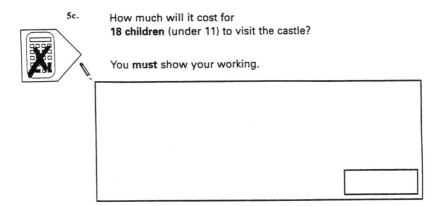

Here are the admission charges for the Château de Versailles

Château de Versailles	
Price per person	
Adults	24,50F
Children (over 11 years)	13F
Children (under 11 years)	9,50F

5c. How much will it cost for **18 children** (under 11) to visit the castle?

You **must** show your working.

Figure 8.7

The English approach to this item was very different, as Figures 8.8–8.11 illustrate. English children used a range of independent strategies. These included: long multiplication – 5 out of 36 English children compared to 15 out of 36 French children used long multiplication. In those scripts there were many more examples of serious computational errors – 9 out of 36 English children compared to 0 out of 36 French children made serious errors in their multiplications. For example

$$\begin{array}{r} 95 \\ 18 \times \\ \hline 7.80 \\ 6 \end{array}$$

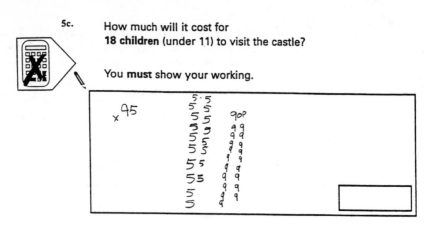

Figure 8.8

where the child incorrectly thought that $5 \times 8 = 60$, and 95 was not multiplied by 1 as well.

Also included were these strategies:

(a) repeated addition; for example see Figure 8.8. Of English children, 21 per cent compared to 0 per cent of French children used repeated addition in this question.
(b) use of tallies; for example see Figure 8.9.
(c) $18 \times £1$; minus $18 \times 5p$; for example see Figure 8.10.
(d) a very independent example of a strategy, used by a girl, which showed an intuitive leap in calculating $90p \times 18 + 18 \times 5p$ which she conceptualized as $90p \times 19$ (see Figure 8.11).

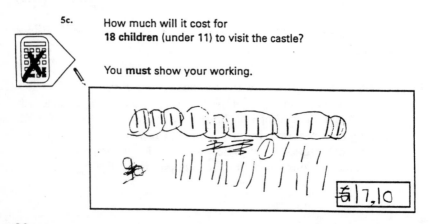

Figure 8.9

5c. How much will it cost for
     18 children (under 11) to visit the castle? \7pounds +5p

You **must** show your working. *cut*

> there 18 chidren + it Cost 95p.
> So you say you had 1pound that
> will come to 18 pound 1F take
> 45 p- off it will Be
> 71 pound 50

Figure 8.10

5c. How much will it cost for
     18 children (under 11) to visit the castle?

You **must** show your working.

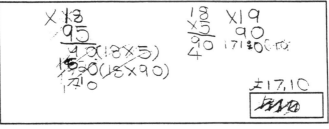

Figure 8.11

(e) the separation of the computation in Maths A Q7 into more manageable sections
   so that the units and tens were first multiplied separately and then added together:

8 × 3 = 24
3 × 3 = 9
80 × 3 = 240

> *240*
> *+9*
> ―――
> *249*

> '*3 times 3 is nine and 80 times 3 is 240 and 240 plus*
> *9 is 249. 249 converted into pound is £2.49*'

Thus these two test items in particular show the different mathematical worlds in
which English and French children were working. Most English children understood

the problem and developed a range of individual strategies to find a solution. However, they were disadvantaged by their inadequate skill in carrying out multiplication and division and their inability to distinguish between efficient and inefficient strategies. Most French children approached the problem with the confidence that came from a strong structural and technical background. They knew how to use multiplication, but some children lacked the skill to interpret the data correctly which prevented them from knowing which numbers to multiply.

A similar pattern emerged when the children were asked to multiply and divide by 10 and 100. The analysis of children's scripts showed that some of the reasons behind the much better performance of French children at such questions was first that more French children appeared to be moving the decimal point in order to arrive at a correct answer. However, this can only be inferred from the numbers of children in the sample who produced the correct answer with no written evidence of having carried out an algorithm, as shown in Table 8.7.

Table 8.7

	No. of English correct answers (out of 36) with no written algorithm	No. of French correct answers (out of 36) with no written algorithm
Maths A Q2a	5	16
Maths A Q2b	3	15

Secondly, French children achieved more correct answers since they were more likely, even when they did not move the decimal point, to carry out the required multiplication or division successfully. In the sample of French scripts 12 French children carried out the following long multiplication correctly, compared to the success of only 5 English children (Figure 8.12).

2.

a)   Work out this multiplication sum.

7 . 1 4 x 1 0 0 =

Figure 8.12

Once again there was plenty of evidence to show that English children understood which algorithm to use but that they did not have the necessary skill to carry it out. In this question, 12 English children attempted unsuccessfully to carry out a long multiplication, compared to only 3 unsuccessful French children.

English errors were serious ones, to take three examples from Maths A Q2a:

e.g.	100	e.g.	7.14	e.g.	14
	× 14		× 100		× 100
	1400		700		104

In the division question (Figure 8.13), there were 9 English children who made unsuccessful attempts to do a long division, compared to only 6 French children's lack of success.

b)   Work out this division sum.

$$325.6 \div 10 =$$

Figure 8.13

English errors illustrated the problems children experienced in setting out a division algorithm:

$$\frac{325.6}{\div 10}$$

and problems again in reversibility:

$$325.6\overline{)\frac{325.60}{10}}$$

In conclusion, the children's scripts in number indicated that French children mostly performed better at number because they were more likely to use traditional algorithms effectively. French children were at a higher level in number; for example, they had moved beyond an interpretation of multiplication as repeated addition and tallies, and they showed no problems with reversibility in subtraction and division. Most French errors in number were related to the process of using algorithms. Their more serious errors involved handling data – choosing the relevant numbers, and choosing the appropriate algorithm to use.

English children, in contrast, often demonstrated an understanding of what the test item required of them and applied a range of efficient, and all too often inefficient, strategies to answer the question. There was considerable differentiation between the level and efficiency of strategies used. Higher-achieving children used efficient strategies which allowed them to make intuitive leaps, but lower-achieving children used inefficient strategies of repeated addition and tallies instead of multiplication. They did not demonstrate that they had learned to distinguish between efficient and inefficient strategies. Where English children did use standard algorithms their skills were considerably less developed than those of French children.

Overall, this comparison of children's performance in relation to arithmetic problems which involved computations, horizontally- and vertically-presented algorithms, language problem-solving computations and multiplication and division by 10 and 100, showed that the gap between the performance of English and French children was at its greatest when the computations required were at a high level.

This kind of detailed analysis of children's performance in number is important not only for what it tells us about *why* English children were not performing as well as French children but also because it tells us something about *how* they were performing. It gives us insights into two different mathematical worlds. English children were using a more experimental and individualized approach, thinking for themselves, trying to find their own solutions to problems. French children, coming from a mathematical background where there is more coherence and consensus about mathematics education, were using a common more technical and structural approach. This cultural difference can also be seen in maths text books from England and France (Harries and Sutherland, 1998) and is illustrative of the different maths cultures which characterize European countries (Burton, 1994). This has important implications for global comparisons.

WHAT DIFFERENCES AND SIMILARITIES DID ENGLISH AND FRENCH CHILDREN DEMONSTRATE IN USING AND APPLYING MATHS?

The story in relation to using and applying maths is somewhat different. Our overall test results had indicated that English children performed better at the more open-ended test paper (Maths C) which involved an investigation into odd and even numbers (Figure 8.14).

A more detailed scrutiny of children's answers revealed that English and French children were using different approaches which were consistent with those that they had used in number. English children were more likely to approach this maths investigation using individualistic strategies; for example, see Figure 8.15.

This example shows a child thinking for him- or herself and finding his or her own way of expressing understanding of the concept of odd and even numbers. Some English children were also able to take the investigation to a higher level (reflecting English classroom differentiation); for example, see Figure 8.16.

You will need to spend about 20 minutes on this Maths problem.

Some children investigated what answers they got when they did sums with odd and even numbers. They made these comments on what they found.

David:
When I add two odd numbers together I always get an even answer.
For example, 3 + 5 = 8   and   9 + 11 = 20

Sarah:
When I add an odd number to an even number I always get an odd number for an answer.

Megan:
I think that an even number multiplied by an odd number might sometimes be even and sometimes be odd.

Farshad:
Taking away an odd number from an even number always gives me an odd answer.
For example, 12 - 9 = 3

1   **Which of these children do you agree with and which do you disagree with? Say <u>why</u> you think they are right or wrong.**

2   What other general statements could you make about calculating with odd and even numbers? Say why you think they are true.

Figure 8.14 *An investigation into odd and even numbers*

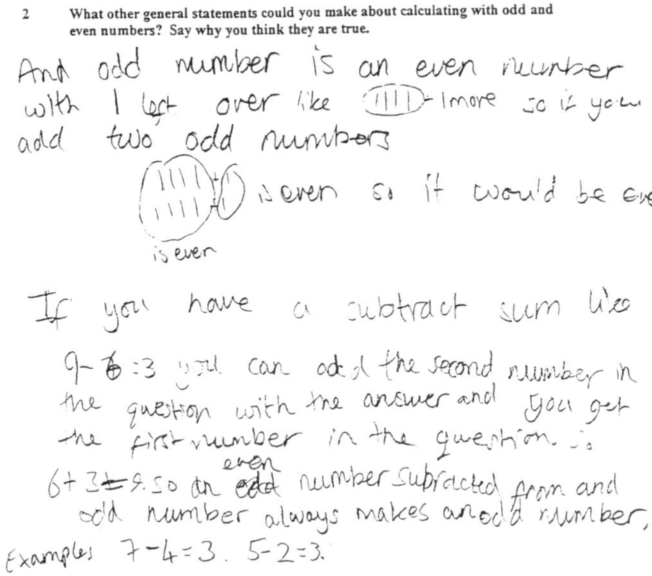

2   What other general statements could you make about calculating with odd and
     even numbers? Say why you think they are true.

And odd number is an even number
with 1 left over like (IIII)–1more so if you
add two odd numbers

(IIIII) is even   so   it   would   be   eve.
is even

If you have a subtract sum like

9–6=3 you can add the second number in
the question with the answer and you get
the first number in the question. ∴
6+3=9. So an ~~odd~~ *even* number subtracted from and
odd number always makes an odd number.
Examples 7–4=3. 5–2=3.

Figure 8.15 *An example of an English child's response to Maths C, showing the use of individual strategies*

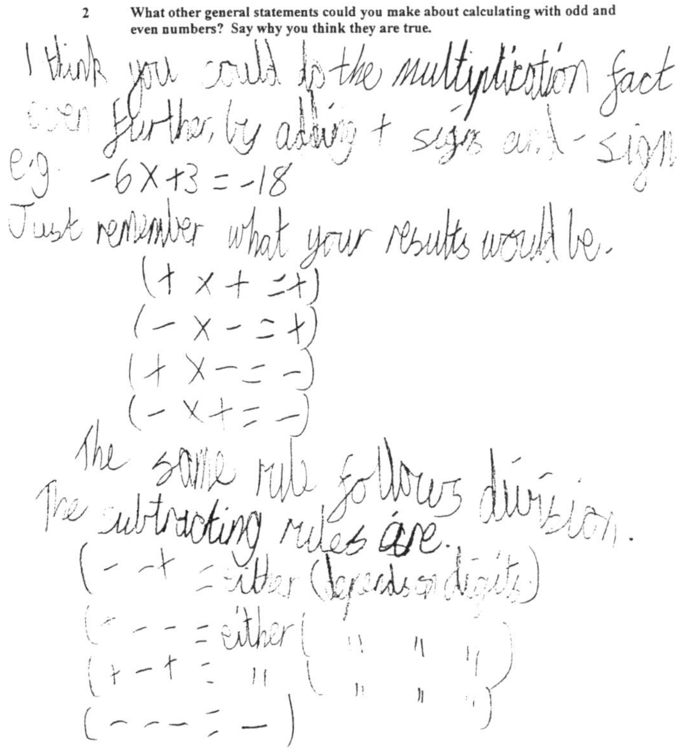

2   What other general statements could you make about calculating with odd and
     even numbers? Say why you think they are true.

I think you could do the multiplication fact
even further, by adding + signs and – signs
e.g. –6 X +3 = –18
Just remember what your results would be.
(+ x + =+)
(– x – =+)
(+ X – = –)
(– x + = –)
The same rule follows division.
The subtracting rules are.
(– –+ = either (breaks or digits)
(– – – = either (,, ,, ,,)
(+ – + = ,, (,, ,, ,,)
(– – – = –)

Figure 8.16 *An example of an English child's high level of analysis in Maths C*

There were no examples of French children performing at a level 6.

French children on the whole had more difficulty in making a response to this unfamiliar type of maths exercise, but where they did respond they were more likely, first, to repeat and rework the given test item statements about odd and even numbers – they seemed reluctant to commit themselves to making general statements. Secondly, their responses often alluded to rules giving definitions of odd and even numbers (Figure 8.17).

2   Qu'est-ce qu tu pourrais affirmer d'autre sur le calcul des nombres pairs et impairs en général? Explique pourquoi tu penses que c'est vrai.

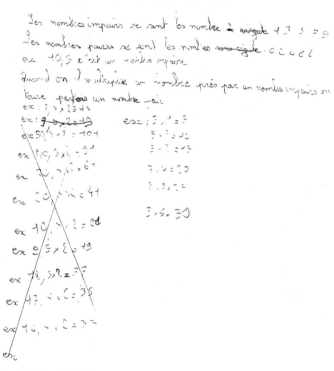

Figure 8.17 *A typical French child's response to Maths C*

Thirdly, they used a more technical approach rather than thinking around the problem in the way that English children tended to do, as Figure 8.18 shows. French children also tended to express their findings in a more formal style (Figure 8.19).

Another difference between the scripts was that English children, when unable to respond mathematically, showed more freedom of expression. Written English comments ranged from the cheeky (Figure 8.20), the anthropomorphic (Figure 8.21), to the absolute:

The calculator is true because it gives you lots of help with your maths and I think calculators are true.

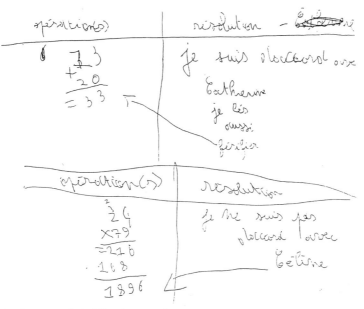

Figure 8.18 *The more technical French approach*

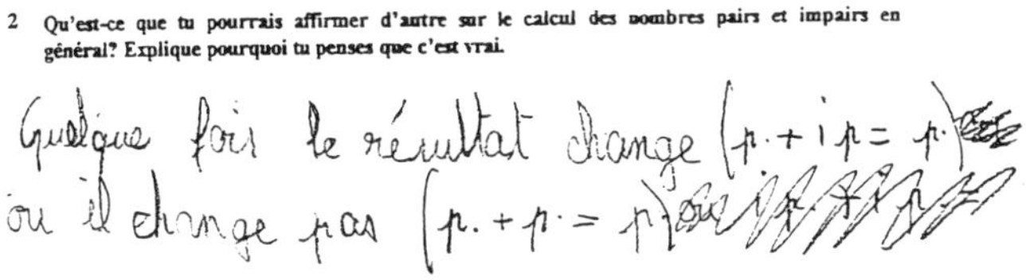

2   Qu'est-ce que tu pourrais affirmer d'autre sur le calcul des nombres pairs et impairs en général? Explique pourquoi tu penses que c'est vrai.

Quelque fois le résultat change $(p. + ip = p.)$
ou il change pas $(p. + p. = p.)$

Figure 8.19 *The more formal style of French responses*

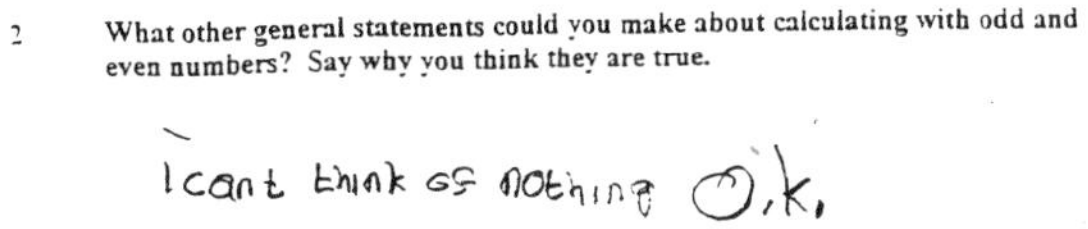

2   What other general statements could you make about calculating with odd and even numbers? Say why you think they are true.

I cant think of nothing O.k.

Figure 8.20 *A cheeky English response*

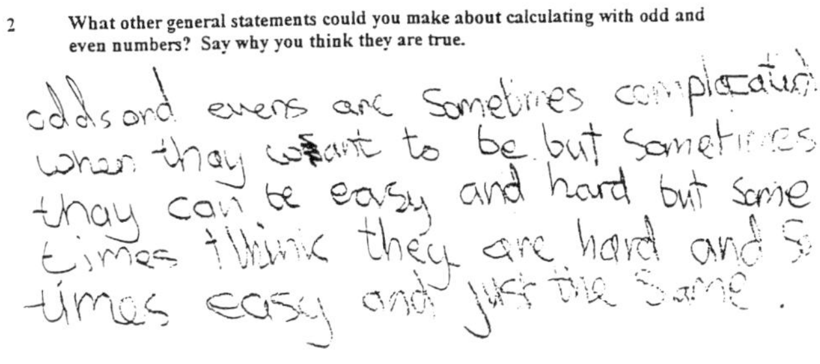

2   What other general statements could you make about calculating with odd and even numbers? Say why you think they are true.

odds and evens are sometimes complicated
when they want to be but sometimes
thay can be easy and hard but some
times I think they are hard and s
times easy and just the same.

Figure 8.21 *An uncommitted English response*

Thus an analysis of answers to this question once again showed a difference in mathematical approach between the two countries. French children tended to use more mechanistic and routinized strategies, English children used a more individualized and 'creative' approach. Quantitative assessment not only revealed *how* the children's performance was different, it also provided some reasons for the different performance levels. English children performed relatively well at this question because the English individualized approach was more suited to the open-ended nature of this mathematical task.

IMPLICATIONS OF THE QUALITATIVE ANALYSIS

It is frequently assumed that maths is a culturally neutral subject and that cross-cultural assessment in maths is therefore straightforward, valid and reliable. However this is far from being the case (Burton, 1994). Even in Europe mathematical notation varies from one country to another; for example, $70.4 \div 22 = ?$ is expressed in France as: $70,4:22 = ?$ In Hungary multiplication is written as a dot: $3 \cdot 5 = 15$. The type of mathematical notation and the computational procedures favoured by different countries are but the tip of the iceberg. Children learn maths through the mediation of what Vygotsky called cultural 'tools' – for example maths procedures – and 'mediated action' – for example, maths teaching. Mathematical learning is, therefore, like other subjects, also social and cultural learning. There are important mathematical cultural differences between England and France. These include: curricular differences (Howson, 1991), national test differences (Planel, 1996), differences in classroom contexts (Osborn and Broadfoot, 1992 and Chapter 6 in this book). These contextual differences produce significant variations in English and French children's approaches to maths. Our data clearly showed that in number and in using and applying maths, English children had a more individualized approach. French children were more routinized and technical in their approach. English children could be characterized as 'explorers' in their maths strategies, French children as 'technicians'. Furthermore, the evidence of the last two chapters suggests that English and French children were conforming to two different learning 'frames' in both maths and language. In Chapter 7 we suggested that for reading comprehension, English children used more *empathetic* skills, whereas French children used more *mechanistic* skills. In story-writing, English children conformed to a model which emphasized *content*, French children conformed to a model which prioritized *form*. It can therefore be argued that children's output in maths and language shared the same underlying cultural preoccupations. The English cultural frame appears to favour wide-ranging content, individualization and experimentation. The French cultural frame by contrast emphasizes structure and technical skill.

The identification of this kind of culturally-informed model of what constitutes 'learning' is significant as it shows the degree to which like is not being compared with like. It challenges the validity and reliability of much international assessment not only in language but also in what superficially at least might have appeared to be the more culturally neutral subject area of maths.

This kind of comparative assessment of English and French children's performance in maths also has important implications for teaching and learning. By comparing children's performance the relative strengths and weaknesses of the two national samples have emerged. These differences ought to inform policy discussions. If English children perform better at open-ended tasks and French children perform better in narrower, but more technically advanced, tasks, our findings give detailed indications about the learning areas in each country which need reinforcing. They also imply that children's performance reflects the maths aims of a country and that it is these aims which need to be clarified before changes in teaching are introduced.

Chapter 9

What Makes a Difference? Social Disadvantage, Gender and National Context

In previous chapters the main focus has been on national comparisons of children's perceptions of learning and schooling and on their sense of pupil, school, and national identity. This chapter, however, seeks to examine *intra*-national differences – particularly those deriving from differences in socio-economic status, gender and, to some extent, ethnic identity. It considers the relative significance of such personal and local environmental differences in influencing children's perceptions of schooling and their achievements compared with the influence of the *inter*-national differences which were documented in previous chapters.

The negative relationship between material and social disadvantage and educational attainment is well established in empirical national and international research findings (Wedge and Prosser, 1972; Davie, Butler and Goldstein, 1972; Rutter and Madge, 1976; Mortimore and Blackstone, 1982; Pilling, 1990). In both England and France, socio-economic and family background factors have been shown to be important influences upon pupils' educational achievement at all stages of education (Duru-Bellat *et al.*, 1993; Obin, 1993; OECD, 1996). By the age of five, children are already very differently placed in terms of the benefit they can derive from primary education and, so far, policy-makers, educationists, and schools have found this link between disadvantage and educational performance very difficult to break. The odds are still stacked against schools in poorer areas, although some schools have been able to succeed in spite of this (National Commission on Education, 1996).

Of course, there is an important distinction to be made between children's perspectives on school and learning, their actual behaviour and their learning outcomes. On the whole, the research evidence for a link between social disadvantage and attitude to learning is less conclusive than that for the link between social disadvantage and learning outcomes. A number of British studies suggest that pupils from socially disadvantaged backgrounds may not have markedly poorer attitudes to school and learning than those from more favoured backgrounds (Cox, 1983; Fogelman, 1983; Keys and Fernandes, 1993). However, Blatchford (1996), in a study of British black (Afro-Caribbean) and white pupils in predominantly disadvantaged areas of inner London found that at age 11 almost all pupils felt that it was important to do well at school but by age 16, white pupils had less positive attitudes to school and to their own achievement than black pupils. A recent MORI survey of the attitudes to learning of a sample of British schoolchildren carried out on behalf of the Campaign for Learning (1998) also found that black and minority ethnic-group pupils were more likely to express an enjoyment of learning than white boys.

The research evidence for gender differences in attitudes to learning is similarly inconclusive, although the disparity in achievement between girls and boys is well documented; for example, in the annual report of the Chief Inspector of Schools (OFSTED, 1998). This report highlighted the poorer academic achievement of boys compared to that of girls, particularly in GCSE examinations, and linked it to an 'anti-achievement' culture among boys. Murphy and Gipps (1996) have reviewed a number of studies which document the lower educational motivation of boys compared with that of girls in the English system. However, Blatchford, in the study cited above, found few significant differences between boys and girls in their attitudes to school. Keys and Fernandes (1993) found only a slight tendency for girls in Years 7 and 9 to show more positive attitudes to school than boys.

DISADVANTAGE AND EDUCATIONAL POLICY IN ENGLAND AND FRANCE

In addressing the issues of educational opportunity, social disadvantage and inequality, the education systems of England and France have evolved very different approaches. In France where the educational system has developed constitutionally, and where there is a strong tradition of republicanism, the origin of which may be traced back to the works of Condorcet, it has been considered morally unacceptable to treat pupils differentially. In the discourse of government and indeed in individual teachers' discourse the idea that all citizens should be seen to have equal rights under the law recurs repeatedly as a fundamental principle. Schools have consequently been expected to provide the same curriculum and pedagogy to all pupils regardless of who they are, where they live, or even (within limits) of their ability level (Holmes, 1985; Sharpe, 1992a). Traditionally, therefore, the French education system has avoided differentiation and has, in principle, adopted a policy of equal entitlement for all pupils. Ideologically at least, there is great emphasis placed on the goals of equal opportunity, reduction of inequality, preparation for citizenship and, of course, secularity. This emphasis on the 'public good' aspects of education is enforced by strong centralization and a pre-eminent role for the state in educational decision-making and control.

In contrast, the English educational system has developed historically in a far more 'piecemeal' fashion, based on what is 'customary' rather than on constitutional principles (Archer, 1979). Unlike France, where the Revolution and subsequent Napoleonic era had led to a formal national commitment to a unified system of provision, English education was strongly influenced in the past by voluntary agencies and the Church, and by a tradition of diversity and individualism evolving from a variety of local initiatives. Religious education and concern with the personal and social development of children has always formed part of the remit of schools. Consequently a concern with the development of individual potential recurs as a theme both at the level of national policy discourse and in teachers' classroom and staffroom discourse. The English primary education system in particular has enshrined the notion of differentiated teaching according to the perceived needs of children. In this view, greater equality within education cannot be achieved without understanding that children start school from rather different points and therefore require different teaching approaches.

In neither case, however, has the approach adopted substantially affected the strong linkage between social class, educational attainment and life chances which has existed in both systems over a period of many years (Halsey, Heath and Ridge, 1980; Banks *et al.*, 1992; Bourdieu and Passeron, 1977; Baudelot and Establet, 1971; Charlot *et al.*, 1992).

Thus in both countries, schools are seen in the main to be simply reproducing the social conditions prevailing in the wider society (Bourdieu and Passeron, 1977). In England, concern about low standards and low teacher expectations in inner-city schools was documented in several HMI reports (Thomas, 1985; Bolton, 1988). A survey of schools in disadvantaged urban areas carried out by OFSTED, the government inspectorate, found that across the system as a whole, the residents of these areas were 'poorly served by the education system' and that pupils had 'only a slim chance of receiving sufficiently challenging and rewarding teaching throughout their educational career' (OFSTED, 1993).

In England, this concern has led to a number of Government policy initiatives such as the privatization of some schools deemed to be 'failing', handing over the management to a consortium of professionals and business people whose responsibility would be to 'turn the school round' (DFE, 1992; OFSTED, 1998). The Education Reform Act of 1988 providing for the implementation of a National Curriculum and National Assessment, and subsequent reforms such as the introduction of a national system of 'quality assurance' of schools through OFSTED inspections, could also be seen as attempts to provide equal entitlement for all children, although there were undoubtedly many other government intentions underlying these reforms (Ball, 1994).

In contrast, in France, there was government and public concern expressed about the inflexibility of the education system, and the failure rate of children in the inner city, as well as the rate of *redoublement* (repeating the year) which resulted in a damaging loss of self-esteem according to some critics (*Le Monde de l'Education*, 1995), although other research found little evidence of this (Robinson, 1990, 1992). A number of recent policy initiatives in France, in particular the Jospin reforms in the late 1980s (*Loi de l'Orientation sur l'Education*, 1989), have attempted to address this problem by introducing the notion of more differentiated teaching according to the needs of the child and by attempting to make the system more flexible to local needs (Jospin, 1989; Corbett and Moon, 1996).

Previous work by the Bristol team has demonstrated how this disparity of goals within the two educational systems has resulted in a significant difference in the beliefs and teaching methods adopted by teachers working in areas of disadvantage in the two countries (Osborn *et al.*, 1997). Teachers in France emphasized equal entitlement and a transmission-enlightenment model of education. Their values were 'universalistic'. They were concerned to treat all children in exactly the same way in order to achieve justice and educational results, and aimed to transmit the same academic body of knowledge to all pupils, taking little account of the risk of alienating some children. In contrast, English teachers in disadvantaged areas were characterized as 'rescuers' who were strongly protective of children's needs. Their discourse emphasized the needs of disadvantaged children as different from the mainstream and requiring a different response from schools. They talked of 'providing education relevant to children's needs and a caring, thoughtful environment' and they placed an emphasis on 'relevant and meaningful' curriculum and teaching methods, rather than on teaching all children in exactly the same way.

Even after the recent educational reforms in both countries, outlined above, which were intended to shift teachers' emphases and pedagogy and, arguably, to bring the goals of both closer together, the research suggested that the strong emphasis by French teachers on 'enlightenment' and 'entitlement' had not changed, nor had English teachers' strong belief in differentiating according to children's needs. The findings demonstrated that teachers' values are not easily changed by reforms imposed from above. This chapter therefore sets out to examine how these national goals, mediated as we have seen by teachers' values, are subsequently received and filtered by children's own perceptions.

PERCEPTIONS OF BOYS AND GIRLS IN RELATION TO SCHOOLING AND LEARNING

When we analysed the responses of boys and girls in each country to elements of the questionnaire concerned with attitudes to schooling and learning, we found some noticeable differences between the attitudes to school and the apparent motivation of boys and girls in both England and France. On most of the measures used, English girls were more strongly positive than English boys towards teachers, school and learning. The pattern for French boys and girls was more variable. Sometimes French girls were slightly more positive, but on the whole there were relatively few differences in attitude between the sexes. However, there were fewer statistically significant gender differences than there were national differences. Those differences which were statistically significant were less strongly significant than the differences between the two national contexts. In other words, although gender did make a difference to attitudes this difference was not so important as the difference attributable to national context. To take one example where the differences *were* statistically significant, in both France and England it was girls more often than boys who agreed strongly that they liked their teacher (Table 9.1a). Where overall agreement was compared (i.e. 'strongly agree' and 'agree' were combined) many of the differences between French girls and French boys disappeared but the differences between English girls and English boys were still striking. In all the gender

Table 9.1 *Gender differences by country in attitude to school*

(a) *'I like my teacher.'*

	England %			France %		
	Girls	Boys	Whole cohort	Girls	Boys	Whole cohort
Strongly agree	36.7	22.4	29.2	73.4	55.1	63.2
Agree	34.9	37.5	35.8	20.7	32.7	27.2
Disagree	3.3	4.3	3.8	0.5	0.9	0.7
Strongly disagree	1.9	8.2	5.1	1.6	3.7	2.7
Not sure	23.3	27.6	25.9	3.7	7.5	6.2
Numbers	208	223	431	181	200	381

(Signif. p = 0.001)   (Signif. p = 0.005)

(b) *'My friends think it's important to do well.'*

	England %		France %	
	Girls	Boys	Girls	Boys
Strongly agree	23.7	19.2	45.9	52.9
Agree	43.7	33.5	27.0	26.2
Disagree	6.8	11.8	9.5	7.0
Strongly disagree	4.7	11.8	4.1	3.5
Not sure	21.1	23.6	13.5	10.5
Numbers	190	203	148	172

(Signif. p = 0.001)   (Signif. p = 0.005)

(c) *'I keep working even if the teacher leaves the room.'*

	England %		France %	
	Girls	Boys	Girls	Boys
Strongly agree	18.8	18.4	61.3	63.1
Agree	43.8	32.7	22.7	25.3
Disagree	15.9	18.8	3.3	3.0
Strongly disagree	7.2	13.5	9.4	6.1
Not sure	14.4	16.6	3.3	2.5
Numbers	208	223	181	200

(Signif. p = 0.001)   (Signif. p = 0.005)

comparisons it was English boys who were the least positively motivated towards teaching, learning and school.

In the questionnaire we also explored the perceived attitudes of the pupils' peer group in order to explore what influence the group might have had on the individual's attitude to school. The responses of the pupils to the statement 'My friends think it's important to do well' were revealing (Table 9.1b). In England significantly more girls than boys agreed with this but, in France there was very little difference between the sexes. If anything boys were more likely to be in agreement. French pupils as a whole were far more likely than English pupils to have a peer group with a positive orientation to school. This would seem to lend some support for the notion that some of the low motivation of boys may be linked to an anti-school peer-group influence.

Similarly, in response to the statement 'I keep working even if the teacher leaves the room' English girls were significantly more likely to be in agreement than English boys, whereas in France the responses of both boys and girls were very similar (Table 9.1c). Overall, French pupils were far more likely to say that they kept on working even if their teacher left the room. This pattern was repeated throughout the responses to the questionnaire items.

SOCIAL DISADVANTAGE AND PERCEPTIONS OF SCHOOLING AND LEARNING

We knew from our previous research that there was a noticeable difference in the goals which primary teachers set themselves in different social environments in England, with inner-city teachers particularly emphasizing a caring approach and evincing an 'ideology of rescue', whereas French teachers tended to share more or less the same objectives for the children regardless of the social environments in which they worked, expressing an ideology of 'entitlement' and 'enlightenment' (Osborn *et al.*, 1997). As we have already seen in Chapter 4, those differences were to some extent reflected in the children's descriptions of their school, with English children in disadvantaged areas emphasizing a caring approach and French children in similar areas emphasizing the importance of good behaviour and academic success.

Overall, the social-class differences in pupils' attitudes to schooling, to learning, and to achievement in the two countries may help to explain what has been referred to as the 'long tail of underachievement' in England. The French educational system's emphasis on 'equal entitlement' compared with the English emphasis on "differentiation" was reflected in children's perceptions. There were relatively few differences in attitude between children in different socio-economic areas in France, whereas there were many significant socio-economic differences in England. These differences in England indicated that middle-class children were more positive about school in some respects, but that children in areas of low socio-economic status valued the affective, personal and social dimensions of school more highly. They were more likely to see school as useful for social and non-academic reasons such as 'helping you to get on with people' or 'learning how to use your spare time' (Table 9.2a). They were also

Table 9.2 *Social class differences by country in attitudes to school*

(a) *'School helps you learn how to use your spare time.'*

	England %		France %	
	Low SES	High SES	Low SES	High SES
Strongly agree	19.0	7.1	29.6	20.3
Agree	29.6	25.3	25.8	32.4
Disagree	12.8	27.6	14.5	16.9
Strongly disagree	12.8	12.4	11.8	15.5
Not sure	25.9	27.6	18.3	15.0
Numbers	276	172	192	211

(Signif. p = 0.00009)   (Non-significant)

(b) *'I like being at school.'*

	England %		France %	
	Low SES	High SES	Low SES	High SES
Strongly agree	21.7	17.0	53.5	43.3
Agree	33.1	33.9	31.6	28.6
Disagree	12.9	20.6	2.1	6.7
Strongly disagree	15.1	8.5	3.2	8.6
Not sure	17.3	20.0	9.6	12.9
Numbers	276	172	192	211

(Non-significant)   (Signif. p = 0.01401)

(c) *'The best part of my life is the time I spend in school.'*

	England %		France %	
	Low SES	High SES	LowSES	High SES
Strongly agree	15.9	6.4	27.9	13.7
Agree	10.5	7.6	14.7	12.3
Disagree	22.8	33.7	14.7	24.6
Strongly disagree	27.5	30.8	16.3	26.1
Not sure	23.2	21.5	26.3	23.2
Numbers	276	172	192	211

(Signif. p = 0.00719)   (Signif. p = 0.00551)

more likely than middle-class children to say that they had fun and enjoyed most lessons, reflecting the particular concerns of teachers in English disadvantaged areas with engaging children's interest and valuing their contribution.

Children from disadvantaged areas were more instrumental in their reasons for wanting to do good work. For example, they said that when they wanted to do good work it was either in order to be praised, or not to be shouted at, or so that parents would be pleased and so that they would get a good mark or sticker. There was more evidence of an anti-school sub-culture in English schools in disadvantaged areas than anywhere else, with these children most likely to say that they had friends who fooled around in class and who made fun of them or teased them if they did really good work.

Socio-economic differences in French children's responses were rarely statistically significant although it was children in *low* socio-economic status areas in France who were more likely to say that they liked being at school (Table 9.2b).

In both countries, it was children in areas of low socio-economic status who said that they wanted to do well so that their parents would give them a treat or some money. However, English children living in these areas were more likely to say that their parents would punish them if they did not do so well. Charlot *et al.* (1992) have suggested that the relative importance of intrinsic motivation in learning and its relationship to social class may explain socio-economic differences in achievement. They argue that children from lower socio-economic status families may be disadvantaged since they are more likely to be extrinsically than intrinsically motivated. These findings lend some tentative support to this link.

Strikingly, there was one exception to the pattern of evident socio-economic differences in attitude in England and the lack of differences in France. Similar social-class differences in both countries emerged in response to the statement 'The best part of my life is the time I spend in school' (Table 9.2c). Children in disadvantaged and low socio-economic status areas in both countries were far more likely to agree with this, although French children were more strongly in agreement. This is a cogent comment on the quality of their lives outside school and suggests that in this respect at least, the impact of poverty and economic inequality was similar in both countries.

GENDER AND SOCIAL DISADVANTAGE IN RELATION TO PERFORMANCE ON MATHS AND LANGUAGE

Chapters 7 and 8 compare the overall performance of French and English pupils on the maths and language assessments, details of which are given in Appendices 1–10. The relationship between gender and performance in the language skills was not always clear-cut, however. On the whole girls performed better than boys. English and French girls outperformed boys in all aspects of story-writing, that is, purpose and organization (in 1997 the average score for English girls was 53 per cent, English boys 44 per cent, French girls 43 per cent, English boys 40 per cent), grammar, style and spelling; English and French girls had higher scores in handwriting than did the English and the French boys (in 1996, 67 per cent of English girls and 91 per cent of

Table 9.3a *Percentages of correct answers by gender for reading comprehension in 1996*

	English girls %	English boys %	French girls %	French boys %
Q5a	47	40	54	41
Q5b	45	43	56	47
Q5c	51	57	39	29

Table 9.3b *Percentages of correct answers by socio-economic scale of school in reading comprehension in 1996*

	English high SES %	English low SES %	French high SES %	French low SES %
Q5a	75	27	50	44
Q5b	70	31	60	42
Q5c	76	42	34	30

French girls achieved a level 3 compared to 56 per cent of English boys and 75 per cent of French boys). However, although French girls performed consistently better than French boys in inferential reading comprehension, English boys outperformed English girls at one of the questions, as shown in Table 9.3a.

The role played by the socio-economic zone of the school in children's performance in language skills was much more clear, with children from high socio-economic-zone schools performing substantially better. Between the performance of English children from schools of low socio-economic status and those from schools of high socio-economic status, there was a greater gap than there was in the performance of French children between the two zones. For example, the scores for inferential reading comprehension were as shown in Table 9.3b.

This greater gap in performance levels according to socio-economic zone of school in England could also be seen in handwriting, with the ratio of high SES level 3 to low SES level 3 being 87 per cent to 48 per cent in England and 87 per cent to 78 per cent in France.

As in the language tests, the results for maths not only increased our understanding about the relative performance of English and French children but also gave some insight into the effect of gender and social class. The relationship between gender and performance was not a straightforward one in 1996 and 1997. English and French boys performed slightly better at both Maths A and Maths B in 1996, but in 1997 English and French girls tended to perform better than boys.

The relationship between performance and gender in Maths C was not very clear-cut either. In 1996 girls performed better and there was a bigger English gender gap, whereas the differences in gender were not so pronounced in 1997, as shown in Table 9.4b.

The performance of English and French children was clearly influenced by the socio-economic zone of the school, particularly in England where children from

Table 9.4a *Average scores by gender for Maths A and Maths B in 1996 and 1997*

	1996		1997	
	Maths A %	Maths B %	Maths A %	Maths B %
English girls	42	38	46	63
English boys	44	42	39	57
French girls	57	31	36	34
French boys	59	33	37	31

Table 9.4b *Percentage of English and French pupils achieving levels 1, 2 and 3 by gender*

	1996			
	English boys %	English girls %	French boys %	French girls %
< level 3	16	10	8	7
= level 3	43	41	66	64
> level 3	40	49	25	27

	1997			
	English boys %	English girls %	French boys %	French girls %
< level 3	15	14	17	8
= level 3	45	46	48	54
> level 3	39	38	33	36

schools in high socio-economic zones performed considerably better than those in low socio-economic zones. As was the case in the language areas of reading comprehension and handwriting, there was a greater spread of achievement between socio-economic zones in England than in France, for example in Maths A and Maths B, as shown in Table 9.5a.

Similarly the results for Maths C showed that English and French pupils from lower SES schools performed less well than those from higher SES schools, and that there was a greater spread of achievement in England than in France, as shown in Table 9.5b.

To summarize, just as the spread in terms of attitudes to schooling, learning, and achievement of boys and girls and of children of different socio-eonomic status was greater in England than in France, so too was the spread in terms of performance in maths and language. The differences were particularly marked in terms of socio-economic status. Consistently there was a greater gap between the performance of English children from schools of lower and higher socio-economic status than there was in the performance of French children from the two types of catchment area. The sections which follow first examine the more qualitative data from children's

Table 9.5a *Average scores by socio-economic zone of school (SES) for Maths A and Maths B in 1996 and 1997*

	1996		1997	
	Maths A %	Maths B %	Maths A %	Maths B %
English low SES	36	31	38	32
English high SES	56	57	54	48
French low SES	53	29	57	29
French high SES	64	35	69	41

Table 9.5b *Percentage of English and French pupils achieving levels 1, 2 and 3 in Maths C for 1996 and 1997 by SES of school*

	1996			
	English low SES %	English high SES %	French low SES %	French high SES %
< level 3	19	1	14	2
= level 3	39	46	63	67
> level 3	40	52	22	29
	1997			
	English low SES %	English high SES %	French low SES %	French high SES %
< level 3	15	13	15	6
= level 3	55	20	53	48
> level 3	29	65	30	45

writing and then present profiles of individual children which lend further support to the findings above.

THE 'LADDER OF PROGRESS THROUGH SCHOOLING': THE INFLUENCE OF NATIONAL CONTEXT, GENDER AND SOCIAL DISADVANTAGE

It was suggested in Chapter 4 that French children had a clearer notion of a ladder of progress through their education than did English children; that they had a clearer idea of their goals and of how to achieve them. The argument was that French children were able to accept and to derive meaning from a learning environment which to an English child might have appeared austere and severe, because of their understanding of where their learning was taking them and that it was for their own good. An eleven-year-old French girl argued

Elle crie mais ça rentre dans la tête . . . c'est pour notre bien . . . plus tard on verra que c'est à cause d'elle . . .
(She shouts but it goes into our heads . . . she does it for us . . . later on we'll know that it's thanks to her . . .)

It was therefore important to find out more about the nature of English and French children's understanding of their ladder of progress at school to further explore the relationship between systems of education and children's achievements. Could the relative success of French children at the more formal elements of learning be partially explained by French children being more motivated by a school system such as the French one which is clearer and more comprehensible than some others?

During the second phase of fieldwork we asked English and French pupils to write about the most important things they saw themselves doing during the next ten years. There were 153 English children and 101 French children in the last year of primary school who completed this exercise in their classrooms. The eight schools in this phase were chosen from the sixteen schools of the original sample on the basis of matching socio-economic criteria.

As background, we note here that in France pupils' year levels are decided on the basis of pupil achievement rather than pupil age. Pupils attend 'collège' from about 11 years to about 16 years. Pupils are then selected on the basis of their educational progress for academically or vocationally orientated 'lycée' which prepares most pupils for a hierarchy of academic and vocational Baccalauréats. The 'Collège' year terminology is 'la Sixième' (Year 7), 'la Cinquième' (Year 8), 'la Quatrième' (Year 9), 'la Troisième' (Year 10), after which pupils may go on to the 'Lycée' years of 'la Seconde' (Year 11), 'la Première' (Year 12) and 'la Terminale' (Year 13).

ENGLISH AND FRENCH CHILDREN'S UNDERSTANDING OF THE LADDER OF PROGRESS THROUGH THEIR RESPECTIVE EDUCATIONAL SYSTEMS

The children's scripts were first coded for whether they had included a vague or a clear understanding of their progress through school. It should be emphasized that the children were not actually asked to refer to their time at school but only to 'important things in the next ten years'. It was thus assumed that a reference to school was a reflection of its importance in the children's lives.

The following two examples from the English context illustrate what was meant by a 'clear understanding' of the ladder of progress:

During the next ten years I will be moving to my secondary school. I will work hard there and get about an hour's homework a night. In my first or second year of secondary school I will be going to France and staying there for about a week. In my fifth and fourth year I will be focusing on my GCSEs which will be very happy but hard years. I hope to get at least 3 A's and 3 B's at least. In my sixth year of school I will be starting on my A-levels which will be very hard and probable very stressful. I will probably be going to university and I would like to study architecture, and that is when I will be choosing my career, which will be one of the most important things in my life. I would relay like to be an architect. (Boy, High SES)

In the next ten years I see myself going to secondary school. I'm looking forward to that but I am also dreading it. I see myself doing GCSEs and my A-levels. I already think I know what to do but I might change. I want to do Dance, Drama and English. I want to do those because I want to be an actress and I enjoy dancing. I also see myself going to university to do a degree in Drama. (Girl, High SES)

Two examples from the French context also illustrate clarity in the ladder of progress:

Je voudrais, en 6°, être dans une très bonne école et être avec des professeurs gentils. Je voudrais aussi ëtre plus attentif pour mieux réussir ma 6°. Si je passe en 5° je serais contente et je ferai comme en 6°, j'écouterai mieux et je ferai ça jusqu'à je réussisse à arriver à ce que je veux, et ce que je veux c'est avoir un très bon travail et ne plus redoubler car je sais que la 4°, la 3° et la 2° seront difficile et qu'il faudra que je travaille sans penser à autre chose, et si je veux rentrer à la 'Fac' il faut que je m'accroche. (Girl, High SES)*
(I'd like in Sixième to be at a very good school with good teachers. I'd like to concentrate more so I do my Sixième better. If I go up to Cinquième I'll be pleased and I'll do like in Sixième, I'll pay more attention and I'll go on like that until I succeed at getting at what I want, and what I'd like is a really good job and not have to repeat a year, because I know that Quatrième, Troisième and Seconde will be difficult and that I'll have to work and not think about anything else and that if I want to go to university I'll have to really get going.)

Pour moi, quand je serai plus vieux, ce qui sera très important, c'est de bien travailler en classe, suivre les leçons, bien écouter le maître, bien apprendre, réfléchir, me souvenir. Bref, faire du bon travail à l'école et passer du CM2 jusqu'en terminal sans avoir de problèmes. Aux études pour avoir son diplôme, je vais essayer d'être archéologue comme j'aime bien l'histoire. Ma mère dit qu'on gagne beaucoup d'argent. J'espère vraiment réussir mon diplôme car je n'aimerais vraiment pas être sans travail, à la rue. (Boy, Low SES)
(What will be very important for me when I'm older is to work hard at school, to keep up with the lessons, listen to the teacher properly, learn things properly, think and remember things. In short, work hard at school and go right up from CM2 to Terminal without any problems. In the way of qualifications I'd like to be an archaeologist because I like History. My mother says you can earn lots of money. I'd really like to get qualified because I relay wouldn't like to be out of work, in the streets.)

A 'vague understanding' can be illustrated by these two examples from the English context:

I think after my primary school I would go to secondary school and do my exam tests and then I would like to find a job. (Girl, Low SES)

After school I will like to go to college to learn some more stuff before I get a job. (Girl, Low SES)

Two examples from the French context also illustrate a 'vague understanding':

J'aurai un booster le jour de mon anniversaire à 14 ans. A 16 ans je vais avoir le Bac Pro. de docteur. Ensuite je travaillerai, je serai très bon docteur, je m'acheterai un superbe appartement. (Boy, Low SES)
(I'll get a scooter on my 14th birthday. At 16 I'll get the Bac Pro to be doctor. Afterwards I'll work, I'll be a good doctor, I'll buy a wonderful flat.)

J'espère pouvoir continuer mes études et sinon travailler dans la médecine pour pouvoir aller dans les pays et soigner les malades. (Girl, Low SES)
(I hope to be able to continue studying, otherwise I'll work in medicine so I can go to other countries and look after ill people.)

Table 9.6 *Socio-economic differences in children's vision of their future progress*

	Children showing an understanding of the ladder of progress %
English low socio-economic status	32.8
English high socio-economic status	46.4
French low socio-economic status	42.8
French high socio-economic status	87.1

The percentage of children from the different social groups in each national sample giving a vague or clear mention of a ladder of progress through school suggested clear socio-economic differences in the children's understanding (Table 9.6). The higher social groups from both countries wrote more about the ladder of progress in their scripts but the French high SES group wrote the most. The findings also show that French children from both social classes included more references to the ladder of progress than English children from both social groups.

Analysis of the children's scripts also showed other characteristics which when put together provide an English child's and a French child's profile of their understanding of their future education:

English child's profile	*French child's profile*
Less understanding of the ladder of progress	More understanding of the ladder of progress
Importance of A-levels and GCSEs to high SES and Asian children	Importance of Baccalauréat to children from all social classes
Less value placed on learning and studying	More value placed on learning and studying
Marks, standards and exams of greater importance	Fear of repeating a year
	Age of less importance

Inevitably there were some children's scripts which were exceptions and did not fit into such a clear-cut pattern. The profiles represent general characteristics.

Not only did the French children have a clearer understanding of a ladder of progress through school but they also emphasized that the primary purpose of school was to pass the Baccalauréat. There was a perception that without the Baccalauréat the children would not find any work:

Il y a le Bac qui est important: plus la moyenne est bonne on a un meilleur boulot. Pour certaines personnes le Bac il est très dur, donc ils ne le passent pas et ils n'ont pas de travail. Si on n'a pas de boulot on n'a pas d'argent. Si on n'a pas d'argent on a rien . . . (Girl, Low SES)

(There's the Bac which is very important. The higher mark you get the better job you'll get. For some people the Bac is very difficult so they can't get it and they don't get any work. If you don't have any work you don't have any money. If you don't have any money you've got nothing . . .)

As a boy from the same Zone wrote:

Il faut déjà passer le Bac avant d'avoir un métier.
(You've got to get your Bac before you can get a job.)

The Baccalauréat is seen to be of prime importance for all jobs:

'*Je voudrais continuer l'école primaire, ensuite le collège, la Sixième, Cinqième, Quatrième, Troisième, le lycée aussi, puis l'université, jusqu'à mon Bac. Mon plus grand rêve c'est de devenir chanteuse.* (Girl, low SES)
(I'd like to continue primary school, then secondary school, Sixième, Cinquième, Quatrième, Troisième, and the lycée, then university, until I get my Bac. What I really dream of doing is being a singer.)

The Baccalauréat assumed far more importance in French children's vision of the future than that given to the importance of A-levels by English children. Of the French children, 25 per cent made reference to the Baccalauréat whereas only 16 per cent of the English children wrote about A-levels. More revealing is the relationship between these two qualifications and socio-economic status in the two countries. With the exception of inner-city ethnic-minority children, French children from all social groups considered the Baccalauréat important. However, an emphasis on the importance of the role of A-levels and even GCSEs in English children's futures seemed to be restricted to English high-SES children and the primarily Asian children from one of the lower-SES schools.

In the French context, studying and learning were also given prime importance, irrespective sometimes of the desired career:

Je voudrais essayer de devenir cuisinier en faisant de longues études. Je vais lire beaucoup de choses sur la cuisine. Je vais aussi apprendre des textes sur la cuisine. Je vais faire des tas de plats comme les lasagnes, les cannelonis . . . (Boy, High SES)
(I would like to be a cook after years of studying. I'll read all about cookery. I'll learn cookery texts. I'll do lots of dishes, like lasagne, cannelloni . . .)

A career which in England would be seen as vocational and non-academic is in this boy's case portrayed as requiring years of intense study.

The value placed on studying and learning in the French context can also be seen in the written discourse used by the French children. The phrases 'faire des études', 'réussir les études' and particularly 'continuer les études' occurred repeatedly. Of French pupils, 42 per cent included these expressions in their scripts. The nearest English equivalent appeared to be 'to get a good education' and 'to do well'. The former phrase was most frequently used by English lower-SES children; education was sometimes referred to as a commodity, as something which was just acquired:

In ten years time I would probably get my education and go to a new school. (Boy, Low SES)

When I am 16 I am going to get an education, smoke and get a job. (Boy, Low SES)

Also of note is the understanding in France that studying lasts for many years and that the pupil's age does not matter:

Je continuerai mes études jusqu'à vingt ans. (Girl, High SES)
(I shall continue my studies until I'm twenty.)

Je voudrais continuer l'école jusqu'à l'âge de 21 ans, plus si ce n'est pas assez. (Girl, Low SES)
(I'd like to stay on at school until I'm 21, or more if that isn't enough.)

The French pupil discourse reflects the reality in French education of some pupils who may stay on at a lycée and only pass the Baccalauréat at the third attempt.

In contrast to the accepted '*longues études*' that French pupils realized lay before them, English pupils were often happy to leave school at 16:

When I grow up to 16 I will be just leaving school. Then looking for a job with computers. (Boy, Low SES)

Education in England was sometimes presented as an alternative to a job rather than as a necessary prelude to one:

If I don't get a job before I leave school I will stay on at school. I want to be a hairdresser when I grow up because I like doing people's hair. (Girl, Low SES)

Whereas the French children referred to the process of studying in their discourse about their future education, the English children referred more to the institution or place of study. Of English pupils, 36 per cent wrote about 'college' or 'university'. Only 3 per cent of French pupils wrote about '*la faculté*', '*l'université*' or '*une école*'. Only 16 per cent of French children mentioned secondary school, compared to the 45 per cent of English children who did so. It is interesting that French discourse refers to the actual process of studying whereas English discourse concentrates more on the type of establishment where learning takes place.

The greater importance accorded to learning and education in France is also seen in the more frequent references that the French children made to their own future children's education. In the same mode as the original script from the first Language test, the French children wrote:

Je veux être marié à une belle femme et avoir deux enfants, très gentils et bien éduqués et assez bon en classe. (Boy, High SES)
(I want to get married to a beautiful woman and have two children who are very good, well behaved and do well at school.)

J'aimerais que mes enfants soient bon en classe et que plus tard ils on un bon métier. (Girl, High SES)
(I'd like my children to do well at school and to later get a good job.)

The English children also wrote about their own children, enumerating the number of girls and boys, but they rarely referred to their education:

... and I would like to grow up and get married and have a baby and my baby will grow up and have a good time. (Girl, low SES, low set)

French high-SES children in particular had a clearer understanding of the difficulties that lay ahead of them and of the effort that they would have to make if they were to do well at school. Of French high-SES children, 41 per cent referred to the difficulties of the task that lay ahead of them, compared to only 8.3 per cent of French low-SES children. There was less of a difference between English socio-economic groups. Of English high-SES children, 18 per cent wrote about their difficulties, compared to 12.7 per cent of English low-SES children.

SUMMARY

These findings suggest that the sample of French children from all socio-economic groups are motivated at school by their need to pass the Baccalauréat and by their knowledge that it is important to learn and study for as long as this will take. There was more disparity between social groups for English children's academic objectives. The English high-SES and Asian children aimed at A-levels, GCSE and college or university more than English working-class children. English low-SES children made less reference to academic goals than French children from lower socio-economic areas. It could be argued that the relative simplicity of the French secondary school system may partly account for the greater degree of homogeneity between socio-economic groups of the French children. The Baccalauréat is (at least) presented as one qualification which is open to all French students, unlike A-levels which are beyond the reach of many English students. Perhaps the Baccalauréat and the relatively high status accorded to learning in France function as a glue binding together primary and secondary school populations from different groups with one common aim.

Not only did the French children seem more motivated by a common aim but they also conveyed a clearer understanding of how that aim was to be achieved. They were aware of the progression from one year to another in the secondary system, and some children conveyed their acute understanding that this progression was not automatic but depended on the effort they made. English children, not surprisingly given the greater complexity of the English secondary school system, did not convey such a clear understanding of their progress through the system; indeed for some low-SES children education was seen as something which occurred almost automatically at the age of 16.

The findings suggest that the relative simplicity or complexity of educational systems may affect children's motivation. Perhaps a simpler system which has one common goal may be easier for both pupils and parents to understand and may motivate children more. It should also not be assumed that all pupils share the same access to information about their school system. More disadvantaged children, particularly those in England, need to be more informed about the secondary school system and to have a better understanding of the ladder of progress at secondary school. For French children the existence of this unifying goal together with a clear understanding of how it may be achieved may mean that if you know where you are going and you know how to get there you may be likely to arrive at your destination.

Individual pupil profiles

The eight profiles of individual children which follow support these arguments about the ladder of progress and the broad generalizations made elsewhere in this chapter.

RICHARD	English low-achiever

Eleven-year-old Richard attends an urban school on the edge of a large city in western England. There are many social problems within the families of this area.

Richard's social background is not known, but his attitude to school is quite clear. He does not like school; he finds it boring and does not think that school work is very useful or that it will help him find a job. According to him a good school provides 'lots of things that make us happy' and his school fits the criteria. His parents' attitude towards his school or his work is unclear. His friends like fooling around and do not think that school is important. All this confirms Richard's lack of motivation towards school in general.

His two best subjects are art and P.E. and his two worst ones are English and maths, but he recognizes their importance because 'when you're older like, you're always putting down the wrong words' (i.e. spelling) and 'you might not know, when it says you must pay this amount of money and it adds all up and you don't know what it means'.

School does not play any part in his future. He mentions 'trying to get a job and getting a lot of money'; he is aware that his teacher would like him 'to get a good education' but knows that he gets confused in class and needs to ask for explanations which he does by getting in the queue to see his teacher.

'I'm not too good in maths', says Richard. This is confirmed by his test scores which were very poor: 4/16 in the French test, 4/21 in the English test and very low marks in the investigation. His computational skills are low (A Q1d); he uses written algorithms accurately for addition and subtraction presented in traditional form but does not attempt an addition when it is set in a 'puzzle' format. He finds it difficult to transfer his computational skills to help him solve problems. In a simple problem where the price of biscuits had to be calculated using a multiplication, he says 'I gested' and appears to have done an addition: 83 biscuits + 3 pence = 86 pence. In another problem where a long multiplication was involved Richard uses repeated addition and some sort of tally system but gets the wrong answer (B Q5c). He has limited understanding of geometry, can only find very basic information in a table, is able to answer a simple question of probability or symmetry but does not understand fractions or decimal numbers. In the investigation he has difficulties with simple statements on odd and even numbers and does not attempt any generalization.

In the language tests he scored slightly better marks, which confirms his impression that 'I'm doing all right in my English'. He is able to find only some factual information in a text (A Q3a. b.) but is unable to use inferential skills. His spelling is quite good in the grammar test where he only makes mistakes in the use of 'there', 'their' and 'they're', and it is also fairly consistent in the creative writing. His punctuation is rather poor in the set exercise but better in his story-writing. He can use joined-up handwriting in an exercise but does not when he writes freely, although his writing is still neat and legible. His story-line is very simple with basic vocabulary and no paragraphs. He uses direct speech to make his story more lively but the suspense comes to an abrupt end and leaves the reader unsatisfied.

Richard says that an ideal pupil should be 'a brainy kid' but concludes that he is 'not a lot' like that child.

1d)

$$\begin{array}{r} 4.28 \\ \times \quad 3.5 \\ \hline 13\overset{.}{:}40 \\ 14 \end{array}$$

5c.   How much will it cost for
18 children (under 11) to visit the castle?

You **must** show your working.

£6.00

3. a   Who did Tom live with when he was a little boy?

...His grandfather, sir Gregory.

b   Who did he live with afterwards?

...Greenthorpe a town in
forestry commission.

Figure 9.1 *An example of Richard's work*

CHRISTINE   English low-achiever

Christine is eleven and attends a traditional working-class school set among council houses in a town of southern England. Approximately one-third of the children in the school receive free school meals.

Her parents are divorced. Her mother is a housewife and according to Christine's teacher 'never comes to parents' evenings'. Christine does not know whether her father works or not as she does not live with him.

Christine is a 'nice, sensible girl ... but she can be stubborn and occasionally nasty', says her teacher. She has a good relationship with her teacher and with her friends but can sometimes bully them. Her future does not involve school: 'I would not stay on at school' and she thinks that 'my job will be to work in a shop'. She does not know her position in the class: 'I think I'm in the middle ... I'm quite good at topics (history or science)' which, to her, is the most important subject with P.E. She is sometimes worried about her work especially 'when I'm doing maths, that's my horridest ... in case you get some sums wrong and the teacher has a go at you because she's explained them to you'.

Her marks in the maths tests, 2/16 (French test), 4/21 (English test), and in the investigation confirm the reasons for her fear. Her computational skills are very poor. She rarely uses written algorithms and when she does, for example in the traditional addition, she forgets the decimal point. Although she tries to use a written algorithm to solve a subtraction, she does not succeed (A Q1b). She never uses trial-and-error, but sometimes some sort of tally system, to help her calculate a 'puzzle' multiplication, without any success. Her problem-solving skills are also poor. In the 'price of biscuits' problem where a multiplication is involved she justifies her answer by saying 'because I added', but her result does not bear any relation to either an addition or a multiplication (A Q7). In the 'price of tickets' problem she does not use any sort of written algorithm or method and comes up with an answer which once again does not fit any pattern. She has limited understanding of geometrical terms, can handle simple data and draw a symmetrical shape but does not understand or attempt averages, probability, the pie-chart problem, decimals, fractions or visual questions involving perimeter and areas. Her approach to the investigation sometimes involves new examples but she does not come up with any kind of generalization.

In the language tests her reading comprehension skills are almost non-existent (1/6 in the French test, 0/6 in the English test) (B Q1. 2. 3.). Even the name of the main character is wrong. In the grammar exercise her spelling is quite good and in the creative writing it is very good. In the punctuation exercise her performance is adequate but in the story-writing her punctuation is erratic; she makes use of speech marks and commas but not always appropriately. Her handwriting is neat but not always joined-up. She has difficulties with the alphabet. Her story is simple but structured although the ending is disappointing and the vocabulary very basic.

In spite of her disappointing results Christine thinks that her school is quite special because she has been there for some time and because 'the teachers are nice'.

7.

During morning break 83 biscuits were sold by a group of 4 children. Each biscuit cost 3 pence.

What was the total price of all the biscuits sold?

Write your answer in the box:

$$200$$

✗

Can you explain how you worked this out?

Because I added

1b)

$463 - 167 = 246$

$$
\begin{array}{r}
3\overset{15}{\cancel{4}}\overset{13}{\cancel{6}}3 \\
1\ 6\ 7 \\
\hline
204\ 6
\end{array}
$$

1. What was Gita's opinion on first hearing about the family outing to Bokeham?

Gitas opinion she said yes ✗

2. Which words tell you this?

'mom anouced a bookfar at Bookham maro ✗

3. How had Gita's opinion changed by the end of the report?

She did But dosent now. ✗

Figure 9.2 *An example of Christine's work*

ELOISE   English high-achiever

Eloise is an eleven-year-old girl attending a 'middle class' school in a fairly affluent urban area.

Her father works as a solicitor and her mother is a housewife who is involved in voluntary work. She has a brother who is deaf.

Eloise is highly motivated and realizes that her school work will be better if she behaves well. Her parents support her and her friends also think that it is important to do well at school. But her school life is still not the best part of her life.

She achieved good results in the French maths test (10/16), a very high score in the English test (17/21) and very good marks in the investigation. Although Eloise is able to do additions, subtractions and divisions (A Q1c) she has difficulty in setting out long multiplications (A Q1d) and gets confused when there are decimal points. However, she does know her times tables and is able to apply her knowledge to solve problems.

She has a good grasp of geometry but does not seem familiar with the concepts of perimeter and area. She also understands probability and the difference between odd and even numbers, and is ready to investigate various approaches to see how these numbers work when they are added, subtracted, multiplied or divided.

Eloise appears to have a good overall understanding of mathematics but does not feel very confident in this subject, especially in exam situations: 'I'm good at tables . . . I'm not good at maths tests'.

English is one of her favourite subjects, which is reflected in her very high scores in the two language papers. Her reading comprehension exercises were almost perfect (B Q5c). This can be easily explained as she says that a good day at school is when she is 'reading books as usual' and when she has 'lots of spare time (for reading)'.

She scored top marks in the grammar/spelling exercise and was able to use varied and appropriate vocabulary, spelt almost without any mistake, in her creative writing. Her story was well structured with a good story-line enhanced by the use of clear paragraphs and relevant punctuation. Eloise was certainly able to transfer mechanical techniques, such as clear handwriting, punctuation and spelling from specific exercises to more complex tasks involving a whole range of skills.

Eloise considers that she is a fairly good pupil: 'I think I'm doing quite well'. She selects English ('spellings, punctuation, speech marks') and maths as important subjects, English 'so, if you're writing to someone important they understand it' and maths 'because it could help you in the future'. She is well aware of moving on to secondary school and continuing school after compulsory age: 'I don't think I'll leave school when I'm 16, in fact I'm sure I won't.' Reading will remain an important part of her life 'using reading to help me learn more, instead of just reading for pleasure', 'finding books that I can enjoy for a while, rather than reading lovely books that don't last for long', . . . 'when I'm 18, 19, 20 or 21 I think I'll probably still like reading'. But she is not just engrossed in her books. When she is older, she thinks that she might get her ears pierced and have contact lenses instead of having to wear glasses!

1c)

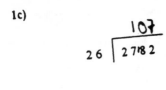

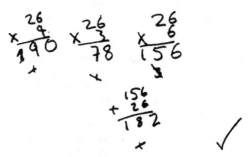

1d)

```
    4.28
x   3.5
    _____
   38.24?.
```

```
   4.28
x 3.50
 _____
  0.00
 21.40
 12.84
 _____
 34.?2?
```

3. **(5c)** How had Gita's opinion changed by the end of the report?

*She thought that it was a really
good fun place and that it was
really interesting.*

Figure 9.3 *An example of Eloise's work*

TIMOTHY   English high-achiever

Timothy is eleven. He attends a large traditional working-class school set among council houses and close to a new detached-houses estate in a town situated in southern England. About one-third of the pupils receive free school meals.

His social background is not known but he has a supportive family. Timothy says that his parents help him with his school work.

According to his teacher, Timothy 'loves learning'. A good teacher, says Timothy, should 'be nice as well as teaching something', she should also be fair, explain things well and make the work interesting. Timothy does not enjoy being at school very much, but he realizes the importance of school. He wants to do well because school is useful and will help him get a job. His friends also think that it is important to do well and do not like fooling around. Timothy modestly says that he is in 'the middle' compared to the other children in the class although they know he usually comes first or second. In fact, he is aware of his position thanks to 'the marks she [the teacher] gives us'. His favourite subjects are maths and science and the ones he likes least are English and history. 'In ten years time I will probably see myself getting a job and probably be in university' says Timothy. He has a realistic awareness of moving from secondary school to university and then looking for a job: 'something to do with the RAF'.

His maths results are excellent: 13/16 for the French test, 18/21 for the English test and very good scores for the investigation. His level of computational skills is high; he uses written algorithms for additions, subtraction, long multiplication set in traditional form and divisions set in traditional or puzzle form successfully. He has more difficulty with a long multiplication presented in puzzle form (B Q3a); although he realizes that it is the reverse of a division and uses trial-and-error as well as a written algorithm, he does not find the correct answer. He uses written algorithms for multiplication and division of decimal numbers by 100 and 10 successfully. He also uses trial-and-error and written algorithms correctly for a simple 'puzzle' sum involving a multiplication followed by a subtraction. His problem-solving skills are equally good and are helped by his confident and accurate calculations. He only makes one error, probably due to carelessness, in the 'price of tickets' problem when he sets out his long multiplication correctly but forgets to add both parts of the multiplication (B Q5c). His knowledge of geometry seems inconsistent: he understands simple as well as more abstract terminology but appears to have gaps in his knowledge, e.g. the meaning of 'angle' or 'right angle'. He can calculate an average, handle data, work out a complex pie-chart problem involving fractions, and can work out a probability problem reasonably well; he also has an excellent understanding of decimals and fractions, of symmetry, perimeter and area; he is willing to try new examples in his investigation.

His language scores are also very good. He uses contextual and inferential skills very well (B Q5c), his spelling is excellent in the set exercise as well as in the creative writing. His story is simple but well structured and imaginative with a good range of adjectives but a rather limited sentence structure. His punctuation is almost perfect but he does not use any paragraphs. Timothy also has a great sense of humour especially when he describes himself: 'My teeth are out of line and my nose looks like a pig's nose'!

$$323 \times \boxed{8}7 = 1518\boxed{1}$$

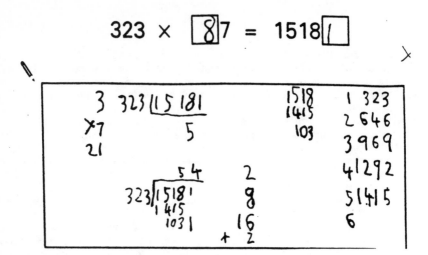

5c.   How much will it cost for
18 children (under 11) to visit the castle?

You **must** show your working.

18
95
90
1620
7

£16·20

3. (5c) How had Gita's opinion changed by the end of the report?

..In...the end she recomends it.......
..and says it was good....... ✓
....

Figure 9.4 *An example of Timothy's work*

MARCEL   French low-achiever

Eleven-year-old Marcel attends a fairly large traditional 'working-class' school in a town in northern France.

Marcel comes from a split-up family. He lives with his mother who is a housewife. His father is a lorry driver. He has one brother and one sister.

According to his teacher Marcel *'n'a pas conscience de l'importance des études'* (he has not realized the importance of learning). He is one of the leaders in the gangs of the playground. He has a good relationship with his teachers but needs to be put back in his place. His teacher anticipates problems of behaviour and achievement in his secondary school. Marcel knows how well he is doing: *'je suis dans les cinq derniers, à peu près 24ème'* (I am among the last five in the class, about 24th (out of 28)). He is aware of this, thanks to his *'classement'* (ranking) which is not always officially stated but can be easily worked out with his *'moyenne'* (average). His last one was 3.22 out of 10. The most important subjects, to him, are *'l'orthographe parce que je fais tout le temps des fautes . . . et les conjugaisons . . . c'est pour savoir plus faire de fautes'* (spelling because I always make mistakes . . . and conjugations . . . so you know how not to make any more mistakes). He has some awareness of progression through school *'je voudrais passer toutes mes classes, mon bac et après cela, à 20 ans je voudrais avoir un boulot . . . éboueur'* (I'd like to always move on to the next class, pass my bac (A-Level), and after, when I'm 20 I'd like to have a job . . . dustman).

In maths, Marcel's scores were: 6/16 in the French test, 2/21 in the English test and rather low results in the investigation. He uses written algorithms successfully for traditional and puzzle additions (with a careless mistake for the decimal point). He also provides a good explanation of how to carry numbers from units, to tens, to hundreds (B Q2b). He works out accurately a traditional subtraction, a traditional division (with a good way of checking how many times 26 go into 182, A Q1c) and a traditional multiplication. But he does not attempt the puzzle division or the puzzle multiplication: *'c'est impossible'*. He uses written algorithms for the sequenced sum and for the division of decimal numbers by 10 correctly, but ignores the word *same* in the first instance and moves the decimal number wrongly in the second example. His problem-solving skills are inconsistent. He uses written algorithms accurately to solve the 'price of biscuits' and the 'price of tickets' problems. But although he selects the right sum, he chooses the wrong numbers for the 'number of bottles on a shelf' question. For the 'picture frame' problem he uses the wrong strategy. He has a poor knowledge of geometry, some understanding of area, but not of perimeter. He does not attempt symmetry, the handling of data, or the pie-chart problem, and gives the wrong answers for the average, the probability and the ordering of decimals and fractions. In the investigation he agrees with the statements for which there are examples and disagrees with the others.

In the language tests his contextual and inferential skills are extremely poor and he does not attempt the 'English' reading comprehension. His spelling is poor in the grammar exercise as well as in his story. In the punctuation exercise he misreads the question, and instead of copying the text and adding the missing punctuation he writes his own text inserting his own punctuation. In the story-writing, most sentences are demarcated by full stops, but his use of commas is usually inaccurate. His handwriting is joined-up and fairly neat. His story is complicated and not always very clear; there are no paragraphs and the vocabulary tends to be basic and colloquial.

Despite his apparent lack of interest in school Marcel shows a surprising maturity: *'Mais maintenant c'est pas facile la vie . . . pour avoir tout ce que je veux il faut que je me mette au travail maintenant.'* (But life is not easy nowadays . . . to have all I want I need to get down to work now.)

1c)

$$26 \\ \times 6 \\ \overline{156} \\ +26 \\ \overline{182}$$

2782 | 26
26
182 | 107 ✓

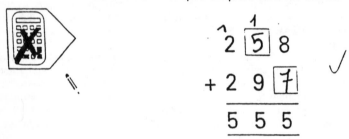

2b. Ecris les chiffres qui manquent dans les carrés.

$$\overset{\curvearrowleft}{2}\ \overset{1}{\boxed{5}}\ 8$$
$$+\ 2\ 9\ \boxed{7}$$
$$\overline{5\ 5\ 5}$$ ✓

j'ai trouver j'ai fais 8 pour arriver
a 5 sa fait 7 est la retenue
5 + 9 + 1 = 15 mais le 1 je le mais
avec les 2 + 2 + 1 = 5 -

Figure 9.5 *An example of Marcel's work*

ANAIS   French low-achiever

Anais says that she is 11 but in reality she is at least 14. She attends an inner-city school in a large town of southern France. A very large proportion of pupils comes from ethnic minorities.

Anais lives with her aunt. Her father washes up in a restaurant.

According to her teacher, Anais works well but she worries a lot and is bothered by racism. She quite likes school and thinks that it is useful and that it will help her find a job. To her mind, a good teacher should '*être gentille avec tous les élèves comme Mme X ou Mme Y*' (be nice to all the pupils like Mrs X or Mrs Y). Her teacher expects them to have good marks, to understand because it will help them throughout their lives, and to have better results. Anais does not single out any one subject as more important than the others but her favourite ones are French and 'la mesure'. She does not know exactly how well she is doing as there is no ranking, but she says: '*je travaille mieux en français qu'en maths*' (I am doing better in French than in maths), and she knows this is because of the marks she gets and the tests they do to see if they have understood. Anais has some awareness that she needs to carry on studying in order to work in the health sector: '*J'espère pouvoir continuer mes études et faire un travail dans la médecine pour pouvoir aller dans les pays et soigner des malades.*' (I'd like to continue studying so that I can practise medicine and go to other countries to care for the sick.)

Her maths results were: 7/16 in the French test, 9/21 in the English test and average scores in the investigation. She uses written algorithms for all traditional and puzzle sums except for the puzzle multiplication. Her computational skills are usually good but she cannot do a traditional long multiplication (A Q1d). She is careless with decimal points. In the sequenced sum she uses mental arithmetic to work out the correct solution but ignores the word *same*. She uses a written algorithm correctly for the multiplication of decimal numbers by 100, but does not attempt the division of decimal numbers by 10. Her problem-solving skills are mixed. She can solve the 'number of bottles' and 'picture frame' problems but does not attempt the 'price of biscuits' problem, and hesitates as to which algorithm to use for the 'price of tickets' problem (B Q5c). She does not attempt to draw a geometrical shape but has a good understanding of geometrical terms. She cannot calculate a perimeter but understands areas; she has difficulties with an average. She can handle data and do a simple probability question but does not attempt symmetry, the pie-chart problem or the ordering of decimals and fractions. In the investigation she agrees with all the statements and cannot generalize.

Her contextual and inferential skills are quite good in the reading comprehensions. She is not good at spelling in either the grammar exercise or the story-writing. Her punctuation is erratic. Her story is imaginative but somewhat confused, without paragraphs. It is made more lively by use of asides to the reader: '*Curieuse comme elle est je vous laisse imaginer*', '*Vous n'imaginerez jamais ce qu'il y avait . . .*' (You can imagine how curious she is), (You'll never guess what there was . . .) and by good, varied vocabulary.

A good pupil should not talk too much, should work hard and be quiet but Anais does not think that she is like that child because she talks too much: '*Je suis trop bavarde.*'

1d)

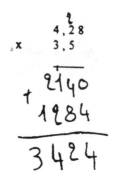

$$
\begin{array}{r}
4,\overset{2}{2}8 \\
\times \quad 3,5 \\
\hline
\overset{1}{2}140 \\
+ \; 1284 \\
\hline
3424
\end{array}
$$

5c. Quel sera le tarif d'entrée pour **18 enfants** (de moins de 11 ans)?

Montre tes calculs.

$18 \times 9,50$

851

Figure 9.6 *An example of Anais' work*

ODILE   French middle-achiever

Odile is 11½. She repeated one year in the early part of her primary schooling. She now attends a traditional 'working-class' school in a town of northern France.

She comes from a split-up family. Her mother is a housewife. Her stepfather has just finished a training period to enable him to work in a factory. According to her teacher, her parents do not look after her very much and she has become very independent.

Odile wants to learn and to have good marks. Her relationship with her male teacher has improved but there are still tensions with the other girls in the class. According to her an ideal school is '*où il y a une cour, des paniers de basket et des classes*' (where there is a playground, where you can play basketball and where there are classrooms). She thinks that her school is good because '*il y a un bon maître, il nous fait rire à pleurer*' (there is a good teacher, he has us in stitches). Her parents think that it is important to do well at school, and so do her friends although they also like to fool around in class. The most important subjects to her are history and science because she wants to be a surgeon or an archaeologist, but she recognizes the role of French '*quand on écrit, si on a une lettre à faire*' (when you're writing, if you have a letter to write). She knows her average mark, 7.35 out of 10 and her position in the class, 9th out of 28. She is also aware of how well she is doing through her marks, the tests and the written and oral comments she gets from her teachers.

In maths her results were: 9/16 in the French test, 11/21 in the English test and fairly good scores in the investigation. Her computational skills are very good for the traditional and the puzzle sums; she uses written algorithms for all of them except the puzzle division. For the sequence sum she uses trial-and-error but misreads the question and tries to do an addition instead of a multiplication (B Q 3b). She does the multiplication and division of decimal numbers by 100 and 10 correctly, without written algorithms. Her problem-solving skills are inconsistent: in the 'price of biscuits' problem she chooses the correct algorithm and the right numbers but gives the wrong answer. She is aware of the irrelevance of some of the numbers given in the problem (A Q7). Again, for the 'number of bottles' question, she chooses the right sum but the wrong numbers. But for the 'picture frame' and the 'price of tickets' problems she uses written algorithms correctly. She has quite a good knowledge of geometry, of areas, symmetry, average and simple probability but she cannot work out a perimeter, complete a table or do a pie-chart problem. She can order decimals but not fractions. In the investigation she checks all the statements with her own examples but cannot generalize.

In the language tests she demonstrates very good contextual and inferential skills. Her spelling is good in the grammar test but generally poor in her story. Her punctuation is adequate in the set test and most sentences in her story are demarcated by full stops. She uses commas and speech marks quite well. Her handwriting is joined-up and neat. Her story, based on traditional fairy tales, is written in the past historic but with few adjectives and no paragraphs.

She thinks that she is an ideal pupil because she works hard and she does not cheat or steal.

7.

A la récréation de 10 heures, 83 petits pains ont été vendus par un groupe de 4 élèves.
Chaque petit pain a été vendu 3 F.

Quel est le montant total de cette vente ?

Ecris ta réponse dans le cadre :

> 284 F

Explique ta réponse :

on fait 83 × 3 = la réponse
10H00 et le groupe de 4 élèves   ✗
ont en n'a pas besoin

3b. Il manque le même chiffre dans chaque carré de cette opération.

$$\begin{array}{r} 6\overset{1}{0} \\ -\ 4\ 2 \\ \hline 1\ 8 \end{array}$$

Ecris le chiffre qui manque dans les carrés.

$\Box \times \Box - \Box = 42$

$$\begin{array}{r} 6\overset{1}{\cancel{0}}\,\overset{1}{8} \\ -\ 1\ 8 \\ \hline 4\ 2 \end{array}$$

$$\begin{array}{r} 2\,1 \\ +\,2\,1 \\ \hline 4\ 2 \end{array} \qquad \begin{array}{r} 30 \\ +30 \\ \hline 60 \end{array}$$

42   30 + 30 = 60 - 18 = 42

Figure 9.7 *An example of Odile's work*   4

ALAIN   French high-achiever

Alain, a 10½-year-old, attends a fairly large middle-class school set on the outskirts of a large town in southern France.

According to his teacher he comes from '*un milieu très correct*' (a very good social background). His father teaches furniture-making in a secondary school and his mother is a secretary.

Alain has '*un comportement bizarre*' (a strange behaviour), '*il vit dans son monde à lui*' (he lives in a world of his own), according to his teacher, but he has a good relationship with her. He is the best in the class and is well aware of his position thanks to his reports which state his average marks. It is then easy for him to work out whether he is among the first or the last in the class by asking the other children what their marks are. Alain is well motivated; he wants to be the best in the class but his work is not for fear of punishment or to please his parents or his teacher. He is extremely conscious of the importance of school and knows precisely what he wants to do: '*Je vais travailler à fond pour aller au lycée où je vais travailler pour avoir une bonne moyenne et passer mon baccalauréat et je ferai des études de chimie.*' (I will work very hard to go to the lycée where I will work to get a good average and pass my baccalauréat and then I will study chemistry.) His friends are also aware of the importance of school and do not laugh at him when he gets things wrong or if he works very well. There does not seem to be any anti-school culture among his peers.

In all his maths tests Alain achieved excellent results: 16/16 in the French test, 19/21 in the English test and very good marks in the investigation. He is excellent at computational maths and uses written algorithms with or without decimal points to work out long multiplications or division as well as to solve problems of varying degrees of complexity, but he never wastes time on non-standard methods of calculation even when sums are set in an unfamiliar way. He has a very good understanding of geometry, although it is his worst subject, according to him. He is capable of handling data accurately, confident in dealing with visual questions and excellent at probability as well as putting decimal numbers in order. The only thing he could not do was to put fractions in order, although he showed a good understanding of the meaning of fractions. Alain is also willing to experiment with investigation, to try new examples to check the accuracy of mathematical statements and to take risks by trying new sums in order to attempt generalization (C Q2).

In the two language papers as well, his scores were very high. Alain uses contextual skills well to retrieve information from a text but has more difficulty with inferential skills, although this could be partly due to the translation of the original English question (B Q1. 2. 3.). His spelling is perfect in the grammar exercise as well as in his story-writing. He uses punctuation effectively, chooses his vocabulary with care and writes a well-structured story containing some suspense.

Even though Alain is a strong high-achiever and the best in his class, he is not very fond of school: '*L'école, je suis obligé d'y aller alors j'y vais.*' (I go to school because I have to.) His best time at school is the day before they break up for the holidays!

2 Qu'est-ce qu tu pourrais affirmer d'autre sur le calcul des nombres pairs et impairs en général? Explique pourquoi tu penses qu c'est vrai.

Quand je divise un nombre impair par un nombre pair, je n'obtien jamais un résultat sans virgule car 9:2=4,5 quand je divise un nombre pair par un nombre pair j'obtiens quelquefois une nombre pair ou impair car 10:2=5 ou 20:2=10

1. Quel était l'avis d'Aisha quand on lui a dit qu'elle allait visiter Pierreclos avec sa famille?

...Elle n'aveit pas envie d'y aller... ✓

2. Quels sont les mots qui vous l'indiquent?

...J'aurais bien voulu qu'il se mette à tomber des cordes... ✓

3. De quelle manière est-ce qu'Aisha a changé d'avis à la fin de son reportage?

...Elle a brutalement changé d'avis... ✗

$$\frac{4}{6}$$

Figure 9.8 *An example of Alain's work*

Summary of profiles

These profiles suggest striking differences between the lower-SES as well as the lower-achieving case-study pupils in the two countries. Like all French children they had a clear notion of school as providing them with a ladder of progress through the educational system and into future careers. Both Anais and Marcel stated this quite clearly: 'But life is not easy nowadays ... to have all I want I need to get to work now.' These children had a clear idea that it was important for them to study for and pass the baccalauréat (equivalent of A-levels). In contrast, Richard and Christine in England did not see school as playing much of a part in their lives. For Richard, for example, one of the main purposes of school was to provide an environment where pupils could be happy. In France, the lower-achieving and the lower-SES children, like the rest of the French children, had a strong awareness of school as a place where pupils had to work hard and make an effort.

CONCLUSION

The findings presented here are drawn from a number of different sets of data both quantitative and qualitative, collected as part of the QUEST study. Yet in all cases, whether it is children's responses from the questionnaire, their individual interviews (used in the profiles), their assessment papers or their writing about their future at school, one fairly consistent conclusion may be drawn. In both countries, gender and social disadvantage *do* make a difference to our sample of children's attitudes, motivation, and achievement at school. However they make a great deal more difference in England than they do in France. In this sense, national context is a far more important influence that the intranational differences considered. In England the gap in attitudes and achievement between boys and girls and between children of different socio-economic backgrounds is far greater and more significant. In both countries, but particularly in England, there are a substantial number of lower-achieving pupils who are not being well served by their current educational systems. In our sample, French boys and girls from all social backgrounds had a more positive attitude to teachers, school, and learning; were less likely to be affected by anti-school attitudes from their peers; and had achievements which, overall, were more comparable than those between children of different sexes and socio-economic backgrounds in England.

We identified the clearer understanding shared by the whole of French society about progress through the educational system, together with a national emphasis, very clearly taken on board by teachers, on equal entitlement and on bringing all children to a common level rather than on differentiation and individualization as factors which might make a difference to the narrowing of this gap in France, although it is beyond the scope of this study to identify which of these might be the most significant influence.

These findings lend some support to the notion of the 'long tail of under-achievement' in England in relation to some boys and to some more disadvantaged groups of children. They suggest that a culture unsupportive to learning is thriving more strongly in England, both inside school, through the existence of an 'anti-achievement' culture among some pupils, and outside school, through a lack of shared understanding about the purpose of education in the wider society.

Chapter 10

Overview of the Study Findings

WHY QUEST?

In the light of the growing international interest in raising educational standards and in comparing national levels of achievement, there has recently been a rash of policy initiatives in England, as elsewhere, aimed at enhancing pupils' learning. However, as we argued in Chapter 1, it is currently difficult to predict whether or not such initiatives will achieve their intended outcome, because they are not grounded in an explicit understanding of how pupils learn in a given cultural context.

It was in an attempt to address this issue that the study that forms the basis of this book was initiated. Chapter 2 provided a detailed rationale for this kind of comparison of the various influences on pupils' learning in two different national contexts – England and France – which have very different educational traditions. Although we already knew from previous research by members of the research team (see, for example, Bristaix, STEP, Sharpe, Planel *et al.*, 1996) that there were major differences in both the priorities and the practices of English and French primary school teachers, we lacked the research to establish the significance of such national differences in educational organization and practice for the potential impact of attempts to enhance learning outcomes.

The goal of our study was thus to explore the extent to which such culturally-located educational differences are significant in explaining variations in pupils' learning outcomes. In this case the particular focus was England and France but the goal was a much more general one. We hoped that this particular empirical study would make it possible to identify the factors which are likely to influence the impact of changes in aspects such as teaching style, classroom organization or curriculum content *in any particular context*. We also hoped that our adoption of a socio-cultural theoretical perspective would lead to more general insights concerning the relationship between culture and learning.

The fundamental principle that has informed our study is Bronfenbrenner's (1979) argument that the quality of learning that takes place is not necessarily a result of the 'objective' features of a learning situation. Rather it is a product of the ways in which the various interventions that take place are construed and interpreted by the people involved in that particular culture and setting. Thus we anticipated that

- particular educational practices might well have *quite different* effects in different cultural settings
- there is no absolute relationship between e.g. a highly authoritarian, didactic teaching style and a particular pupil response
- pupils' reaction to different opportunities to learn is not a constant of their role as pupils, but is just as much a product of their culturally-informed expectations of what is both normal and desirable.

We chose to focus on England and France for this study because of their superficially similar, but in many ways fundamentally different, educational traditions. We anticipated that the marked cultural differences between these two countries would be reflected in contrasts in pupils' attitudes, in their perceptions and in their styles of learning. In Chapters 2 and 3 we highlighted some of the most significant of these differences in our brief analysis of the defining characteristics of the two systems. We anticipated, for example, that the formal, didactic style of teaching characteristic of French primary schooling would foster a passive, authority-dependent style of learning among pupils, and that French pupils might typically perform better on tasks which required the careful application of learned formulae; whereas English children, who had experienced a style of pedagogy which gave more emphasis to pupil autonomy and individual development, might typically perform better on tasks which required problem-solving skills and creative independent thinking. We anticipated that such different emphases in educational practice were likely to be a reflection of more general features of the two national cultures. We described how in France the national emphasis is on the role of education in inducting children into their role as future citizens, whereas the English tradition is one of decentralization and individual choice. We anticipated that these differences would be reflected in English pupils having a much less clear sense of their educational goals and indeed of their national identity more generally.

Thus the aim of the study was both to compare primary-school learning outcomes in England and France and to explain the source and significance of these in terms of the different educational environments which pupils had experienced. It was hoped that by so doing, the study would throw light on the way in which current UK Government pressures for change in teachers' classroom practices are likely to affect the quality of pupils' future learning. Starting from a recognition that schools are embedded in their local and national communities, the study sought to establish and explain the significance of cultural factors for pupils' attitudes to education and their learning outcomes. In short, the research was designed to build on what was already known about characteristic styles of curriculum *delivery* in England and France to investigate the effects of these differences on the processes of curriculum *reception* by pupils.

In Chapter 2 we also described the variety of research methods that the research team adopted to achieve this goal, how we explored pupils' attitudes to their classroom experiences and the social world of school in the two countries through a combination of open and fixed-response pupil questionnaires. These were supplemented by 'focus-group' discussions with small groups of pupils which allowed us to explore the significance of the national context in more depth. Systematic and informal observations of classrooms in both countries allowed us to identify key differences in practice. Last but not least, we designed a series of assessments in language and maths which allowed us to link pupils' learning outcomes in the two countries with the data we had collected on their attitudes and experiences.

THE REALITY OF DIFFERENCE

Having set the scene in terms of the goals of the study, its rationale and methodology in the initial chapters of this book, the rest has been devoted to reporting and analysing our findings concerning differences in pupil perspectives and their educational experiences in the two countries. Chapter 4 is the first of two chapters in which we presented evidence of the striking differences in beliefs and attitudes that characterized our two national groups. Although findings from the questionnaire survey and from the more in-depth pupil interviews suggested that children in both countries share the role and structural position of 'pupil' in common, and develop many common strategies and responses to schooling as a result, there are nevertheless striking differences in their perceptions of what it means to be a pupil.

Although, as we report in Chapter 6, English teachers typically made much more effort than was observed in France to motivate children through arousing their interest, protecting their self-esteem, and avoiding negative feedback, it was French children who were significantly more positive about school. Despite experiencing a typically more formal and authoritarian classroom, they were more likely to see teaching as helpful and useful to them and appeared to be more highly motivated toward educational success and academic goals. We also reported that the personality and personal characteristics of the teacher were of less concern to French pupils than to their English counterparts. Most important was that he or she should make them work hard!

This emphasis on teachers who give hard work and who ensure that the curriculum is covered was strongly associated with the perception held by French children that school work is important as a preparation for adult life. A clear delineation between work and play within school and the explicit and immediate feedback given to pupils, helped to emphasize the school's educational function in French pupils' minds. Closely associated with these more positive perspectives on the part of French pupils, we suggested, was the noticeable absence of a negative peer-group influence opposed to school values, unlike circumstances in England.

These findings emphasize the importance of understanding attitudes to learning, schooling and achievement within a wider cultural context. Our findings suggest that French pupils, their parents and the wider society all share a common understanding of the organization and content of schooling and a clear appreciation of its importance. The existence of a publicly understood ladder of progress through school and the valuing of educational success and intellectual endeavour by politicians, the media and the wider society in France, have a clear influence on what takes place in school. The existence of explicit, well-understood, and widely-shared goals for education helps to explain why French children were more positive in their attitudes to school.

But importantly, we argued, these positive attitudes are also related to the nationally-derived assumption that educational success is based on effort, rather than ability; on a separation of the 'self' as a whole from the business of learning so that negative feedback is perceived in relation to the quality of the work and the effort expended, rather than to the pupil's very self. In England, where the emphasis on innate ability is so deeply ingrained in the individualist educational discourse, lack of progress is more likely to be perceived by pupils as a result of their being 'thick' or 'dummies'. This helps to explain their apparently lower self-esteem in an educational environment in which teachers strive to be supportive. Equally, the strong French tradition of national conformity may help to explain the absence of the fear of being a 'goodie' in French primary schools which is such a characteristic feature of the same schools in England.

These and other findings which we reported in Chapter 4 suggests that policy-borrowing which simply involves importing one limited aspect of another country's educational system without taking into account this wider cultural context is unlikely to resolve the problem it is designed to solve.

In Chapter 5, the second of the two chapters dealing with pupils' attitudes, we explored variations in French and English children's sense of national identity and their perceptions of themselves as future citizens. Here the contrast between the children was even more marked than in relation to their attitudes to school. We reported significant differences in the extent to which they identified themselves with their country and had a sense of 'belonging' to it; the importance they attached to having a particular nationality; and how well they felt their primary schooling had prepared them for future citizenship in their society. French pupils had much higher levels of national pride than English pupils. They appeared to have a much clearer idea of what it meant to be French and were much readier to declare that they considered themselves to be very French. While many French children expressed feelings of attachment to, and affection for, France, the characteristic response of English children was to think pragmatically about why being English might be a good thing. Where French children were emotional, English children were practical, focusing on the benefits of living in England, its high standard of living, its possession of the major world language and its sporting achievements.

While interesting in themselves, these differences in English and French pupils' attitudes to their country arguably reflect a more profound difference between the two national cultures.

In France there appears to be a greater homogeneity of values. Social and educational realities are more readily taken for granted. Notions of what teaching is, what learning is, and what the purposes of schooling are seem to be widely shared and, to a large extent, treated as unproblematic. In this sense, the relative absence of anti-school pupil sub-cultures, the common commitment of teachers and pupils to 'getting through' to the next national scholastic level in the 'ladder of progress', and the readiness to employ learnt, authoritatively-taught strategies in mathematical and language tasks appear to be based on the same kind of willingness to accept authority as the unquestioned and unconditional assumption that being French is 'naturally' something to be proud of.

In England, by comparison, there seems to be a much greater heterogeneity of values and a much greater preparedness to question and render issues problematic. The response of English pupils to their learning role was found to vary widely, and to be much more affected by the vagaries of pupil sub-cultures. English pupils demonstrated more individual variation and 'independence' in both their general attitudes to schooling and in their response to specific mathematics and language tasks, especially in the areas of problem-solving and creative writing. It surely cannot be coincidence that this greater readiness to 'stand apart', and to take an individual detached view in both responding to questions about attitudes and in undertaking assessment tasks, occurred in the same national sample that demonstrated a more independent and conditional approach to feelings of national identity. There is no doubt that children's growing understanding of their national identity is significantly shaped by the 'national context' in which they are schooled, and this has important implications for current English policy initiatives in the area of citizenship education. (See, for example, Crick, 1998.)

Our findings in this area have implications for current developments in Europe and for 'globalization' more generally. They suggest that it will be a long time before differences in ideology and discourse which are clearly the product of *national* cultures can be blended to become a more common European or global culture. They also suggest that in a country such as France, whose earlier political upheavals have resulted in a deeply-embedded commitment to inclusivity and universalism, these principles profoundly shape the way both individuals and government see the world. In England, different historical experiences have contributed to the emergence of a culture which is characterized by differentialism and particularism – a culture in which individuality is the central principle. It is individuals' *different* needs, rights and responsibilities, rather than their common membership of a well-defined national community, which is most characteristic of English culture. As we argued in Chapter 5, our evidence suggests that the nation state continues to exercise a powerful influence over hearts and minds, values and attitudes. In efforts to improve education, we ignore these at our peril since, to be effective, education policies need to take account of the social realities which affect pupils' and teachers' daily lived experience.

One of the important aspects of the QUEST project was its efforts to cross-validate findings by collecting a range of different kinds of data. Thus, as well as exploring pupils' perspectives, we also observed them in their classrooms. Although it would be dangerous to generalize too much from a relatively small amount of classroom observation data, in Chapter 6 we documented some potentially important differences and similarities between the two countries which this part of the study revealed.

We reported, for example, that French children were more likely to be 'task-engaged' in the classrooms we studied, with English children correspondingly more likely to be apparently distracted. We argued that such differences could be explained both by French children's typically higher levels of motivation across all types of schools and also perhaps by the greater prevalence of whole-class teaching which we observed in France. French teachers were more likely than their English counterparts to be engaged in formal instruction – a finding that perhaps reflects the ubiquitous use of the traditional French 'leçon' which involves teacher exposition followed by individual practice and a final whole-class evaluation and feedback session.

However, we observed something arguably more important than the amount of any particular activity undertaken by teachers: the nature and content of the interaction between teacher and pupil. In the brief extracts from two lessons, one English and one French, which we presented in Chapter 6, we illustrated the profound ideological and culturally-rooted differences of pedagogical approach which exist in the two countries. The French teacher's goal is, quite simply, that pupils should master the material being taught, whereas the English teacher's emphasis is on encouraging the children to think for themselves, and on the promotion of understanding and knowledge through problem-solving. Thus, we argued, it is possible to trace a clear link between national attitudes to the role of education, teachers' pedagogic approaches, and pupils' learning outcomes.

STRENGTHS AND WEAKNESSES

The significance of these differences was clearly demonstrated in the national patterns that distinguished pupils' performance in the language and maths tests that we gave them (these are reported in Chapters 7 and 8 of the book). The significant variations in the profile of pupil competencies in the two countries, which we documented in detail in these chapters, were not a function of what is often termed 'opportunity to learn' – that is, the time devoted to these two subjects in the classroom. Virtually the same time was given to language in both countries with only a marginal difference in maths, with other subjects occupying roughly similar marginal amounts of time in both. However these apparent similarities masked important differences in emphasis within the subjects which reflected the different emphases of the two countries' national curricula. The different national patterns of pupil performance also reflected their degree of familiarity or unfamiliarity with a particular style of test item. We reported that English pupils had access to a wider range of skills but often at a lower level. Conversely French pupils were often at a higher level but in a narrower field. Thus although differences in performance could often be traced to differences in pedagogy it could not always be assumed that this was the case.

In Chapter 7 we showed that, in the results from all the three maths tests that we set, each national sample outperformed the other sample at its own test. The performance of English pupils was stronger on investigation, averages, handling data, probability, fractions and visual questions taken from the English maths tests. But English pupils also outperformed French pupils in items from the French maths test which involved interpreting geometric language, area and perimeter and visualization.

French pupil performance was better in the French maths test in computation, geometrical drawing skills and terminology and problem-solving. Moreover, French pupils outperformed English pupils on those items in the English maths test which involved the application of the four rules of number and decimals. Indeed in Chapter 7 we presented evidence to suggest that many English pupils had not grasped the concepts of multiplication or division, though they were stronger than French pupils at handling data and in using and applying maths.

In Chapter 8 we documented the significant differences that emerged in pupils' language skills. English pupils performed significantly better at inferential reading questions and in many other aspects of language including spelling, punctuation and creative writing. They were both more able to infer meaning from a text and more willing so to do.

The overall picture which emerged from the assessment results was that English pupils had a more individualistic approach to maths and language, which could be categorized as 'thinking for themselves', over a wider range of topics. While this had clear advantages in areas such as inferential reading comprehension questions and maths investigations, there were definite disadvantages in other areas where a deep level of understanding and knowledge of techniques were required, as in computation, decimal place value and some problem-solving questions. We reported that English pupils were more likely to use 'trial-and-error' and showed more willingness to attempt unfamiliar items. The approach of French pupils was more mechanized and routinized than that of English pupils, and their skills were limited to a smaller range of topics.

It is important to recognize the combination of intellectual and affective dimensions which appears to underpin these differences in performance. If French children apply their learning more mechanistically than their English counterparts, it is because this is the way they know, but it is also because they do not feel confident in departing from tried and tested procedures. The strong French tradition of conformity and of the acceptance of authority inhibits them from feeling that they can come up with their own strategies to solve a problem. If modes of thinking are cultural, as we argue in Chapter 7, in weighing up the significance of these differences in national performance in English and maths, it is important to consider the kind of approach adopted by pupils as well as the overall level achieved. Moreover, it underlines the desirability of more qualitative culturally-informed comparisons of pupil achievement, since only studies of this kind can make clear the important contextual factors that help to determine the impact of different pedagogic strategies.

In Chapter 9, the last of the three chapters reporting aspects of pupils' learning outcomes, we drew attention to the relative significance of differences between schools and pupils within each country and the significance of these in comparison with the national differences reported earlier.

Significant socio-economic differences were found in pupils' attitudes to schooling, to learning and to achievement in the two countries. Contrasts between the French educational system's ideological emphasis on 'equal entitlement' and the English system's increasing emphasis on 'differentiation' were reflected to some extent in children's perceptions. For example, English children in areas of low socio-economic status particularly valued the affective, personal and social dimensions of school more highly, while French children in similar areas emphasized the importance of good behaviour and academic success.

Significantly, in view of the current debate about boys' under-achievement in England, in all the gender comparisons we made, English boys were the least positively motivated towards teaching, learning and school. The pattern for French boys and girls was more variable. Overall the gap in attitudes to school and achievement between boys and girls and between children of different socio-economic backgrounds was more substantial and significant in England than in France. In our sample, French boys and girls from all social backgrounds had a more positive attitude to teachers, school, and learning; were less likely to be affected by anti-school attitudes from their peers; and had achievements which, overall, were more closely comparable than those between children of different sexes and socio-economic backgrounds in England. One explanation of this lack of a male anti-school peer culture may be the tendency of French education to separate 'the pupil' and 'the person' and to emphasize academic factors such as effort, rather than personal characteristics such as ability, as determinants of achievement. One consequence of this seems to be the location of peer culture largely outside the school in French society rather than within it. We also identified the clearer understanding in French society generally of a ladder of progress through the educational system together with the emphasis on bringing all children to a common level of achievement which might make a difference to the narrowing of this gap in France.

The detailed case-studies of individual children which we presented in this chapter made it apparent that French and English children share many features in common, as might be expected. Moreover, the profiles illustrate the very significant differences in both countries between the educational experiences of 'successful' pupils and those of 'lower-attainers' and how these affect their subsequent motivation, confidence and aspirations. The case-studies provide an in-depth illustration of the national differences to which we have drawn attention in illuminating how, in both countries, but more particularly in England, there is a substantial number of lower-achieving pupils who are not being well served by their current systems.

Thus in summary, we have suggested that there are significant educational differences between the two countries and that these may be explained by the influence of cultural factors of various kinds. First, our study has revealed that the French education system places great value on the learning of established procedures and following rules, in contrast to the English system which gives greater prominence to children thinking for themselves and developing their own solutions to problems. These differences were clearly reflected in the national tests set by each country which in turn also help to reinforce them. Secondly, we suggested that these fundamental differences in educational ideology are reflected in differences in the curriculum and teaching approach of the two countries. Thirdly, we traced the influence of these cultural differences in the pattern of strengths and weaknesses evidenced by English and French children, the latter typically performing better where the task required the application of a known procedure and the former doing better on more open-ended tasks where the procedure to be followed was less obvious. Fourthly, we linked these learning strategies and outcomes to classroom processes and pupil attitudes to education, in order to demonstrate more clearly the links between national educational goals, school and classroom factors and individual pupil learning styles.

Perhaps the most important general finding of the study was that English pupils' achievements in these two key areas of maths and language compared favourably in many respects with their French counterparts. Their combined results on all the QUEST tests which included both English and French National Assessment items showed that English pupils were outperforming the French in many aspects of language and maths. In particular, there were significant national differences in pupils' levels of confidence and their willingness to 'have a go' and to take risks. English pupils were much stronger in this respect, whereas French pupils seemed to be constrained by their desire to avoid making mistakes and to refer constantly to authority. Our detailed comparative analysis of the pattern of errors made revealed that the source of these differences in orientation, as well as performance, could be traced back through differences in pupils' classroom experiences, as well as to the particular traditions and assumptions about education of the two national cultures. Furthermore, given that both sets of pupils performed better on their own national tests, this suggests the importance of curriculum validity and task familiarity as influences on pupil achievement, and raises questions concerning how meaningful international 'league-tables' of national comparisons really are.

We have suggested that English pupils' willingness and ability to tackle unfamiliar tasks would seem to reflect the well-established differences in pedagogic approach between the two countries. In France, the underlying educational philosophy is one of the 'induction' of pupils into established bodies of knowledge, a process that we refer to in Chapter 3 as 'catechistic'. French teachers are often 'drillers', their model of the goals of education largely a convergent one. The French emphasis on correct performance was reflected in weaker pupils' not always knowing which approach to take in order to solve a particular problem, as well as their demonstrating a fear of getting a wrong answer by not answering questions to which they did not know the answer.

By contrast, the established pedagogic tradition in English primary schools has been one that emphasizes discovery and the search on the part of each pupil for a solution to a given problem. Pupils have been encouraged to think for themselves, and their efforts have been valued in these terms. The effects of these different emphases, which of course vary in degree from teacher to teacher and school to school, are reflected in maths, for example, by our finding that some English children tried to develop their own strategies to do long multiplication tasks involving decimal points. High-achieving children in particular were able to develop their own efficient strategies in number and investigative maths. They also had a better sense of the correctness or otherwise of their answers than French children. However, the other side of the coin is English pupils' tendency to use inefficient non-standard procedures in relation to numeracy, and their lower level of expertise than French pupils in the use of standard arithmetical procedures. It is particularly this weakness that the Numeracy Hour initiative, which was formally launched on 16 March 1999, is designed to address.

In language too, French pupils were typically 'technicians' applying skills they had been taught, often in a decontextualized way, whereas English pupils were more likely to be 'explorers' coping well with tasks where the route was not clearly laid out. Indeed our language findings are significant in this respect, with English pupils consistently outperforming their French counterparts. It would seem that, although French pupils may undertake extensive exercises in grammar, this knowledge is not readily transferred when required to be applied in a holistic way in, for example, writing a story. It would seem that the English emphasis on teaching language through using it, rather than the French emphasis on more mechanistic methods, has significant advantages.

It is important to recognize the strengths of the English tradition. While paying due regard to the limitations of any measures used to judge comparative national performance in terms of both validity and familiarity, it is nevertheless clear from our research that English children have some significant strengths both in terms of their general approach and their skills in language and in maths which perhaps have not been sufficiently well recognized either in more conventional international tests or in current government policy. It is also the case that some of the important skills and attitudes that English children possess are also some of the most difficult to measure by conventional means and hence are often not recognized for this reason.

IMPLICATIONS FOR POLICY

Our research provides strong support for the conduct of more 'diagnostic' comparative studies which use detailed analyses of pupils' test performance in different national settings both to explore the relative strengths and weaknesses of a particular educational system and to link these to the content of the curriculum and teachers' classroom practice. However, it has also underlined the fact that pupils are not a 'tabula rasa' but come to the classroom with expectations and attitudes rooted in their broader cultural experiences. By their nature, such cultural experiences cannot easily be influenced or changed. Their important influence on the educational process rather needs to be recognized as largely a 'given' which both affects the way in which individual learners respond to particular teaching strategies and colours the collective life of teachers and pupils in the classroom. It is equally important to recognize that teachers, too, are heirs to such cultural traditions and are likely to share the same broad expectations and assumptions about education as their pupils. Thus, particular pedagogic strategies and their consequences cannot be conceived as absolutes. The way in which the content of the curriculum and particular teaching approaches impact on pupil learning outcomes also needs to be understood as culturally specific. The implications of our research for national policy need to be considered in this light with both caution and understanding concerning the extent to which they may be generalized.

Our study suggests that English primary education is still very different from that of other countries. Despite the introduction of a national curriculum, at the time of the QUEST study during 1996 and 1997 it was a system that remained characterized by diversity, although recent initiatives, such as the National Literacy and Numeracy strategies may be reducing this somewhat. Furthermore, the choice of curriculum content and pedagogic strategy, in maths in particular, appeared to be more grounded than in France in an individualized and differentiating approach, rather than in social constructivist theories of learning. The English approach appears to reflect the assumption that if pupils are interested and busy, learning will follow. Where other countries provide children with a clear vision of the journey in which they are engaged and a map describing how it is intended they will get there, this is less easy to discern in the English curriculum, which has been criticized for being overcrowded and lacking in any unifying rationale. Equally, in England, every effort is made to make the learning experience in maths as entertaining as possible for pupils – lively lessons, colourful and attractive books – but these may well disguise the lack of a clear rationale concerning the contribution of a given task to the overall journey.

The current emphasis on differentiation is also a significant and rather different characteristic of English education. As we have seen, the French education system is informed by the pervasive commitment to equality which is deeply rooted in French culture. This is translated into the reality of a common educational experience for all pupils. It is also clear that the association of curriculum coverage with particular year groups, rather than levels, assumes that there is a common goal for all pupils. Moreover, the French emphasis on *effort*, rather than *ability*, as the explanation of differences in performance helps to prevent pupils being discouraged from trying at an early stage in their school career.

There would therefore appear to be strong arguments for giving consideration as to how the structure and goals of a revised National Curriculum may be made more accessible to pupils and parents, as well as to teachers. Linked to this is the question of whether the introduction of specific common targets for each year group, which is a practice widely used in other countries, would focus more attention on how the class as a whole can be helped to reach these targets through the use of differentiation for a more collective purpose.

The French National assessments are conducted at the *beginning* of the key stage and their purpose is to provide teachers with diagnostic information about their pupils' strengths and weaknesses. They are not 'high-stakes' in the way that the English Key Stage 2 national tests are. Their timing and purpose therefore allow them to be constructed primarily to provide information for national monitoring on the one hand and for informing classroom instruction on the other. However, although their timing and purpose would allow them to introduce more emphasis on problem-solving and creativity, this opportunity is not taken.

By contrast, the high-stakes nature of the English tests means that reliability has to be at a premium. This makes it difficult to assess and to adequately reflect the full range of English pupils' 'strengths', in particular their greater willingness to take risks in learning, their problem-solving skills and their creativity in writing, all of which arguably are significant 'lifelong learning' skills.

The French maths tests used more traditional items than the English national test. This both reflected and reinforced the French pedagogic and curriculum emphasis on practising the application of number skills. In order to improve English children's computational skills, there would seem to be a case for incorporating into the English maths test a mixture of both the investigational items currently used and some more traditional, conventionally laid-out items in which the emphasis is on correct application of the procedure indicated rather than, as at present, requiring the pupil to find out which procedures could be applied.

The English National Curriculum tests cannot, by their nature, test the creative and problem-solving skills which are strengths of the English system. In Pacific Rim countries and in many other parts of the world, there is a move toward more emphasis on autonomous and independent learning. It is important not to lose these aspects of learning from the English system, and teacher assessment clearly has an important part to play in this.

THE WAY AHEAD

Our findings suggest that despite the clear pressures towards greater convergence in educational systems as a result of Europeanization, the pressure of global economies, and international youth culture, the influence of national context and national cultural traditions remains important and leads to significant differences in both pupils' attitudes to education and in their learning outcomes. Our research demonstrates the need for a more holistic understanding of the cultural context in which motivation and learning outcomes are situated. By giving a voice to primary pupils it also represents an attempt to highlight the differences between the intended and the experienced curriculum in both countries, between what policy-makers and teachers intend when planning curriculum tasks and what pupils actually experience in the classroom.

We believe therefore that the findings which we have reported in this book can make a unique contribution to national-policy debates in England and France about how to improve the quality of primary education. We believe that our study has also contributed more generally in challenging the validity of international comparisons of achievement that only focus on outcomes and in highlighting instead the need for, and potential value of, rigorous, culturally-contextualized comparative studies.

In Chapter 1, we argued that the growing prominence of comparative studies of pupil achievement represented a potentially misleading and dangerous abuse of a powerful research technology if the results are taken out of their cultural context. In this final chapter we return to this theme but with a rather different purpose. In the light of the findings we have presented in this book we feel emboldened to assert the potentially significant contribution of such studies when properly constructed and used. First of all, such studies underline the limitations of currently fashionable research approaches such as international studies of school effectiveness. Like international comparative studies of pupil achievement, such studies are vulnerable to a range of technical criticisms (Goldstein, 1998) as well as to the influence of political agendas (Bonnet, 1999). They have also been distorted and side-tracked by the 'league table' issue and by commercial interests. Perhaps most important, though, is their failure to recognize the complex causalities associated with schooling and, in consequence, their neglect of the need for more qualitative theoretically-informed studies which focus on pupils and classrooms as well as on the school as a whole. The result has been a dangerous escalation in the tendency to import apparently successful practices from elsewhere. Reynolds and Farrell's influential 1996 report 'Worlds Apart' for example, was both scathing about more conventional comparative studies and all too ready to jump to conclusions about the lessons to be learned from the apparent educational success of other countries compared to that of the United Kingdom. But, as Galton (1999) argues:

> The peculiarities and similarities of different systems are not to be attributed to broad generalized criteria such as interactive whole-class teaching, however loosely that term is defined . . . Whole-class teaching in the UK will therefore not be the same as whole-class teaching in China and the successes of one country cannot, therefore, be easily transferred to another. For this and other reasons, therefore, comparative studies of the kind advocated by David Reynolds and his International School Effectiveness Research Project (ISERP) team are unlikely to yield significant or useful findings on pedagogy (Galton, 1999: 182).

What we need instead are studies of pupil achievement – national and international – that are designed to be explicitly diagnostic in nature (see, for example, Jones, 1996). There needs to be careful pairing or grouping of similar countries both through statistical analyses as a basis for further enquiry (Zabulionis, 1998) and by looking at different cultural groups within one educational setting (Cortazzi, 1998). Alexander (1999) underlines the need for 'micro-comparative studies which are designed to compare the meanings and interpretations of participants in a range of national classroom settings'. Ideally, the QUEST project will have helped to establish the potential value – indeed necessity – of including culture as part of the analytic framework. As the international focus of educational policy and practice shifts increasingly toward learning rather than teaching, so the need to understand the various elements that impact upon that process becomes more pressing. Pupils are neither a 'black box' nor a 'tabula rasa'; the way in which their attitudes and aspirations, cognitive styles and attributions, hopes and fears interact with those of the teacher to encourage or inhibit learning, urgently needs to be both understood and accepted as central to the business of education. Figure 10.1 represents in graphic form the many different influences that impact upon individual learners' careers within the overarching mediation of culture.

The force of this model is well demonstrated by the systematic national differences our research has identified and which we have traced to deeply-rooted national discourses. We have argued that there is a close link between learning outcomes, pupils' perspectives and the underpinning cultural epistemology which quite literally defines the taken-for-granted assumptions about education at every level of society. This is the 'deep structure' of education; without understanding its defining influence, efforts to manipulate the surface structure of teaching methods, curriculum and so on are likely to run into the sand of professional values and understanding which

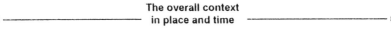

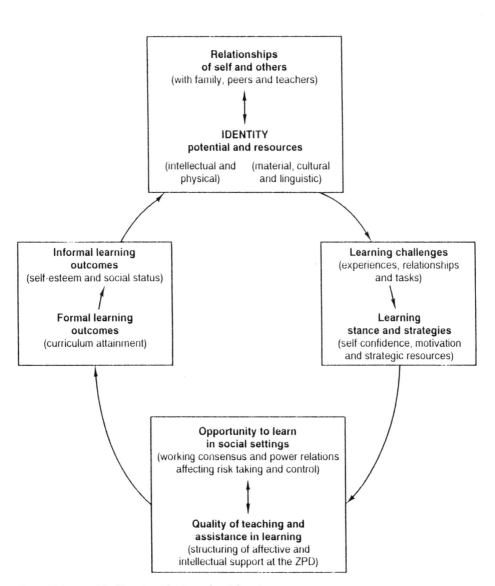

Figure 10.1 *A model of learning, identity and social setting*
(Adapted from Pollard, A.: *The Social World of Children's Learning* (1995: 97) Cassell)

fundamentally affect their realization. There is already considerable evidence to this effect in England (Pollard *et al.*, 1994) and in France (Broadfoot, 1998).

What will the learners of the twenty-first century require? Adaptability in the face of constant change; a hunger for learning; skills to take advantage of the plethora of new opportunities that will be available to them: they are some of the most frequently-expressed aspirations. Such qualities imply the need to equip learners to be divergent rather than convergent in their approach, those learners being willing to cope with ambiguity and to try out different solutions to problems, taking responsibility for their own learning and enjoying it. Few if any education systems have yet found the key to unlocking this potential; they are still heavily constrained by a model of schooling which emphasizes the transmission of established bodies of knowledge in largely didactic ways, knowledge whose acquisition is measured by forms of assessment that put a premium on the reproduction of the correct answer and on those aspects of learning that can be tested most reliably with the technologies currently available.

The French education system arguably represents an excellent example of this tradition. For several centuries it has produced a nation with a profound respect for scholarship and individuals who feel committed to both learning and their country. But there are signs that this tried and tested formula is breaking down under the pressure of social change. While the problems and consequent policy responses at primary school have been relatively modest, secondary schools − both the lower secondary 'collège' and the upper secondary 'lycée' − are currently the focus of major government reforms. Central to these reforms is the desire to build more autonomy and responsiveness into the system so that schools and teachers can engage pupils in different ways according to their varying needs and interests and equip them for the demands of the twenty-first century. But it is clear that this is not easy. The scale of dissaffection of some pupils continues to result in major problems of violence in some schools and in teachers who feel inadequately-trained and equipped to cope with them (Note d'information, 99.01, Ministere de l'éducation nationale).

In England there are also problems. These centre more on the perceived need to raise standards at the present time. Important as this agenda is, it is in serious danger of obscuring the very considerable strengths of English education:

> At the very time when English teachers are being urged to adopt the methods of their allegedly more successful Asian counterparts, the latter are being urged to become more like their English colleagues. Countries such as Singapore and Hong Kong are looking to increase the proportion of co-operative group work within the curriculum and to encourage a greater degree of critical thinking (Morris, 1998, cited in Galton, 1999).

Over the last twenty years or so, the quality, standards and accountability agenda has arguably become so powerful in Britain that it has effectively eclipsed our national capacity to ask more fundamental questions about educational practice. One of the great strengths of comparative educational studies, as Mark Bloch pointed out (Judge, 1999), is to provide the contrast needed in order to question taken-for-granted assumptions. What concepts of the mind and of learning are currently informing English education? What vision of society underpins our educational efforts? At the present time we are arguably in grave danger of reducing a social problem to a technological problem because of our collective failure explicitly to engage with these questions (Sander, 1999). If, as Dawkins (1989) 'argues', culture is the tutor of our unconscious assumptions, it is only by stepping outside of our own cultural arena to 'make the familiar strange' that we can hope to achieve a more dispassionate appraisal of our imputed goals, our strengths and weaknesses and the nature of the prevailing discourse.

It is perhaps for this reason that we seem to have failed to recognize in recent years the great strengths of English primary education; that instead of tackling acknowledged weaknesses of the system within an overall understanding of its strengths, government policy has been obsessed with driving it back to familiar and reassuring educational territory based on a convergent approach to learning at the very time when this model is subject to profound challenge in other parts of the world.

The deeply-embedded professional tradition of teachers in this country leads them to be almost unique internationally in both their willingness and their ability to take responsibility for responding to pupils' needs at classroom level. In our study we have shown that the English tradition of teaching 'the person' rather than simply 'the pupil' is a very high-risk strategy given its potential to make pupils vulnerable to a sense of failure. This tradition requires the most sensitive response by teachers to the hearts as well as the minds of their pupils. Nevertheless, in a world of lifelong learning, it is arguably only by just such an engaging of pupils' emotions as well as their minds that the necessary empowerment of learners will be achieved. In this respect, English teachers and pupils arguably have a head start. It is time to recognize the unique strengths of the English educational tradition; to give English teachers back their vision and to make English primary school teachers once again the envy of the world. If our study makes even a small contribution to this agenda, it will have achieved its purpose.

Appendices

Appendix 1

LANGUAGE 1

Write the name of your school in this box:

Write your name and age in the following boxes:

NAME

AGE

Tick the right box:

GIRL   **BOY**

We hope you enjoy answering these questions.
Your answers will help us. Thank you.

READING COMPREHENSION A

Tom had been living with his grandfather, Sir Gregory, as he was known to the local people, since he was ten years old. So he had been on the estate for nearly five years. A series of quite straightforward events had brought him to this isolated spot, cut off from the rest of the world.

Tom had spent his early childhood at Greenthorpe, a town in the Midlands, with his parents, the Westons. Mr Weston was an official in the Forestry Commission. The family were both happy and comfortably off until Tom fell ill at the age of nine.

For a period of several weeks the boy's health improved but then he suffered several relapses. The doctor and his parents were worried. It was decided that Tom should be entrusted to his grandfather in the hope that a spell in the healthy air of the wild and open countryside would cure him.

Read the passage above, then answer all the questions.

1.   **What is the name of the main character in the story?**

   ....

2.   **Which of the titles below is the correct one?**

   Put a tick in the box which matches the title you have chosen. You can only give one answer.

   The Westons Move House   ☐

   An Easy Life   ☐

   Life Had to Change   ☐

   Tom on Holiday   ☐

3. a   **Whom did Tom live with when he was a little boy?**

   ....

   b   **Whom did he live with afterwards?**

   ....

4.   **Draw a line between 2 of the dots to show the family relationships:**

   a.   Mr Weston is .

   . Sir Gregory's father
   . Tom's uncle
   . Tom's father
   . Tom's grandfather

   a.   Sir Gregory is .

   . Mr Weston's son
   . Mr Weston's grandfather
   . Tom's father
   . Tom's grandfather

A REPORT FROM OUR TRAVEL WRITER, GITA GUPTA, WHO VISITED THE BOKEHAM MANOR ANNUAL BOOKFAIR.

There's only one thing worse than a wet holiday weekend – and that is a hot one. If it is wet we can laze about at home, playing video games, watching T.V. and reading. There's no rush, no routine or stress.

So you can imagine my reaction when Mum announced that, as it was sunny, we were all going out to visit a bookfair at a place called Bokeham Manor. I wished that the skies would open.

Getting to Bokeham was a slow, stifling journey, as we inched our way along the A1 in the usual holiday jams. We had forgotten that sitting in traffic on hot holiday weekends was a national hobby.

Once we arrived, however, it did not take me long to warm to the place. For a start, Bokeham is not like the ordinary type of stately home with cases of dusty vases, wall-to-wall paintings and old-fashioned furniture. The Manor actually recreates life in the 16th century. You don't have to tiptoe about in hushed silence. Bokeham is a lively, noisy place where you can touch and feel everything, and if you want to, you can dress up in Tudor costume and take part yourself.

The main event was a 16th century bookfair. Papermakers, printers, bookbinders and illuminators were all demonstrating their skills. No one could fail to enjoy trying their hand at these crafts or any of the others that were being demonstrated that day.

Visitors in wheelchairs and people with babies had a difficult time, as getting these in and out of the buildings was not easy. In some places it was impossible. I'm not a regular visitor to stately homes, but I'm really pleased that I was taken to Bokeham. It was a great day out and I'd recommend it to most people.

GRAMMAR

Can you find where the words   'they're'
'there'
'their'

should go in the passage below?

Choose the correct words carefully and write one down in each empty box. Use each word only once.

1. In the house at the bottom of our road [ ] are four dogs. [ ] all black labradors and [ ] names are Billy, Blackie, Brutus and Bongo.

In the same way, where would you put   'where'
'were'
'we're' ?

Choose carefully and write one word in each box.

2. The house [ ] the black dogs live is a bit strange and scary. [ ] always daring each other to knock on the door and make the dogs bark. When we [ ] there last week we got caught.

What about   'to'
'too'
'two'?

Write the correct word in each box.

3. A man opened the window and shouted, "What are you doing?" But we were [ ] scared [ ] answer. We ran home.

Questions about Gita Gupta's report

1. What was Gita's opinion on first hearing about the family outing to Bokeham?

....

Which words tell you this?

....

2. ....

3. How had Gita's opinion changed by the end of the report?

....

....

ALPHABET

Look at the envelopes on the next page.

**Put the surnames on the envelopes into alphabetical order.
The first one is ARMSTRONG: so there is a 1 written in the circle under the envelope.**

Can you continue? Write under each envelope the number which you think shows the alphabetical order of the surnames.

Be careful: **do not use the same number more than once!**

Lang1E
03 96

PUNCTUATION AND HANDWRITING

Some of the punctuation in the following paragraph has been left out. Can you correct it?

Read this passage.

the thunder storm lasted all night the thunder rumbled and rolled darkly and endlessly over all the land the lightning struck a pine tree which split and crashed to the ground

Write it out in your neatest handwriting, putting in the missing full stops and capital letters. You will be given a mark for your handwriting.

....

....

....

....

....

....

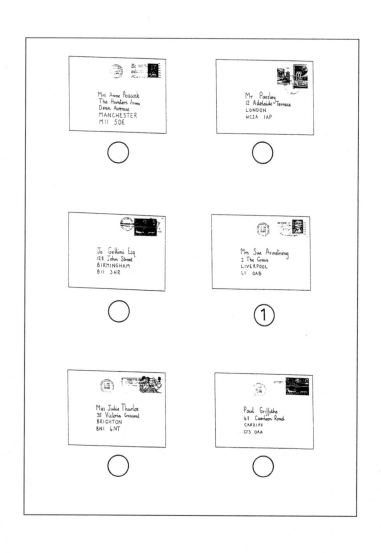

Appendix 2

LANGUAGE 2
STORY WRITING

Write the name of your school in this box:

Write your name and age in the following boxes:

NAME

AGE

Tick the right box:

GIRL   **BOY**

We hope you enjoy answering these questions.

Your answers will help us. Thank you.

Planning Sheet
Story Writing
Levels 1–6

*Have you chosen **one** of the starting points? Now make a note of some of your ideas. You can write them down here, or, if you prefer, turn over and use the guided Planning Sheet.*

A Door Opens

"What's in the room I have never entered?
What's behind the door I have never opened?"

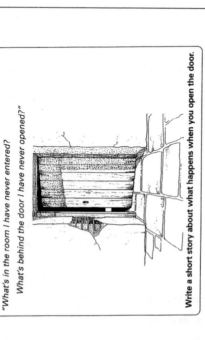

Write a short story about what happens when you open the door.

- **Setting** *(Where and when does it happen?)*

- **Characters** *(e.g. Who are they? What are they like?)*

- What makes the story **begin?**

- What happens **next?**

- How will your story **end?**

LangEng.doc
18 04 96

Appendix 3

MATHS A

Write the name of your school in this box:

Write your name and age in the following boxes:

NAME

AGE

Tick the right box:

GIRL   **BOY**

We hope you enjoy answering these questions.

Your answers will help us.   Thank you.

Appendices 221

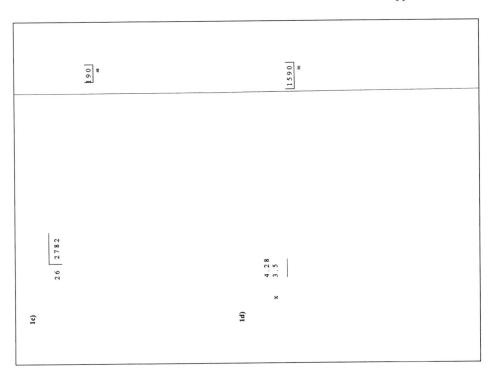

2.

a) Work out this multiplication sum.

7 . 1 4 x 1 0 0 =

| 1 5 6 7 9 0 |
38

b) Work out this division sum.

3 2 5 . 6 ÷ 1 0 =

| 1 5 6 7 9 0 |
40

3. You were away from school and missed some maths.

Your friend telephones you and describes the following geometric shape which you have to draw. This is what he says:

Draw a **rectangle** which is 6 cms long and 4 cms wide.

Draw the two **diagonal lines** of the rectangle and write in **I** at the point where the two diagonals cross over.

Choose one **angle** of the rectangle and call it **A**.

Draw a **circle** which has **A** at its centre and which goes through point **I**.

FIGURE

| 1 9 0 |
60

| 1 2 3 9 0 |
61

| 1 3 5 9 0 |
62

5.

a) What is the perimeter of this shape?

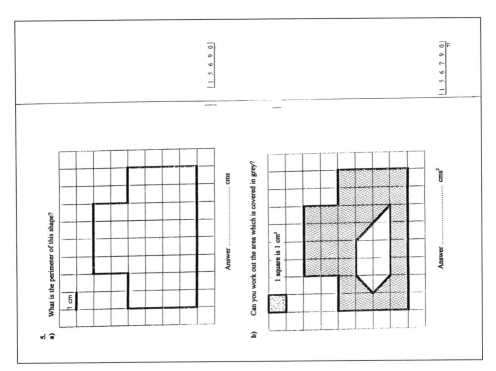

1 cm

Answer .... cms

b) Can you work out the area which is covered in grey?

1 square is 1 cm²

Answer .... cms²

4.

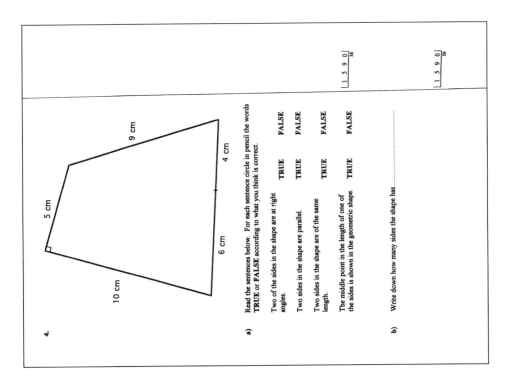

10 cm
5 cm
9 cm
6 cm
4 cm

a) Read the sentences below. For each sentence circle in pencil the words TRUE or FALSE according to what you think is correct.

Two of the sides in the shape are at right angles.	TRUE	FALSE
Two sides in the shape are parallel.	TRUE	FALSE
Two sides in the shape are of the same length.	TRUE	FALSE
The middle point in the length of one of the sides is shown in the geometric shape.	TRUE	FALSE

b) Write down how many sides the shape has ....

6.

The small rectangles which make up the big rectangle **ABCD** are the same size as the rectangles in the grey square above.

Mark with a tick which one of the answers below is the correct one.

The total area of the rectangle ABCD is:

□ 2½ times that of the grey square.

□ 4 times that of the grey square.

□ 6½ times that of the grey square.

□ 8 times that of the grey square.

□ 10 times that of the grey square.

□ 11 times that of the grey square

□ 20 times that of the grey square

1 5 6 7 9 0 | 34

---

7. During morning break 83 biscuits were sold by a group of 4 children. Each biscuit cost 3 pence.

What was the total price of all the biscuits sold?

Write your answer in the box:

[ ]

Can you explain how you worked this out?

....

....

....

1 5 9 0 | 6

8. A cardboard box containing bottles of lemonade holds 6 bottles of 1.5 litres each.

The supermarket shelf stacker puts 25 of these cardboard boxes in the drinks area.

Tick which one of these sums is the right one to use to work out how many bottles of lemonade were shelved.

□ 25 + 6	□ 25 x 6	□ 1.5 x 6
□ 25 - 6	□ 25 x 1.5	□ 6 - 1.5

1 5 9 0 | 70

FMathE.doc
24 03 96

Appendix 4

MATHS B

Write the name of your school in this box:

Write your name and age in the following boxes:

NAME

AGE

Tick the right box:

GIRL   **BOY**

We hope you enjoy answering these questions.

Your answers will help us.   Thank you.

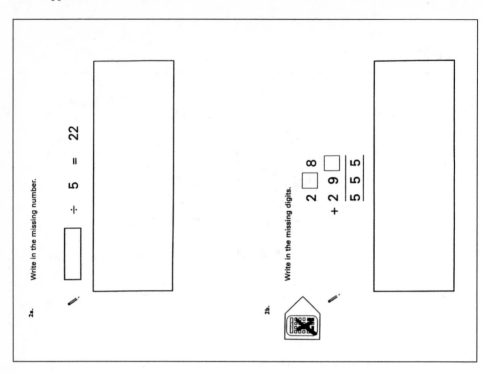

2a.

Write in the missing number.

□ ÷ 5 = 22

2b.

Write in the missing digits.

```
   2 8 □
 + 2 9
   ───
   5 5 5
```

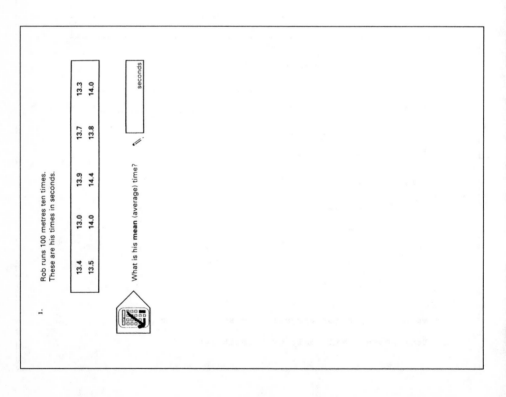

1.

Rob runs 100 metres ten times.
These are his times in seconds.

| 13.4 | 13.0 | 13.9 | 13.7 | 13.3 |
| 13.5 | 14.0 | 14.4 | 13.8 | 14.0 |

What is his **mean** (average) time?

□ seconds

4. Here are some picture frame sizes.

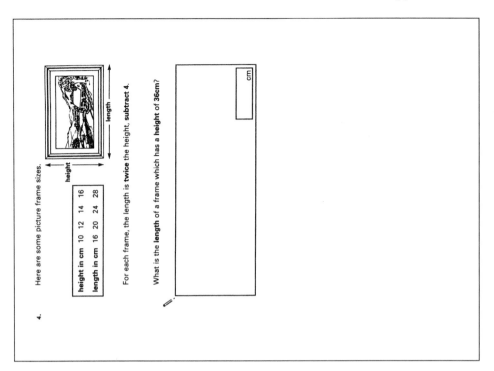

height in cm	10	12	14	16
length in cm	16	20	24	28

For each frame, the length is **twice** the height, **subtract 4.**

What is the **length** of a frame which has a **height of 36cm?**

cm

3a. Write in the missing digits.

$$323 \times \boxed{}7 = 1518\boxed{}$$

3b. This calculation has the **same** number missing from each box.

Write the missing number in the boxes.

$$\boxed{} \times \boxed{} - \boxed{} = 42$$

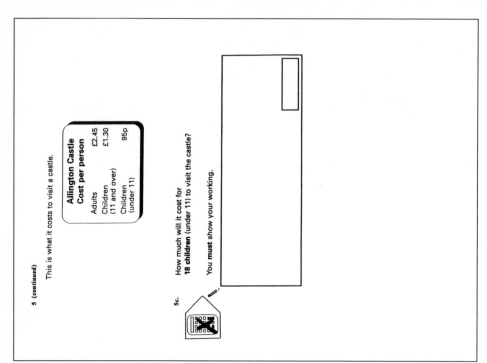

5 (continued)

This is what it costs to visit a castle.

**Allington Castle
Cost per person**

Adults	£2.45
Children (11 and over)	£1.30
Children (under 11)	95p

5c. How much will it cost for
18 children (under 11) to visit the castle?

You **must** show your working.

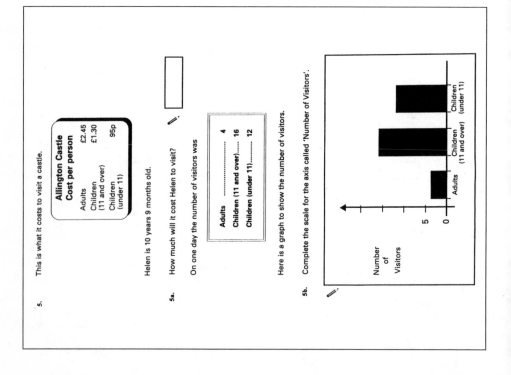

5. This is what it costs to visit a castle.

**Allington Castle
Cost per person**

Adults	£2.45
Children (11 and over)	£1.30
Children (under 11)	95p

Helen is 10 years 9 months old.

5a. How much will it cost Helen to visit?

On one day the number of visitors was

Adults	4
Children (11 and over)	16
Children (under 11)	12

Here is a graph to show the number of visitors.

5b. Complete the scale for the axis called 'Number of Visitors'.

7. Sam has 3 different spinners.

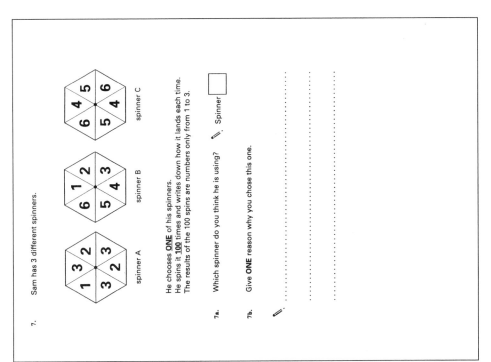

spinner A   spinner B   spinner C

He chooses **ONE** of his spinners.
He spins it **100** times and writes down how it lands each time.
The results of the 100 spins are numbers only from 1 to 3.

7a. Which spinner do you think he is using? ✎ . ... Spinner [ ]

7b. Give **ONE** reason why you chose this one.

✎ : ....

....

....

6. On the table there are 2 packets.

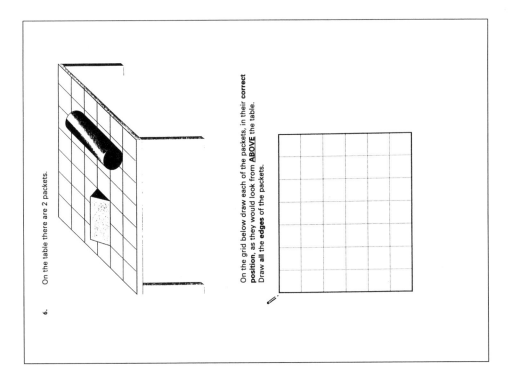

On the grid below draw each of the packets, in their **correct position**, as they would look from **ABOVE** the table.
Draw all the **edges** of the packets.

✎ :

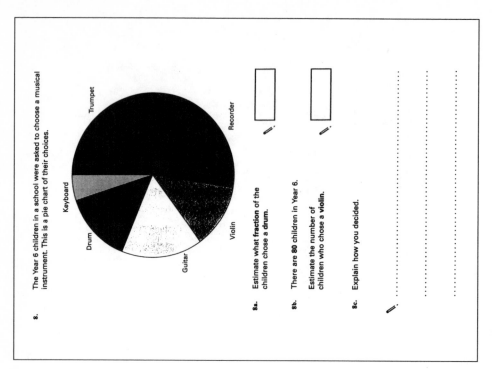

8. The Year 6 children in a school were asked to choose a musical instrument. This is a pie chart of their choices.

8a. Estimate what **fraction of the** children chose a **drum.**

8b. There are **80** children in Year 6.
Estimate the number of children who chose a **violin.**

8c. Explain how you decided.

....
....
....

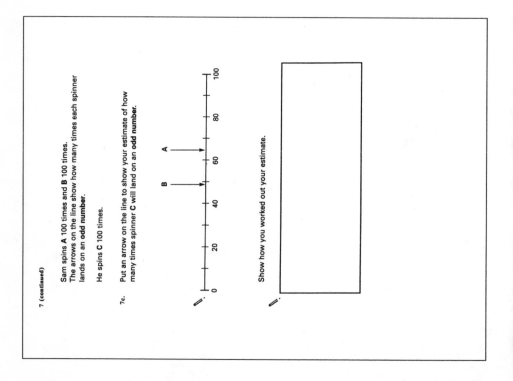

7 (continued)

Sam spins **A** 100 times and **B** 100 times.
The arrows on the line show how many times each spinner lands on an **odd number.**

He spins **C** 100 times.

7c. Put an arrow on the line to show your estimate of how many times spinner **C** will land on an **odd number.**

Show how you worked out your estimate.

10a. Place these numbers in order of size, starting with the **smallest**.

✏️ 0.19   0.9   0.091   0.109

☐ ☐ ☐ ☐

smallest ——————————————— largest

10b. Place these fractions in order of size, starting with the **smallest**.

✏️ $\frac{1}{2}$ $\frac{1}{3}$ $\frac{5}{12}$ $\frac{5}{6}$

☐ ☐ ☐ ☐

smallest ——————————————— largest

EMathEng.doc
30 04 96

9. On the grid, draw the **reflection** of the shape **in the mirror line**.

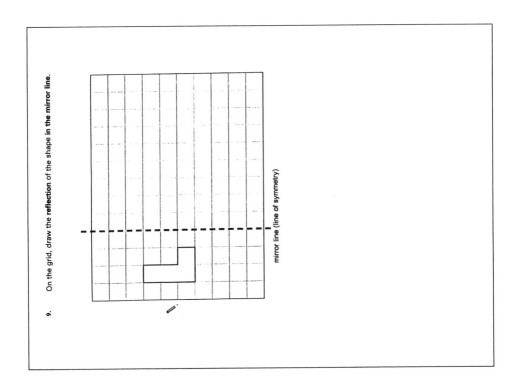

mirror line (line of symmetry)

Appendix 5

MATHS C

Write the name of your school in this box:

Write your name and age in the following boxes:

NAME

AGE

Tick the right box:

GIRL   **BOY**

We hope you enjoy answering these questions.
Your answers will help us.   Thank you.

You will need to spend about 20 minutes on this Maths problem.

Some children investigated what answers they got when they did sums with odd and even numbers. They made these comments on what they found.

David: When I add two odd numbers together I always get an even answer.
For example, $3 + 5 = 8$ and $9 + 11 = 20$

Sarah: When I add an odd number to an even number I always get an odd number for an answer.

Megan: I think that an even number multiplied by an odd number might sometimes be even and sometimes be odd.

Farshad: Taking away an odd number from an even number always gives me an odd answer.
For example, $12 - 9 = 3$

1 **Which of these children do you agree with and which do you disagree with? Say why you think they are right or wrong.**

Please turn to the next page.

---

2 **What other general statements could you make about calculating with odd and even numbers? Say why you think they are true.**

MathCEng.doc
21 05 96

Appendix 6

LANGAGE 1

Ecris le nom de ton école dans ce cadre:

Ecris ton nom et ton âge dans les cadres ci-dessous:

NOM

AGE

Mets une croix dans la case qui convient:

FILLE   **GARÇON**

Tes réponses vont nous aider.   Nous te remercions.

COMPREHENSION DE TEXTE A

Depuis l'âge de dix ans, Alexis habitait chez son grand-père, Monsieur Grégoire, ainsi que l'appelaient les gens du pays. Il y avait donc presque cinq ans qu'il vivait dans le domaine. De très simples événements l'avaient conduit en ce lieu coupé de toute relation avec le monde.

Alexis avait passé son enfance à Pontbaud, une ville du centre de la France, chez ses parents, les Rousselande. Monsieur Rousselande occupait un poste dans l'administration des Eaux et Forêts. La vie de la famille était tout à fait heureuse et aisée, lorsque Alexis, à l'âge de neuf ans, tomba malade.

La santé de l'enfant se rétablissait pendant quelques semaines, et puis c'étaient des rechutes qui inquiétaient aussi bien les docteurs que les parents. On décida de confier Alexis à son grand-père, avec l'espoir qu'un séjour dans l'air salubre (1) d'une campagne tout à fait sauvage lui serait enfin salutaire.

André DHOTEL, *L'enfant qui disait n'importe quoi*

(1) salubre: sain, qui a une action favorable sur l'organisme.

Lis le texte ci-dessus, puis réponds à chacune des deux questions suivantes.

1. **Comment s'appelle le personnage principal du texte?**

....

2. **Parmi les 4 titres ci-dessous, quel est celui qui te convient?**

Mets une croix dans le carré qui suit le titre de ton choix. Donne une seule réponse.

Les Rousselande déménagent ☐

Une existence sans problème ☐

Un changement de vie nécessaire ☐

Alexis en vacances ☐

---

3. **Réponds aux 2 questions suivantes:**

   a. **Chez qui Alexis a-t-il passé les premières années de sa vie?**

   ....

   b. **Chez qui a-t-il vécu ensuite?**

   ....

4. **Indique par une seule flèche quel est, d'après le texte, le lien de parenté:**

   a. Monsieur Rousselande est   . le père de M. Grégoire
   . l'oncle d'Alexis
   . le père d'Alexis
   . le grand-père d'Alexis

   b. M. Grégoire est   . le fils de M. Rousselande
   . le grand-père de M. Rousselande
   . le père d'Alexis
   . le grand-père d'Alexis

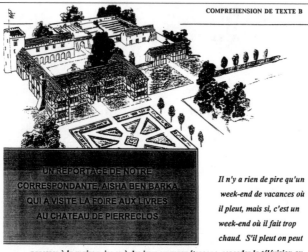

UN REPORTAGE DE NOTRE CORRESPONDANTE, AISHA BEN BARKA QUI A VISITE LA FOIRE AUX LIVRES AU CHATEAU DE PIERRECLOS

Il n'y a rien de pire qu'un week-end de vacances où il pleut, mais si, c'est un week-end où il fait trop chaud. S'il pleut on peut paresser à la maison, jouer à des jeux au magnétoscope, regarder la télévision ou lire. On n'a pas besoin de se dépêcher, il n'y a ni routine ni contrainte.

Alors vous pouvez imaginer ma réaction quand Maman m'a annoncé que, comme il faisait beau, nous allions tous aller à une foire aux livres dans un endroit qui s'appelle le Château de Pierreclos. J'aurais bien voulu qu'il se mette à tomber des cordes.

Il faisait une chaleur étouffante et nous avons mis longtemps pour arriver à Pierreclos à cause des embouteillages habituels sur la N6 pendant la période des vacances. Nous avions oublié que c'était un passe-temps national favori d'être dans sa voiture au milieu des bouchons par un beau et chaud week-end de vacances.

Pourtant, une fois arrivée, il ne m'a pas fallu longtemps pour me sentir attirée par cet endroit. D'abord, Pierreclos n'est pas du tout comme les châteaux imposants qu'on voit d'habitude avec leurs vitrines remplies de vases poussiéreux, leurs murs couverts de tableaux et leurs meubles démodés. Ce château recrée véritablement la vie telle qu'elle était au 16e siècle. Vous n'avez pas

besoin de marcher sur la pointe des pieds sans faire de bruit. Pierreclos est un endroit plein d'animation et de bruits où l'on a le droit de tout toucher, et si l'on veut, on peut se déguiser en costume de l'époque de François I et participer aux évènements.

Le clou de la journée c'était la foire aux livres qui se passait au 16e siècle. Il y avait des fabricants de papier, des imprimeurs, des relieurs et des enlumineurs qui faisaient des démonstrations. Il était impossible de ne pas apprécier la possibilité qu'on avait d'essayer pour soi-même de fabriquer des produits artisanaux en tout genre.

Mais il n'est pas facile de circuler pour les visiteurs en fauteuil roulant ou les personnes accompagnées de bébés en poussette et dans certains cas il est même impossible de pénétrer dans les bâtiments ou d'en sortir. Je ne visite pas très souvent les beaux châteaux, mais je ne regrette pas du tout d'être allée à Pierreclos. J'y ai passé une excellente journée et je recommenderais cette visite à tout le monde ou presque.

GRAMMAIRE

Peux-tu placer les mots suivants   'peux'
                                       'peu'
                                       'peut'

dans le texte ci-dessous?

Choisis les mots qui conviennent et écris un mot dans chaque cadre.
N'utilise pas deux fois le même mot.

1. Il y a ☐ de gens qui connaissent la maison de la sorcière.

On ☐ passer devant sans le savoir, mais moi je ne

☐ pas la regarder sans avoir peur.

A toi maintenant de placer les mots 'a'
                                       'as'
                                       'à'.

Choisis le mot correct pour chaque cadre.

2. Tu n' ☐ jamais vu une maison pareille. Elle

☐ dû être construite il y a longtemps avec

ses petites fenêtres sombres et ses vieux volets délabrés qui ne sont

qu' ☐ moitié ouverts.

Peux-tu placer les mots   'habiter'
                                 'habitait'
                                 'habité'

dans le cadre qui convient?

3. La sorcière a toujours ☐ là. Il paraît qu'elle y

☐ quand mon père était petit. Ma famille voudrait

☐ un appartement juste en face de cette maison. Qu'est-ce

que je vais faire?

Questions sur le reportage d'Aisha Ben Barka

1. Quel était l'avis d'Aisha quand on lui a dit qu'elle allait visiter Pierreclos avec sa famille?

....

....

2. Quels sont les mots qui vous l'indiquent?

....

3. De quelle manière est-ce qu'Aisha a changé d'avis à la fin de son reportage?

....

....

L'ALPHABET

Regarde les enveloppes à la page suivante.

Classe ces enveloppes par ordre alphabétique des noms de famille.
On a mis le numéro 1 sous l'enveloppe qui est la première de la liste: ALVAREZ.

A toi de continuer, en écrivant le numéro qui convient sous chaque enveloppe.

Attention: **n'utilise pas deux fois le même nombre!**

Langalf.doc
23 04 96

PONCTUATION ET ECRITURE

Dans ce paragraphe, une partie de la ponctuation a été oubliée. A toi de la rétablir.

Lis ce texte.

il tonna toute la nuit le tonnerre gronda vraiment, sans se ménager il couvrait de ses roulements sombres toute la campagne la foudre tomba sur un pin qui craqua et s'abattit

D'après H. BOSCO, *L'enfant et la rivière*

Ecris le texte très soigneusement en ajoutant les points et les majuscules qui manquent. Ton écriture et ta présentation seront notées.

....

....

....

....

....

Appendix 7

LANGAGE 2
EXPRESSION ECRITE

Ecris le nom de ton école dans ce cadre:

Ecris ton nom et ton âge dans les cadres ci-dessous:

NOM

AGE

Mets une croix dans la case qui convient:

FILLE   **GARÇON**

Tes réponses vont nous aider.   Nous te remercions.

Expression écrite

Plan

Si tu veux, écris quelques idées sur cette feuille. Ou si tu préfères, tourne la page et sers-toi des suggestions que tu trouveras.

La Porte S'ouvre

"Qu'y a-t-il dans la pièce où je ne suis jamais entré? Qu'est-ce qu'il y a derrière la porte que je n'ai jamais ouverte?"

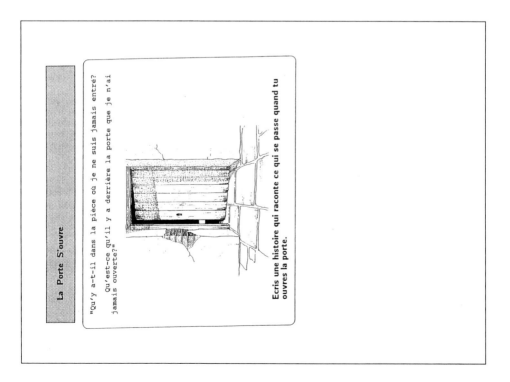

Ecris une histoire qui raconte ce qui se passe quand tu ouvres la porte.

LangFr.doc
18 04 96

Voici quelques notes qui t'aideront à rédiger ton histoire.

- **Situation**   (Où et quand est-ce que l'histoire se passe?)

- **Personnages**   (Qui sont-ils? Décris-les.)

- **Comment commence l'histoire?**

- **Que se passe-t-il ensuite?**

- **Comment se terminera ton histoire?**

Appendix 8

MATHEMATIQUES A

Ecris le nom de ton école dans ce cadre:

Ecris ton nom et ton âge dans les cadres ci-dessous:

NOM

AGE

Mets une croix dans la case qui convient:

FILLE   **GARÇON**

Tes réponses vont nous aider. Nous te remercions.

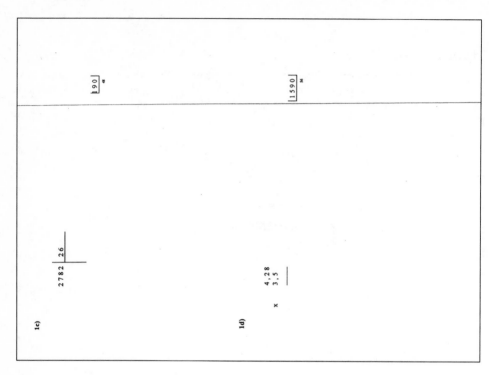

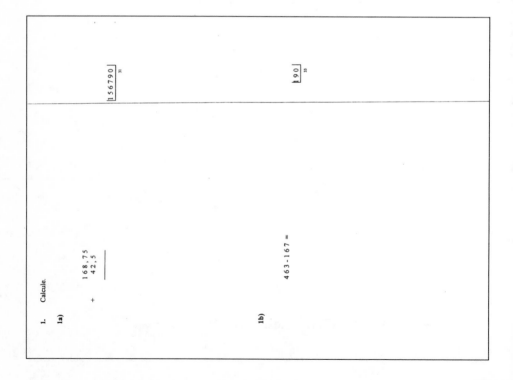

2.

a) Donne le résultat de la multiplication suivante.

$$7,14 \times 100 =$$

| 1 5 6 7 9 0 |
38

b) Donne le résultat de la division suivante.

$$325,6 : 10 =$$

| 1 5 6 7 9 0 |
40

3.

Tu étais absent à la dernière leçon de mathématiques.

Ton camarade te décrit au téléphone une figure de géométrie que tu dois dessiner ci-dessous. Voici le texte:

Dessine un <u>rectangle</u> de longueur 6 cm et de largeur 4 cm.

Trace les <u>diagonales</u> de ce rectangle et appelle **I** le point où les diagonales se coupent.

Choisis un <u>sommet</u> du rectangle et appelle ce sommet **A**.

Trace le <u>cercle</u> qui a pour centre **A** et qui passe par le point **I**.

FIGURE

| 1 9 0 |
60

| 1 2 3 9 0 |
61

| 1 3 5 9 0 |
62

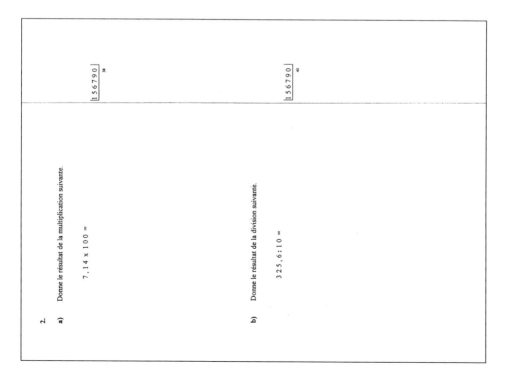

5.

a) Quel est le périmètre de la figure ?

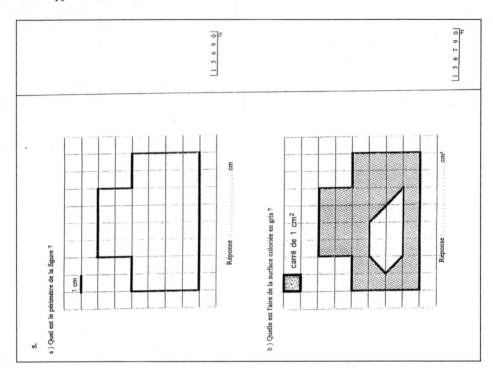

|1 cm|

Réponse : .... cm

| 1 | 5 | 6 | 9 | 0 |
74

b) Quelle est l'aire de la surface coloriée en gris ?

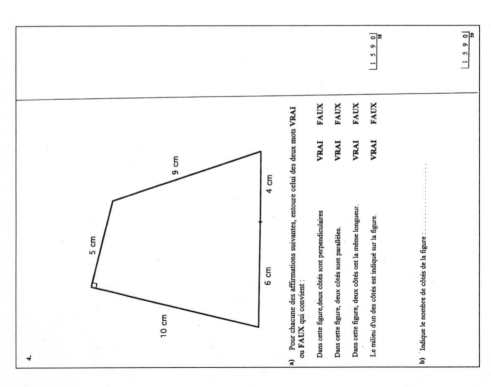

▦ carré de 1 cm²

Réponse : .... cm²

| 1 | 5 | 6 | 7 | 9 | 0 |
75

4.

10 cm

5 cm

9 cm

6 cm

4 cm

a) Pour chacune des affirmations suivantes, entoure celui des deux mots VRAI ou FAUX qui convient :

Dans cette figure, deux côtés sont perpendiculaires   VRAI   FAUX

Dans cette figure, deux côtés sont parallèles.   VRAI   FAUX

Dans cette figure, deux côtés ont la même longueur.   VRAI   FAUX

Le milieu d'un des côtés est indiqué sur la figure.   VRAI   FAUX

| 1 | 5 | 9 | 0 |
58

b) Indique le nombre de côtés de la figure : ....

| 1 | 5 | 9 | 0 |
59

7.

A la récréation de 10 heures, 83 petits pains ont été été vendus par un groupe de 4 élèves.
Chaque petit pain a été vendu 3 F.

Quel est le montant total de cette vente ?

Ecris ta réponse dans le cadre :

Explique ta réponse :

....

....

....

`| 1 | 5 | 9 | 0 |` 6

8.

Un carton d'eau minérale contient 6 bouteilles de 1,5 litre.

Le magasinier range 25 de ces cartons sur son rayon.

Indique par une croix l'opération qui convient pour trouver le nombre de bouteilles rangées.

☐ 25 + 6   ☐ 25 × 6   ☐ 1,5 × 6

☐ 25 - 6   ☐ 25 × 1,5   ☐ 6 - 1,5

`| 1 | 5 | 9 | 0 |` 70

FMathF.doc
24 04 96

6.

A ▢▢▢▢▢ B
▢▢▢▢▢
▢▢▢▢▢
D ▢▢▢▢▢ C

Tous les petits rectangles qui composent le rectangle ABCD et le carré colorié sont identiques.

Mets une croix devant la bonne réponse.

L'aire totale du rectangle ABCD est :

☐ 2,5 fois celle du carré colorié
☐ 4 fois celle du carré colorié
☐ 6,5 fois celle du carré colorié
☐ 8 fois celle du carré colorié
☐ 10 fois celle du carré colorié
☐ 11 fois celle du carré colorié
☐ 20 fois celle du carré colorié

`| 1 | 5 | 6 | 7 | 9 | 0 |` 24

Appendix 9

MATHEMATIQUES   B

Ecris le nom de ton école dans ce cadre:

Ecris ton nom et ton âge dans les cadres ci-dessous:

NOM

AGE

Mets une croix dans la case qui convient:

FILLE   **GARÇON**

Tes réponses vont nous aider.   Nous te remercions.

1. Robert fait une course de 100 mètres dix fois de suite.
Voici ses temps en secondes.

13,4	13,0	13,9	13,7	13,3
13,5	14,0	14,4	13,8	14,0

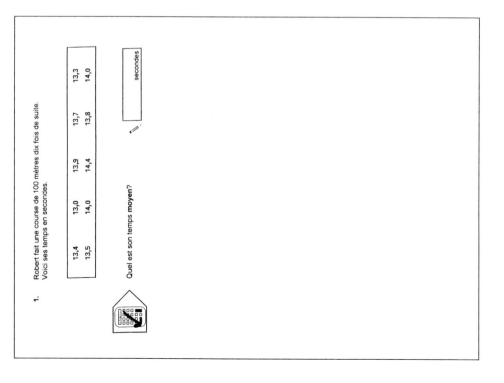

Quel est son temps **moyen**?

[___] secondes

2a. Ecris le nombre qui manque dans le cadre.

[___] : 5 = 22

2b. Ecris les chiffres qui manquent dans les carrés.

```
    2  8
 [ ]
+  2  9  [ ]
 ----------
    5  5  5
```

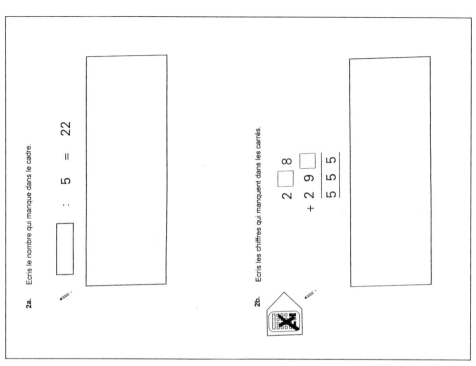

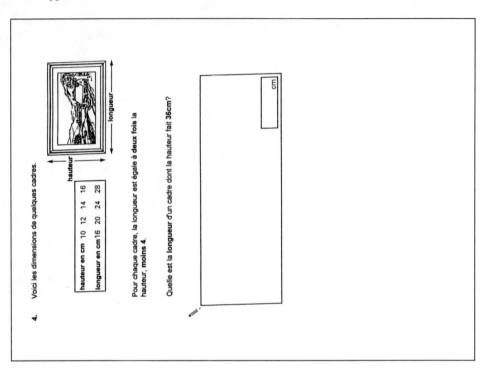

4. Voici les dimensions de quelques cadres.

hauteur

longueur

hauteur en cm	10	12	14	16
longueur en cm	16	20	24	28

Pour chaque cadre, la longueur est égale à **deux fois** la hauteur, **moins 4**.

Quelle est la longueur d'un cadre dont la hauteur fait **36cm**?

cm

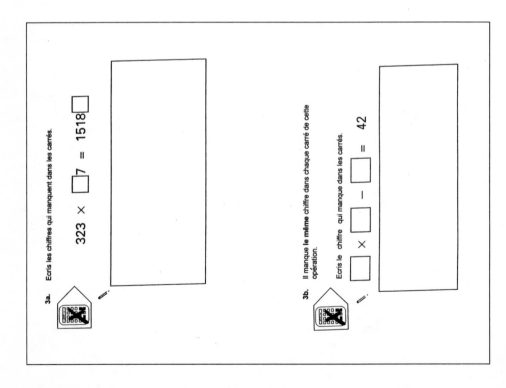

3a.   Ecris les chiffres qui manquent dans les carrés.

$$323 \times \boxed{}7 = 1518\boxed{}$$

3b.   Il manque le **même** chiffre dans chaque carré de cette opération.

Ecris le chiffre qui manque dans les carrés.

$$\boxed{} \times \boxed{} - \boxed{} = 42$$

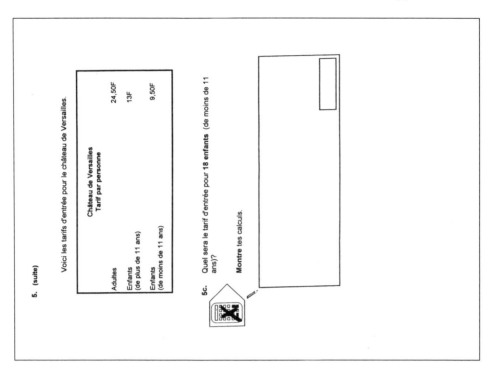

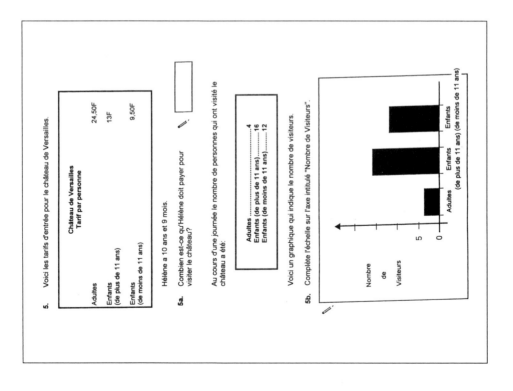

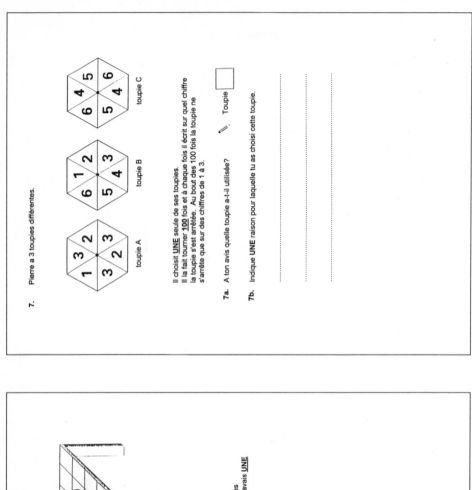

7. Pierre a 3 toupies différentes.

toupie A

toupie B

toupie C

Il choisit **UNE** seule de ses toupies.
Il la fait tourner **100** fois et à chaque fois il écrit sur quel chiffre la toupie s'est arrêtée. Au bout des 100 fois la toupie ne s'arrête que sur des chiffres de 1 à 3.

7a. A ton avis quelle toupie a-t-il utilisée? Toupie

7b. Indique **UNE** raison pour laquelle tu as choisi cette toupie.

....

....

....

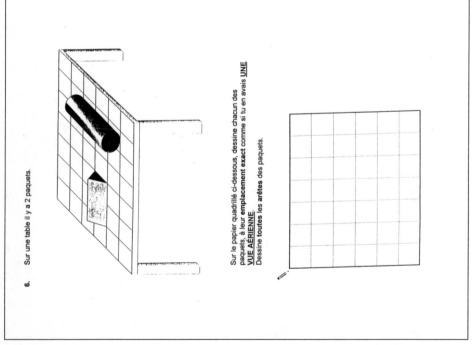

6. Sur une table il y a 2 paquets.

Sur le papier quadrillé ci-dessous, dessine chacun des paquets, à leur **emplacement exact** comme si tu en avais **UNE VUE AÉRIENNE**.
Dessine **toutes** les **arêtes** des paquets.

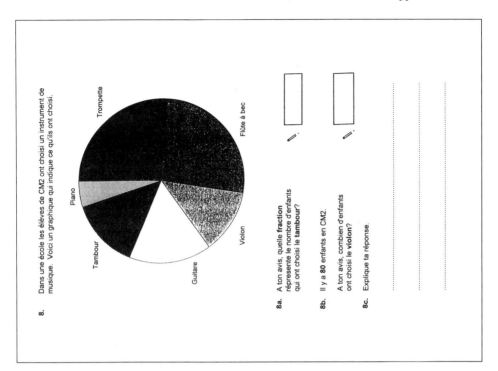

8. Dans une école les élèves de CM2 ont choisi un instrument de musique. Voici un graphique qui indique ce qu'ils ont choisi.

8a. A ton avis, quelle **fraction** représente le nombre d'enfants qui ont choisi le **tambour**?

8b. Il y a **80** enfants en CM2.

A ton avis, combien d'enfants ont choisi le **violon**?

8c. Explique ta réponse.

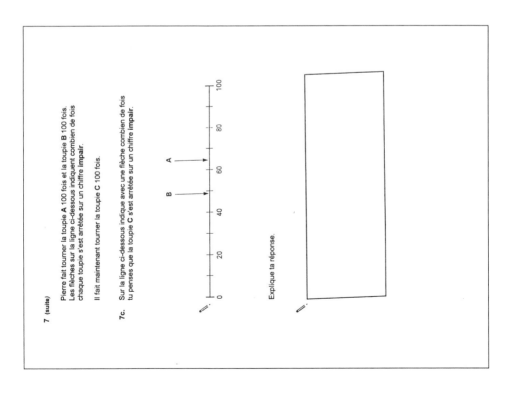

7 (suite)

Pierre fait tourner la toupie **A** 100 fois et la toupie **B** 100 fois.
Les flèches sur la ligne ci-dessous indiquent combien de fois chaque toupie s'est arrêtée sur un chiffre **impair**.

Il fait maintenant tourner la toupie **C** 100 fois.

7c. Sur la ligne ci-dessous indique avec une flèche combien de fois tu penses que la toupie **C** s'est arrêtée sur un chiffre **impair**.

Explique ta réponse.

10a. Mets ces nombres par ordre croissant de taille en commençant par le plus petit.

0.19   0.9   0.091   0.109

plus petit   plus grand

10b. Mets ces fractions par ordre croissant de taille en commençant par la plus petite.

$\frac{1}{2}$ $\frac{1}{3}$ $\frac{5}{12}$ $\frac{5}{6}$

plus petite   plus grande

EMathF.doc
30 04 96

9. Sur le papier quadrillé ci-dessous, trace la **réflexion** de la figure dessinée **par rapport à la ligne de symétrie.**

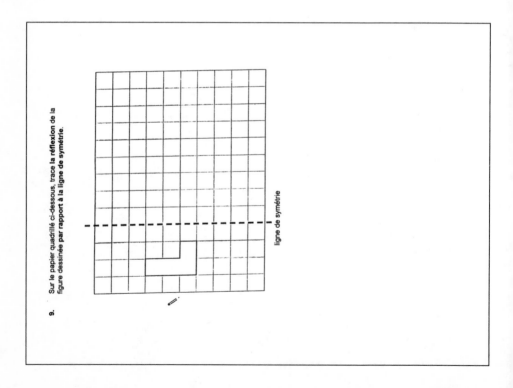

ligne de symétrie

Appendix 10

MATHEMATIQUES C

Ecris le nom de ton école dans ce cadre:

Ecris ton nom et ton âge dans les cadres ci-dessous:

NOM

AGE

Mets une croix dans la case qui convient:

FILLE   **GARÇON**

Tes réponses vont nous aider. Nous te remercions.

Il te faudra environ 20 minutes pour faire ce problème.

Des enfants ont fait des recherches pour voir quelles réponses ils obtenaient en faisant des calculs avec des nombres pairs et impairs. Voici ce qu'ils ont dit à la suite de leurs recherches.

Philippe: Quand j'ajoute deux nombres impairs ensemble j'obtiens toujours un nombre pair comme réponse.
Par exemple, $3 + 5 = 8$ et $9 + 11 = 20$

Catherine: Quand j'ajoute un nombre impair à un nombre pair j'obtiens un nombre impair comme réponse.

Céline: Je crois que quand on multiplie un nombre pair par un nombre impair on peut quelquefois obtenir un nombre pair et quelquefois un nombre impair comme réponse.

Ahmed: Si je soustrais un nombre impair à un nombre pair j'obtiens toujours un nombre impair comme résultat.
Par exemple, $12 - 9 = 3$

1   **Avec lesquels de ces enfants es-tu d'accord ou pas d'accord? Dis pourquoi tu penses qu'ils ont raison ou tort.**

Tourne la page pour la question suivante.

2   **Qu'est-ce que tu pourrais affirmer d'autre sur le calcul des nombres pairs et impairs en général? Explique pourquoi tu penses qu c'est vrai.**

Appendix 11

QUEST

PUPIL QUESTIONNAIRE

SUMMER 1996

Write the name of your school in this box:

Write your name and age in the following boxes:

NAME

AGE

Tick the right box:

GIRL   **BOY**

We hope you enjoy answering these questions.

Your answers will help us.   Thank you.

PART 1

1. Finis la phrase suivante: Un(e) bon(nne) maître/maîtresse devrait...........

_____
_____
_____
_____
_____

2a. Si un nouvel élève arrivait dans votre classe, quel genre d'élève est-ce que tu crois que ton maître aimerait?

_____
_____
_____
_____
_____

2b. Dans quelle mesure est-ce que tu penses que tu ressembles à cet élève?

_____
_____
_____
_____
_____

3a. Qu'est-ce que c'est qu'une bonne école?

_____
_____
_____
_____
_____

3b. Est-ce que tu penses que ton école est une bonne école? Explique pourquoi ou pourquoi pas.

_____
_____
_____
_____

PART 2

MY FEELINGS ABOUT SCHOOL

1 How much do you agree or disagree with the sentences below?

Please tick only one box for each row.

	Strongly agree	Agree	Disagree	Strongly disagree	Not sure
1. I like my teacher.					
2. School helps you to learn how to use your spare time.					
3. School helps you to get on with people.					
4. I like being at school.					
5. You don't need to pass exams to get a job.					
6. School helps you learn how to do things on your own.					
7. I really enjoy most lessons.					
8. School is boring.					
9. I want to do well at school.					
10. The work I do at school is a waste of time.					
11. School-work helps you to get a job.					
12. I don't learn very much at school.					
13. The best part of my life is the time I spend in school.					

IDENTITY

2a Write the four most important things about you in school.

1. _____

2. _____

3. _____

4. _____

2b How much do you agree or disagree with the sentences below?

Please tick only one box for each row.

	Strongly agree	Agree	Disagree	Strongly disagree	Not sure
1. I consider myself to be very English.					
2. I feel very proud of being English.					
3. I think it matters what country I belong to.					
4. In class we learn a lot about the way of life of children whose families come from abroad.					
5. In England everyone is equal.					
6. I have been taught quite a lot about what will be expected of me as a future citizen of England.					

2c A good reason for being proud of being English is _____

_____

2d I think being English means

Please tick only one box for each row.

	Strongly agree	Agree	Disagree	Strongly disagree	Not sure
1. being a hard worker at school.					
2. knowing your country is best.					
3. being proud of what your country has done in the past.					
4. feeling you belong to your country and that your country belongs to you.					

3 How good do you think you are at

Please tick only one box for each row.

	Very good	Good	OK	Not very good	Hopeless
1. maths?					
2. English?					
3. science?					
4. music?					
5. geography?					
6. history?					
7. art?					
8. sport?					
9. computers?					
10. technology?					

4 Do you agree or disagree with the sentences below?

Please tick only one box for each row.

	Strongly agree	Agree	Disagree	Strongly disagree	Not sure
1. Anyone can do well in maths if he or she works hard.					
2. Either you can do maths or you can't.					
3. It doesn't matter how hard they try, some people will never be good at maths.					

5 How do you feel in class?

Please tick only one box for each row.

	Strongly agree	Agree	Disagree	Strongly disagree	Not sure
1. My teacher often praises children for their good work.					
2. It quite often happens that the teacher says somebody's work is bad or wrong in front of the class.					

SCHOOL WORK

6 What do you think about the work you do at school?

For each item below, put a tick to show how you feel.
For example, if you think school work is most often 'fun', put a tick close to the word 'fun', but if you find it most often 'boring', put your tick next to 'boring'.
If you don't think it's 'fun' or 'boring', put a tick in the middle.

School work is something which is most often

fairly difficult	: : : : : : :	fairly easy
takes a long time	: : : : : : :	done quickly
fun	: : : : : : :	boring
done on your own	: : : : : : :	done with others
useful	: : : : : : :	no use
given a mark	: : : : : : :	not given a mark
interesting	: : : : : : :	not interesting
done in silence	: : : : : : :	done when talking with friends
involves finding things out	: : : : : : :	involves learning things by heart

7   How do you most often work?

Tick either the 'True' box or the 'Not true' box to tell us about yourself

When I'm working

	True	Not true
I am most often on my own	☐	☐
I am most often working with a friend	☐	☐
I am most often able to move around	☐	☐
I am most often sitting quietly	☐	☐
I am most often able to talk	☐	☐
I am most often working in a quiet room	☐	☐
I am most often doing practical activities	☐	☐
I am most often listening to or watching the teacher	☐	☐
I am most often answering the teacher's questions	☐	☐
I am most often writing	☐	☐
I am most often able to talk to the teacher on my own	☐	☐
I am most often working in a group	☐	☐
I am most often finding things out	☐	☐

8   When I want to do good work it's because

Please tick only one box for each row.

	Strongly agree	Agree	Disagree	Strongly disagree	Not sure
1. otherwise I might get shouted at.					
2. I like being praised.					
3. it makes me feel happy.					
4. my parents will be pleased.					
5. I want to be the best in the class.					
6. I want to get a good mark or sticker.					
7. my parents will give me a treat or some money.					
8. it's important for me to do well.					
9. it will help me to get a good job.					
10. my teacher will be happy.					

LEARNING AT SCHOOL.

9   What do you think about how you learn things at school?

Please tick only one box for each row.

	Strongly agree	Agree	Disagree	Strongly disagree	Not sure
1. We learn a lot by finding things out.					
2. In class we mostly learn from the textbook the class is using.					
3. At school the teacher likes you to come up with your own ideas.					
4. Most of our work in class is listening to the teacher.					
5. Our teachers like us to find different ways of answering questions.					
6. Most school-work is learning things by heart.					
7. You learn a lot when you work with a friend.					
8. The teacher's job is just to make you learn.					
9. I can choose some of the things I do.					
10. Having tests makes you work hard.					
11. You can learn by playing.					
12. You learn more if the teacher gives you all the same work and you do it all together.					
13. I keep working even if the teacher leaves the room.					
14. My teacher always wants careful and neat work.					
15. It's difficult to concentrate on your work at school because of the noise of other people talking.					
16. Most of the school-work we do is practising something we've already learnt.					
17. You learn most from your teacher.					

ABILITY/EFFORT

10 I think some children do better at school than others because

Tick the three most important reasons

they work harder.

they're clever.

their parents help them more.

they listen to the teacher more.

they think more quickly.

they get more help from the teacher.

they don't mess about so much.

they've got better brains.

they're older.

☐ ☐ ☐ ☐ ☐ ☐ ☐ ☐ ☐

TEACHERS

11 What do you think about teachers?

Tick if the following sentences are like my teacher', 'not like my teacher', 'a bit like my teacher'.

	Please tick only one box for each row.		
	Like my teacher	Not like my teacher	A bit like my teacher
1. My teacher has told us exactly what we should know by the end of the year.			
2. My teacher doesn't mind us talking in class.			
3. My teacher makes us work hard nearly all the time.			
4. My teacher always tells off people who aren't working.			
5. My teacher often has a laugh with us.			
6. My teacher normally gives us interesting things to do.			

12 What are the most important things that a teacher should do?

Put the following into order of importance number 1–8.
For example, if you think the most important thing about a teacher is that he or she should be strict, put a 1 in the box for 'Be strict', but if you think that is the least important thing, put an 8 by that box.

☐ ☐ ☐ ☐ ☐ ☐ ☐ ☐

Be strict.

Always be fair.

Let children choose what they want to do.

Make children work hard.

Explain things well.

Give children work which will be useful when they are adults.

Pay attention to children who find things difficult.

Make the work interesting.

13 Put the following sentences into order of importance from 1 to 5, as you did in Question 12.

When I behave well in class it's because

☐ ☐ ☐ ☐ ☐

I like to be good.

I get on with my teacher and want him or her to like me.

My teacher is strict and makes everyone behave properly.

My teacher punishes people who behave badly.

My school work will be better if I behave well.

SCHOOL ACTIVITIES

14a Which two school subjects do you like best at school?

_____

_____

14b Which two school subjects do you like least at school?

_____

_____

HOW I DO AT SCHOOL

15a How does your teacher know how well you are doing?

_____

_____

15b How do _you_ know how well you are doing?

_____

_____

_____

15c How does your teacher mostly mark your work?

Please tick only one box for each row.

	Always	Very often	Often	Rarely	Never
1. With marks out of 10 or 20.					
2. With comments.					
3. With grades (A, B, C).					
4. With 'levels'.					
5. With ticks.					

15d What do you think about the marking of your work?

Please tick only one box for each row.

	Strongly agree	Agree	Disagree	Strongly disagree	Not sure
1. I like knowing how many marks I've got out of 10.					
2. I like it when the teacher marks my work.					
3. I feel worried when the teacher marks my work.					
4. I like to know how I'm doing in my work.					
5. Teachers aren't always fair.					
6. I find it embarrassing when the teacher says in front of the class that my work is wrong.					

15e What is your position in the class compared to the other children?

_____

PARENTS

16 What part do your parents play in your school work?

Please tick only one box for each row.

	Strongly agree	Agree	Disagree	Strongly disagree	Not sure
1. My parents don't mind if I do well at school or not.					
2. My parents sometimes help me with my school-work.					
3. My parents think school is a waste of time.					
4. My parents think it's important to do well at school.					
5. My parents punish me if I don't do well at school.					
6. My parents reward me if I do well at school.					

FRIENDS

17 What part do your friends play in your learning?

Please tick only one box for each row.

	Strongly agree	Agree	Disagree	Strongly disagree	Not sure
1. My friends like to fool around in class.					
2. My friends think it's important to do well at school.					
3. My friends make fun of me if I get something wrong.					
4. My friends tease me if I do some really good work at school.					

Thank you very much for answering these questions.

QuesEng2.doc
21 05 96

References

Ainley, J. and Bourke, S. (1992) 'Student views of primary schooling', *Research Papers in Education*, **7**(2).

Alexander, R. (1996) 'Other primary schools and ours: hazards of international comparison'. Invitational Lecture given at Warwick University, July.

—— (forthcoming) 'Culture in pedagogy, pedagogy across cultures', in Alexander, R., Broadfoot, P. and Phillips, D. (eds) *Learning from Comparing, vol. 1: Contexts, Classrooms and Outcomes*. Wallingford: Symposium Books.

Alexander, R., Rose. J. and Woodhead, C. (1992) *Curriculum Organisation and Classroom Practice in Primary Schools*. London: DFEE.

Andersson, B.-E. (1996) 'Why am I in school? A study of Swedish adolescents' perceptions of their school situation', *EERA Bulletin*, **2**(2), July.

Andersson, J. and Bachor, D. (1998) 'A Canadian perspective on portfolio use in student assessment', *Assessment in Education*, **5**(3).

Archer, M.S. (1979) *Social Origins of Educational Systems*. London: Sage.

Atkin, J.M. and Black, P. (1997) 'Policy perils of international comparisons: the Timms Case', *Phi Delta Kappan*, September, 22–28.

ATL (1998) *Take Care Mr Blunkett!* London: ATL.

Ayers, W. (1990) 'Small Heroes: In and out of school with ten year old city kids', *Cambridge Journal of Education*, **20**(3), 269–76.

Ball, S.J. (1994) *Education Reform: a critical and post-structural approach*. Buckingham: Open University Press.

Banks, M., Bates, I., Breakwell, G. and Bynner, J. (1992) *Careers and Identities*. Buckingham: Open University Press.

Baudelot, C. and Establet, R. (1971) *L'école capitaliste en France*. Paris: Maspero.

Baumgart, N. (1997) 'Globalisation v. cultural diversity: the role of assessment', London: ICRA Conference.

Bayrou, F. (1994) 'Vingt-quatre propositions sur l'école'. Ministère de l'Éducation Nationale, Paris.

—— (1994) Speech on 'Un nouveau contrat pour l'école'. Ministère de l'Éducation Nationale, May.

Beattie, N. (1997) 'Interview and Concours: teacher appointment procedures in England and Wales and France and what they mean', *Assessment in Education*, **3**(1), 9–28.

Beck, J. (1996) 'Nation, curriculum and identity in conservative cultural analysis: a critical commentary', *Cambridge Journal of Education*, **26**(2), 171–98.

Beishuizen, B. and Anghileri, J. (1998) 'Which mental strategies in the early number curriculum? A comparison of British ideas and Dutch views', *British Educational Research Journal*, **24**(5), 519–38.

Bickner, R. and Peyasantiwong, P. (1988) 'Cultural variation in reflective writing', in Purves, A. (1988) *Writing across Languages and Cultures: issues in contrastive rhetoric*. Sage Publications.

Bierhoff, H. (1996) 'Laying the foundations of numeracy: a comparison of primary school text books in Britain, Germany and Switzerland', London: National Institute of Economics and Social Research.

Blatchford, P. (1992) 'Children's attitudes to work at 11 years', *Educational Studies*, **18**(1), 107–18.

—— (1996) 'Pupils' views on school work and school from 7 to 16 years', *Research Papers in Education*, **11**, 263–88.

Blishen, E. (1969) *The School That I'd Like*. Harmondsworth: Penguin.

Bolton, E. (1988) 'The National Curriculum: an overview'. Paper presented to INOGOV Conference, Birmingham.

Bonnet, G. (1999) 'Commentary', in Alexander, R., Broadfoot, P. and Phillips, D. (eds) *Learning from Comparing*, Wallingford: Symposium Books.

—— (ed.) (1998) 'The effectiveness of the teaching of English in the European Union'. Report of a colloquium, 20–21 October 1997, Paris, Ministère de l'Éducation Nationale.

Bourdieu, P. and Passeron, W.C. (1977) *Reproduction*. London: Sage.

Boyer, R., Bounure, A. and Delclaux, M. (1991) *Paroles de lycéens, les études, les loisirs, l'avenir*. Paris: Editions Universitaires, Institut National Pédagogique.

Bracey, G.W. (1996) 'International comparison and the condition of American education', *Educational Researcher*, **25**(1), 5–11.

Bracey, G.W. (1993) 'The third Bracey report on the condition of public education', *Phi Delta Kappan*, **75**, October, 104–17.

Branwhite, T. (1988) 'The Pass Survey: school based preferences of 500+ adolescent consumers', in *Educational Studies*, **14**(2), 165–75.

Bray, M. and Thomas, M.R. (1995) 'Levels of comparison in educational studies: different insights from different literatures and the value of multilevel analysis', *Harvard Educational Review*, **65**(3), 472–90.

Brighouse, T. (1998) 'Primary targets threat to weaker pupils', *TES*, 29 May 1998, p. 1.

Broadfoot, P. (1985) 'Institutional dependence and autonomy: English and French teachers in the classroom', *Prospects*, **15**(2), 263–71.

—— (1992) 'Assessment developments in French education', *Education Review*, **44**(3), 309–16.

—— (1996) *Education, Assessment and Society*. Buckingham: Open University Press.

—— (1998) *What Makes Primary Education Successful? perspectives from a comparative study in European education*. New York: Sharpe.

—— (forthcoming) 'Not so much a context, more a way of life? comparative education in the 1990s', in Alexander, R., Broadfoot, P. and Phillips, D. (eds) *Learning From Comparing, vol. 1: Contexts, Classrooms and Outcomes*. Wallingford: Symposium Books.

—— and Osborn, M. (1993) *Perceptions of Teaching: primary school teachers in England and France*. London: Cassell.

—— and Pollard, A. (1999) *The Assessment Society*. London: Cassell.

—— and Osborn, M. with Gilly, M. and Paillett, A. (1988) 'What professional responsibility means to teachers: national contexts and classroom constants', *British Journal of Sociology of Education*, **9**(3).

—— and Osborn, M. with Gilly, M. and Paillet, A. (1987) 'Teachers' conceptions of their professional responsibility: some international comparisons', *Comparative Education*, **23**(3), 287–301.

—— Osborn, M., Planel, C. and Pollard, A. (1995) 'Systems, teachers and policy change: a comparison of English and French teachers at a turbulent time'. Paper presented to the European Conference on Educational Research, University of Bath.

—— Osborn, M., Planel, C. and Pollard, A. (1996a) 'Assessment in French primary schools', *Curriculum Journal*, **7**(2), 227–46.

—— Osborn, M., Planel, C. and Pollard, A. (1996b) 'Teachers and change: a study of primary school teachers' reactions to policy changes in England and France', in Winther-Jensen, T. (ed.) *Challenges to European Education: cultural values, national identities and global responsibilities*. Berne: Peter Lang.

Bronfenbrenner, U. (1979) *The Ecology of Human Development: experiments by nature and design*. Cambridge, Mass.: Harvard University Press.

Brown, M. (1998) 'FIMS and SIMS: the first two IEA International Mathematics Surveys', *Assessment in Education*, **3**(2), 193–212.

—— (1996) 'International comparisons and mathematics education: a critical review', *Oxford Studies in Comparative Education*, **3**(2), July.

—— (1990) *Acts of Meaning*. Cambridge, Mass.: Harvard University Press.

Bruner, J. (1996) *Actual Minds, Possible Worlds*. Cambridge, Mass.: Harvard University Press.

Budge, D. (1997) 'Maths failure lingers after curriculum revolution', *TES*, 13 June, p. 20.

Burghes, D. (1996) 'Education across the world'. Presentation to Home Lessons from Abroad: Learning from International Experience in Education. Neil Stewart Associates Conference, Hammersmith, London.

Burton, L. (1984) *Thinking Things Through: problem solving in mathematics*. London: Basil Blackwell.

—— (ed.) (1994) *Who Counts: assessing mathematics in Europe*. Stoke on Trent: Trentham Books.

Caffyn, R. (1989) 'Attitudes of British secondary teachers and pupils to rewards and punishments', *Educational Research*, **31**(3), 210–20.

Callender, C. (1966) 'Cultural-style in multi-ethnic classrooms: the case of African Caribbean teachers and pupils', BERA, Lancaster.

Carré, C. and Head, J. (1974) *Through the Eyes of the Pupil*. New York: McGraw-Hill.

Charlot, B. (1994) *L'école et le territoire*. Paris: Armand Colin.

—— (1997) 'Une école moderne, mais à la française', *Revue Internationale d'éducation*, **15**, 73–83.

Charlot, B., Bautier, E. and Rochex, J.-Y. (1992) *Ecole et Savoir dans les Banlieues et Ailleurs*. Paris: Armand Colin.

Chinapah, V. (1997) *Monitoring Learning Achievement*. Paris: UNESCO.

CNDP (1995) *Programmes de l'Ecole Primaire*. Ministère de l'Education Nationale.

Connolly, P. 'In search of authenticity: researching young children's perspectives', in Pollard, A., Thiessen, D. and Filer, A. (eds) (1997) *Children and Their Curriculum: the perspectives of primary and elementary school children*. London: Falmer Press.

Cooper, P. and McIntyre, D. (1994) 'Teachers and pupils' perceptions of effective classroom learning', in Hughes, M. (1994) *Perceptions of Teaching and Learning*. Clevedon: Multilingual Matters Ltd.

Corbett, A. and Moon, R. (1996) *Education in France: continuity and change in the Mitterrand years, 1981–1995*. London: Routledge.

Cortazzi, M. (1998) 'Learning from Asian lessons: cultural expectations and classroom talk', *Education 3–13*, **26**(2), 42–9.

Coulby, D. and Ward, S. (1990) *The Primary Core National Curriculum: policy into practice*. London: Cassell.

Cousin, O. (1997) 'The experience of pupils in the French educational system'. Paper presented to the European Conferences on Educational Research, University of Frankfurt.

—— (1998) *L'Efficacité des Collèges*. Paris: PUF.

Cowan, R. (1996) 'Last past the post: comparative education, modernity and perhaps postmodernity', *Comparative Education*, **31**(2), 151–70.

Cox, T. (1982) 'Disadvantaged fifteen-year-olds: initial findings from a longitudinal study', *Educational Studies*, **8**, 1–13.

—— (1983) 'The educational attitudes and views about school of a sample of disadvantaged fifteen-year-olds', *Educational Studies*, **9**, 69–79.

Crick, B. (1997) 'The English and the Others', *TES*, 2 May, 15.

Crick, B. (1998) *Education for Citizenship and Teaching for Democracy.* Final report of the advisory group chaired by Bernard Crick. QCA Report, code 98/245.

Croll, P. (ed.) (1996) *Teachers, Pupils and Primary Schooling.* London: Cassell.

Crooks, T. and Flockton, L. (1996) Science: Assessment results 1995, National Education Monitoring report 1, 2 (Art) and 3; Graphs, Tables and Maps. Otago, New Zealand: Educational Assessment Research Unit, University of Otago.

—— Kane, M. and Cohen, A. (1996) 'Threats to the valid use of assessments', in *Assessment in Education,* **3**(3), 265–85.

Crossley, M. and Broadfoot, P. (1992) 'Comparative and international research in education: scope, problems and potential', *British Educational Research Journal,* **18**(2), 99–112.

—— and Murby, M. (1994) 'Textbook provision and the quality of the school curriculum in developing countries: issues and policy options', *Comparative Education,* **30**(2), 99–114.

—— and Vulliamy, G. (eds) (1997) *Qualitative Educational Research in Developing Countries.* New York: Garland Publishing Inc.

Cullingford, C. (1991) *The Inner World of the School.* London: Cassell.

—— (1985) 'Expectations of parents, teachers, children', in Cullingford, C. (ed.) *Parents, Teachers and Schools.* London: Robert Royce Ltd, pp. 131–52.

—— (1986) 'I suppose learning your tables could help you get a good job: children's view of the purpose of school', *Education 3–13,* **14**, 41–6.

—— (1988) 'Children's views about working together', *Education,* **16**, 29–33.

Daugherty, R. (1997) 'National Curriculum assessment: the experience of England and Wales', *Educational Administration Quarterly,* **33**(2), 198–218.

Davie, R., Butler, N. and Goldstein, H. (1972) *From Birth to Seven: a report of the National Child Development Study.* London: Longman.

Davie, R. and Galloway, D. (1996) *Listening to the Voice of the Child in Education.* London: David Fulton.

Dawkins, R. (1989) *The Selfish Gene.* Oxford: Oxford University Press.

Dearing, R. (1993) 'The National Curriculum and its assessment'. Final Report. London, SCAA.

De Beer, P. (1996) 'Le nouveau visage de l'éducation anglaise', *Le Monde de L'Education,* Mai 1996, 43–9.

DFE (1992) *Choice and Diversity: a new framework for schools.* Cm 2021. London: HMSO.

DFEE (1995) *English in the National Curriculum,* London: HMSO.

DFEE (1997) *The National Literacy Strategy.* London: DFEE.

DFEE (1998a) *The National Numeracy Strategy.* London: DFEE.

DFEE (1998b) *Numeracy Matters: the preliminary report of the Numeracy Task Force,* London: DFEE.

Les dossiers d'Éducation et Formations, No 62, February 1996, Ministère de l'Éducation Nationale, Direction de l'évaluation et de la prospective.

Dubet, F. (1991) *Les Lycéens.* Paris: Editions du Seuil.

—— Cousin, O. and Guillemet, J.P. (1996) 'A sociology of the lycée student', in Corbett, A. and Moon, R., *Education in France: continuity and change in the Mitterrand years, 1981–1995.* London: Routledge.

Dupré, J.P., Olive, M. and Schmitt, R. (1988) 'Langue Française: la balle aux mots', CM2, Nathan.

Durkheim, E. (1968) *The Elementary Forms of the Religious Life.* London: George Allen and Unwin.

Duru-Bellat, M. (1996) 'Social inequalities in French secondary schools: from figures to theories', *British Journal of Sociology of Education,* **17**(3), 341–50.

—— and Mingat, A. (1993) *Pour une approche analytique du fonctionnement du système educatif.* Paris: Presse Universitaire de France.

—— and van Zanten, Agnès (1999) *Sociologie de l'école.* Paris: Armand Colin.

Economie et Statistique no 293 1996/3 'L'école, les élèves et les parents', Paris: National Statistics and Economic Studies Institute.

Elliott, J., Hufton, N., Hildreth, A. and Illushin, L. (1999) 'Factors influencing educational motivation: a study of attitudes, expectations and behaviour of children in Sunderland, Kentucky and St Petersburg', *British Educational Research Journal*, **25**(1), 75–94.

Entwhistle, N. and Kozeki, B. (1985) 'Relationship between school motivation, approaches to studying and attainment among British and Hungarian adolescents', *British Journal of Educational Psychology*, **55**(2), 124–37.

—— *et al.* (1988) 'Dimensions of motivation and approaches to learning in British and Hungarian secondary schools', *International Journal of Educational Research*, **12**(3), 243–55.

—— *et al.* (1989) 'Pupil perceptions of schools and teachers', *British Journal of Educational Psychology*, **549**(3), 326–50.

Fairclough, N. (1995) *Critical Discourse Analysis*. London: Longman.

Federal Reserve Bank of New York (1998) Economic Policy Review, March.

Felouzis, G. (1990) 'Filles et garçons au collège. Comportements, dispositions et réussite scolaire en Sixième et Cinquième'. PhD thesis, Université de Provence.

Fletcher, T.V. and Sabers, D.L. (1995) 'Interaction effects in crossnational studies of achievement', *Comparative Education Review*, **39**(4), 455–67.

Firestone, W. (1998) 'A tale of two tests: tensions in assessment policy', *Assessment in Education*, **5**(2), July, 178–93.

—— Winter, J. and Fitz, J. (1998) *Different Policies, Common Practice: mathematics assessment and teaching in the United States and England and Wales*. San Diego: AERA.

Fogelman, K. (ed.) (1983) *Growing up in Britain: collected papers from the National Child Development Study*. London: Macmillan.

Foucault, M. (1979) *Discipline and Punish: the birth of the prison*. London: Penguin.

Fourez, G. (1990) *Eduquer, Ecoles, Ethiques, Sociétés*. Brussels: De Boeck.

Foxman, D. (1992) *Learning Mathematics and Science*. Slough: NFER.

Furet, F. and Ozouf, J. (1977) *Lire et écrire: l'alphabétisation des Français de Calvin à Jules Ferry*. Paris: Les Editions de Minuit.

Galton, M. (1999) 'Commentary: interpreting classroom practice around the globe', in Alexander, R., Broadfoot, P. and Phillips, D. (eds) *Learning from Comparing*, Symposium.

Garfinkel, H. (1967) *Studies in Ethnomethodology*. New York: Prentice Hall.

Gilly, M. (1997) 'Maître–élève: roles institutionnels et représentations', in *Pédagogie d'aujourd'hui*. Paris.

—— (1987) 'Institutional roles, partners, representations and attitudes in educational interactions', in Corte, E. (ed.) *Learning and Instruction*. London: Pergamon Press.

Giust-Desprairies, F. (1989) *L'Enfant Rêve: significations imaginaires d'une ecole nouvelle*. Paris: Armand Colin.

Goldschmidt, P. and Eyermann, T. (1999) 'International Educational Performance in the United States: is there a problem that money can fix?', *Comparative Education*, **35**(1), 27–45.

Goldstein, H. (1995) *Interpreting International Comparisons of Student Achievement*. Paris: UNESCO.

—— (1996) Introduction. *Assessment in Education*, **3**(2), 125–8.

—— (1998) 'A response to Gibson and Asthana', *Oxford Review of Education*, **24**(4), 521–3.

Greaney, V. and Kellaghan, T. (1996) 'Directions in development: monitoring the learning outcomes of education systems', Washington, DC: The World Bank.

Green, A. (forthcoming) 'Converging paths or ships passing in the night: an English critique of Japanese school reform', *Comparative Education*, **36**(3).

Halsey, A.H., Heath, A.F. and Ridge, J.M. (1980) *Origins and Destinations: family, class and education in modern Britain*. Oxford: Clarendon Press.

Hanushek, E. (1989) 'The impact of differential expenditures on school performance', *Educational Researcher*, **18**(4), 45–51.

Hargreaves, E. (1996) 'Learning, teaching and the monster of the Secondary Leaving Certificate', in *Assessment in Education*, **4**(1), 161–71.

Harlen, W. (1998) The new PISA project, OECD Nuffield Assessment Seminar on International Comparisons of Assessments of Achievements. London, 8 June.

Harries, T. and Sutherland, R. (1998) 'A comparison of primary mathematics textbooks from five countries with a particular focus on the treatment of number'. QCA Final Report.

Harris, S. and Ruddock, J. (1994) ' "School's great – apart from lessons": students' early experiences of learning in secondary schools', in Hughes, M. (1994) *Perceptions of Teaching and Learning*. Clevedon: Multilingual Matters Ltd.

Higginson, J.H. (ed.) (1979) *Selections from Michael Sadler: studies in world citizenship*. Liverpool: Northern Design Unit.

Holmes, B. (ed.) (1985) *Equality and Freedom in Education: a comparative study*. London: George Allen and Unwin.

Hopkin, A.G. (1992) 'Qualitative research methodologies: a cross cultural perspective', *Compare*, **22**(2), 133–41.

Howson, G. (1991) *National Curricula in Mathematics*. Leicester: Mathematics Association.

Hughes, M. (1997a) 'The National Curriculum in England and Wales: a lesson in externally-imposed reform?', *Educational Administration Quarterly*, **33**(2).

—— (1997b) 'Whole-class teaching in Maths: Japan and England'. Seminar given to the University of Bristol Graduate School of Education, 20 May.

IAEP (1992) *IAEP Technical Report*. Princeton NJ: Education Testing Service.

I.D.S. Research Reports RR17 (1987) 'Why do students learn? a six-country study of student motivation', University of Sussex: I.D.S. Publications.

L'Institut Louis-Harris (1990) 'Es-tu heureux à l'école?' in *Le Monde de L'éducation*, October.

Jacques, M. (1996) 'Taiwan: a case study'. Presentation to Home Lessons from Abroad: learning from international experience in education. Neil Stewart Associates Conference, Hammersmith, London.

Johnson, N. (1980) *In Search of the Constitution: reflection on state and society in Britain*. London: Methuen.

Jones, L.V. (1996) 'A history of the national assessment of educational progress and some questions about its future', *Educational Researcher*, **25**(7), 15–22.

Jospin Reforms (1989) Loi d'orientation sur l'éducation. See also 'The Loi Jospin extracts', in Corbett, A. and Moon, B. (1996) *Education in France: Continuity and Change in the Mitterrand Years, 1981–1995*. London: Routledge.

Judge, H. (1999) 'What is today about?'. Paper given at 6th ESRC Seminar Series Conference 'Learning from comparing: the uses and abuses of comparative education research: education professionals compared', University of Bristol, 9.3.99.

Kaplan, R. (1988) 'Contrastive rhetoric and second language learning: notes toward a theory of contrastive rhetoric', in Purves, A. (ed.) *Writing across Languages and Cultures, Issues in Contrastive Rhetoric*. California: Sage Publications.

—— (1966) 'Cultural thought patterns in inter-cultural education', *Language Learning*, **16**, 1–20.

Kellaghan, T., Madaus, G. and Raczek, A. (1996) 'The use of external examinations to improve student motivation', Washington, DC: American Educational Research Association.

Keys, W. and Fernandes, C. (1993) *What Do Students Think About School? research into factors associated with positive and negative attitudes toward school and education*. Slough: National Foundation for Educational Research.

Keys, W., Harris, S. and Fernandes, C. (1996) Third International Mathematics and Science Study: first national report. Slough: NFER.

Kincheloe, J.L., Steinberg, S.R. and Gregsson, A.D. (eds) (1997) *Measured Lies: the bell curve examined*. New York: St Martin's Griffin.

King, R. (1978) *All Things Bright and Beautiful*. Winchester: John Wiley & Sons Ltd.

Koretz, D.M. (1991) 'State comparisons using NAEP: large costs, disappointing benefit', *Educational Researcher*, **20**(3), April, 19, 24.

Kozaki, B. (1985) 'Motivation and educational styles in education', in Entwhistle, M. (ed.) *New Directions in Educational Psychology: learning and teaching*. London: Falmer Press.

Lang, V. (1999) *La Professionnalisation des Enseignants*. Paris: Presses Universitaires de France.
Lees, Lynn Hollen (1994) 'Educational inequality and academic achievement in England and France', *Comparative Education Review*, **38**(1), 65–116.
Le Figaro (1999) 'Journal d'un prof de banlieu'. 19 January, p. 1.
Litt, E. and Parkinson, M. (1979) *US and UK Educational Policy: a decade of reform*. New York: Praeger.
Little, A. (1997) 'The diploma disease 1977–1997: a national or global phenomenon?'. Paper given to International Centre for Research. Assessment Conference, Institute of Education, London, July.
Lumbroso, M. (1993) 'Les Enseignants du second degré français et leur conception sur la cause et la fatalité de la réussite (ou de l'échec) scolaire', *European Journal of Teacher Education*, **16**(2).
Macbeath, J. and Weir, D. (1991) Attitudes to School: A Digest of UK Surveys and Polls on Parents', Teachers', and Pupils' Attitudes to School, 1985–1990. Glasgow: Jordanhill College of Education.
McMeniman (1989) 'Motivation to learn', in Langford, P. (ed.) *Educational Psychology: an Australian perspective*. Cheshire: Longman.
McPake, J. and Powney, J. (1995) 'A Mirror to ourselves? The educational experience of Japanese children at school in the UK'. Scottish Council for Research in Education.
Masters, G. and Forster, M. (1997) Mapping Literacy Achievement: results of the 1996 National School English Literacy Survey, Department of Employment and Education Training and Youth Affairs, Canberra, Australia.
Masters, N. (1997) Literacy Standards in Australia. Commonwealth of Australia, Canberra.
Mathematics Assessment at KS2 Project (1996) Error analysis of Key Stage 2 Pupil Performance. School of Education Leeds mimeo.
Measor, L. and Woods, P. (1984) *Changing Schools: pupil perspectives on transfer to a comprehensive*. Buckingham: Open University Press.
Ministère de l'Éducation Nationale (1998) *Education in France*, 8th edn, October.
—— Direction de la prospective (1996) Les Dossiers d'Éducation et Formations, No 62, February.
—— (1998) Comparaison des performances en lecture: compréhensive des élèves en fin de CM2 á dix années d'intervalle (1987–97). Paris.
—— (1998) Observation à l'entrée au CP des élèves du panel 1997. Paris.
Mislevy, R.J. (1995) 'What can we learn from international assessments?', *Educational Evaluation and Policy Analysis*, **7**(4), 419–37.
Le Monde de l'éducation (1995a) 'Le fléau du redoublement: maladie honteuse ou seconde chance?', June, pp. 42–9.
—— (1995b) 'On reform of French primary schools', September.
—— (1996) 'Le mythe de l'égalité', June, pp. 26, 27.
—— (1996) 'Le bonheur d'être prof, et comment on le pratique'. Special issue 237, May, 27–43.
Morris, P. (1998) 'Comparative education and educational reform: beware of prophets returning from the Far East', *Education 3–13*, **26**(2), 5–9.
Mortimore, J. and Blackstone, T. (1982) *Disadvantage and Education*. London: Heinemann.
Mortimore, P. *et al.* (1988) *School Matters*. London: Open Books Publishing Limited.
Murphy, P. (1997) Seminar presented at University of Bristol, 'Assessment and Gender', 3 June 1997.
Murphy, P.F. and Gipps, C.V. (1996) *Equity in the Classroom: towards effective pedagogy for girls and boys*. London: Falmer [and] UNESCO. 1996 Conference Proceedings.
Nash, R. (1976) 'Pupils' expectations of their teachers', in Stubbs, M. and Delamont, S. (eds) *Explorations in Classroom Observation*. London: Wiley.
National Commission on Education (1993) *Learning to Succeed*. London: Heinemann.
—— (1996) *Success Against the Odds*. London: Routledge.
National Statistics and Economics Studies Institute (1996) 'L'école, les élèves et les parents', *Economie et Statistique*, **293**(3).

Obin, J.P. (1993) *La Crise de l'Organisation Scolaire*. Paris: Hachette.

OECD (1995a) *Secondary Education in France: a decade of change*. Paris, OECD.

—— (1995b) *Schools Under Scrutiny*. Paris, OECD.

—— (1996a) *Measuring What People Know*. Paris, OECD.

—— (1996b) *Reviews of National Policies for Education: France*. Paris: OECD.

—— (1997) *Education at a Glance*. Paris: OECD.

—— (1998) Centre for Educational Research and Innovation. *Human Capital Investment: an international comparison*. Paris: OECD.

Office for Standards in Education (1993) *Access and Achievement in Urban Education*. London: OFSTED.

—— (1995) *Teaching Quality: the primary debate*. London: OFSTED.

—— (1998) *The Annual Report of Her Majesty's Chief Inspector of Schools in England: standards and quality in education. 1996–97*. London: The Stationery Office.

O'Leary, M., Madaus, G. and Kellaghan, T. (1997) 'The validity and stability of international comparative findings in Mathematics and Science: the IAEP TIMSS Enigma', ICRA, London, 3–5 July.

Osborn, M.J. and Broadfoot, P.M. (1992) 'A lesson in progress', *Oxford Review of Education*, **18**(1), 3–15.

—— Broadfoot, P., Planel, C., and Pollard, A. (1997) 'Social class, educational opportunity, and equal entitlement: dilemmas of schooling in England and France', *Comparative Education*, **33**(3).

—— Broadfoot, P., Planel, C. Sharpe, K. and Ward, B. (1998) 'Being a pupil in England and France: findings from a comparative study', in Kazamias, A.M. and Spillane, M.G. (eds) *Education and the Structuring of the European Space*. Athens: Seirios Editions, and the Greek Comparative Education Society, for the Comparative Education Society in Europe (CESE).

Pascal, F. (1996) 'L'école et ses images', in *Le Monde de L'éducation*. September, 68–9.

Paulston, R.G. (ed.) (1996) *Social Cartography: mapping ways of seeing social and educational change*. New York: Garland.

Phillips, D. (1989) 'Neither a borrower nor a lender be? the problems of cross-national attraction in education', *Comparative Education* **25**(3), 267–274.

—— (1991) 'Benefits of state-by-state comparisons', *Educational Researcher*, **20**(2), 17–19.

Pilling, D. (1990) *Escape from Disadvantage*. Lewes: Falmer Press.

Planel, C. (1996) 'Children's experience of learning', *EERA Bulletin* (1) March.

—— with Broadfoot, P., Osborn, M., Sharpe, K. and Ward, B. (1998) 'Assessing national assessments: underlying cultural values revealed by comparing English and French national tests papers'. Paper given at European Educational Research Association Annual Conference in Seville.

Pollard, A. (ed). (1985) *The Social World of the Primary School*. London: Cassell.

—— (1987) *Children and their Primary Schools*. Lewes: Falmer Press.

—— (1996) *The Social World of Children's Learning*. London: Cassell.

—— Broadfoot, P., Croll, P., Osborn, M. and Abbott, D. (1994) *Changing English Primary Schools? The impact of the Education Reform Act at Key Stage One*. London: Cassell.

—— Thiessen, D. and Filer, A. (eds) (1997) *Children and Their Curriculum: the perspectives of primary and elementary school children*. London: Falmer Press.

Purves, A., (1988) *Writing across Languages and Cultures: issues in contrastive rhetoric*. California: Sage Publications.

QCA (1998a) *Education for Citizenship and Teaching for Democracy*. Final report of the advisory group chaired by Bernard Crick.

—— (1998b) Standards at Key Stage 1, Yr 4 KS2 and KS3, London, summarized in *TES*. 20.2.98.

—— (1998c) Standards at Key Stage 2: English, Maths and Science. Report on the 1997 National Curriculum Assessments for 11 year olds. Middlesex: QCA Publications.

Reasons for Writing. Course book 4. Oxford: Ginn.

Resnick, L.B., Nolan, K.J. and Resnick, D.P. (1994) 'Benchmarking education standards', *Education Evaluation and Policy Analysis*, **17**(4), 438–61.

Reynolds, D. and Farrell, S. (1996) *Worlds Apart: a review of international surveys of achievement involving England*. London: OFSTED/HMSO.

Richards, M. and Light, P. (1986) *Children of Social Worlds*. Bristol: Polity Press.

Roberts, R. and Dolan, J. (1989) 'Children's perception of work: an exploratory study'. *Educational Review*, **41**(1), 19–28.

Robinson, P. (1989) 'Correlates of low academic attainment in three countries', *International Journal of Educational Research*, **13**, 581–96.

—— (1990a) 'Academic achievement and self-esteem in secondary school: muddle, myths and reality', *Educational Research and Perspectives*, **17**, 3–21.

—— (1990b) 'School attainment, self-esteem, and identity: France and England', *European Journal of Social Psychology*, **20**, 387–403.

—— (1992) 'Redoublement in relation to self-perception and self-evaluation: France', *Research in Education*, **47**, 64–75.

Robinson, P. (1999) 'The tyranny of league tables: international comparisons of educational attainment and economic performance', in Alexander, R., Broadfoot, P. and Phillips, D. (eds) *Learning From Comparing, vol. 1: Contexts, Classrooms and Outcomes*. Wallingford: Symposium Books (forthcoming).

Rudduck, J., Chaplain, R. and Wallace, G. (1996) *School Improvement: what can pupils tell us?* London: David Fulton.

—— Wallace, G. and Day, J. (1997) 'Students' perspectives on school improvement', in Hargreaves, A. (ed.) *Rethinking Educational Change with Heart and Mind. ASCD Yearbook*. Vancouver: ASCD.

Rust, V.D. (1991) 'Postmodernism and its comparative education implications', *Comparative Education Review*, **35**, 610–26.

Rutter, M. and Madge, N. (1976) *Cycles of Disadvantage*. London: Heinemann.

—— Maughan, B., Mortimore, P. and Ouston, J. (1979) *Fifteen Thousand Hours: secondary schools and their effects on children*. London: Open Books.

Sadler, M. E. (1979) *Selections from Michael Sadler: studies in world citizenship*. Compiled by J. H. Higginson. Liverpool: Dejall & Meyorre.

Salter, B. and Tapper, T. (1981) *Education, Politics and the State*. London: Grant-McIntyre.

Sander, T. (1999) 'The politics of comparing teacher education in Europe'. Paper given at 6th ESRC Seminar Series Conference 'Learning from comparing: the uses and abuses of comparative education research: education professionals compared', University of Bristol, 9.3.99.

Scott-Hodgetts, R. (1992) *Learning Mathematics: pupil perspectives*. Open University.

Secada, W. (1998) 'TIMMS: a narrowly-constructed, US-centric view'. Seminar paper given to Institute of Education, 24 June in London.

Sharma, Y. (1997) 'Primary's roll is down – by 4,000', *TES*, 7 February, 16–17.

Sharpe, K. (1992a) 'Educational homogeneity in French primary education: a double case study', *British Journal of Sociology of Education*, **13**(3), 329–429.

—— (1992b) 'Catechistic teaching style in French primary education: analysis of a grammar lesson with seven-year olds', *Comparative Education*, **28**(3), 249–68.

—— (1993a) 'An examination of some conditions of educational homogeneity in French primary schooling'. Unpublished PhD thesis, University of Kent at Canterbury.

—— (1993b) Final report to ESRC on research project, 'A double ethnography of French primary schooling'.

—— (1993c) 'An inspector calls: an analysis of inspection procedures in French primary education', *Compare*, **23**(3), 263–75.

—— (1997) 'The Protestant ethic and the spirit of Catholicism: ideological and institutional constraints on system change in English and French primary schooling', *Comparative Education*, **33**(3), 329–48.

Shorrocks-Taylor, D. (1996) 'Evaluation of the English Test Materials (for 11-year-olds) in reading, writing and spelling'. Paper presented to ECER Conference, Seville.

Silvernail, D. (1996) 'The impact of UK's National Curriculum and assessment system on classroom practice; potential lessons for American reformers'. *Educational Policy*, **10**(1), 46–62.

Simon, B. (1960) *Studies in the History of Education 1800–1870*. London: Lawrence & Wishart.

Stake, R.E. (1991) 'Impact of changes in assessment policy', in Stake, R.E. (ed.) *Advances in Programme Evaluation*, vol. 1, part A. London: JAI Press.

Stedman, L.C. (1997) 'International achievement differences: an assessment of a new perspective', *Educational Researcher*, **26**(3), 4–15.

Steedman, H. (forthcoming) 'Measuring the quality of educational outputs: some unresolved problems', in Alexander, R., Broadfoot, P. and Phillips, D. (eds) *Learning From Comparing, vol 1: Contexts, Classrooms and Outcomes*. Wallingford: Symposium Books.

Stevenson, G. *et al.* (1985) 'Cognitive performance and academic achievement of Japanese, Chinese and American children', *Child Development*, **56**(3), 718–34.

Sutherland, R. *et al.* (1998) Interim Report to QCA on International Maths Textbook Study.

Takala, S., Purves, A. and Buckmaster, A. (1982) 'On the interrelationship between language, perception, thought and culture and their relevance to the assessment of written composition', *Evaluation in Education*, **5**, 317–42.

Tall, D. (1993) 'The transition from arithmetic to algebra: number patterns or proceptual programming'. Proceedings of 2nd Annual Conference on Teaching and Learning, London.

—— (1996) 'Can all children climb the same curriculum ladder?' in *The Mathematical Ability of School Leavers*, Gresham Special Lecture, Gresham College, London.

Tate, N. (1997) Presentation to conference on *Curriculum, Culture and Society*. London: SCAA publications.

Thomas, N. (1985) *Improving Primary Schools*. London: ILEA.

Thompson, J. (1990) *Ideology and Modern Cultures*. Cambridge: Polity Press.

Threlfall, J. (1996) 'The formative use of performance data in maths'. Paper given to ECER, Seville.

Tonnies, F. (1955) *Gemeinschaft and Gesellschaft: Community and Association*. London: RKP.

Vahäpassi, A. (1988) in Purves, A. (ed.) *Writing across Languages and Cultures, issues in contrastive rhetoric*. California: Sage Publications.

Vinuesa, M. (1996) 'Transmission culturelle par le curriculum caché – la socialisation des enfants de 5 à 7 ans à l'école publique en France et en Angleterre'. Unpublished doctoral thesis, Université de Paris XIII.

Vygotsky, L.S. (1978) *Mind in Society*. Cambridge, Mass.: Harvard University Press.

—— (1986) *Thought and Language*. Cambridge, Mass.: MIT.

Watkins, D.A. and Briggs, J.B. (eds) (1996) 'The Chinese learner: cultural psychological and contextual influences', Hong Kong: CERC and ACER.

Webb, R., Vulliamy, G., Häkkinen, K. and Hämäläinen, S. (1998) 'External inspection or school self-evaluation? a comparative analysis of policy and practice in primary schools in England and Finland', *British Educational Research Journal*, **24**(5), 539–56.

Wedge, P. and Prosser, H. (1972) *Born to Fail?* London: Arrow.

Weiler, H. (1988) 'Reform politics in French education', *Comparative Education Review*, **32**(3), 251–66.

Wertsch, J.V. (1991) *Voices of the Mind*. Cambridge, Mass.: Havard University Press.

Whitburn, J. (1996) 'Contrasting approaches to the acquisition of mathematical skills: Japan and England', *Oxford Review of Education*, **22**(4), 415–35.

White, M. (1987) *The Japanese Educational Challenge*. London: Macmillan.

Whiting, B.B. and Edwards, C.P. (1988) *Children of Different Worlds*. Cambridge, Mass.: Harvard University Press.

Wiliam, D. (1996) SCAA Key Stage 3 Diagnostic Software; Statistics and Data presentation\guide. London: Kings College.

—— (1998a) 'Construct-referenced assessment of authentic tasks: alternatives to norms and criteria'. Paper given to 24th annual IAEA conference, Barbados, WI.

—— (1998b) 'New interpretation of validity'. Paper given to 24th IAEA annual conference, Barbados, WI.

Winter, S. (forthcoming) 'International comparisons of student achievement and the Asian educational phenomenon: a critical analysis', *Comparative Education*, **35**(2).

Woods, P. (1990) *The Happiest Days?* London: Falmer Press.

Woronoff, J. (1996) *Japan as Anything but Number One*, 2nd edn. London: Macmillan.

Zabulionis, A. (1998) 'The formal similarity of the maths and science achievement of the countries', Barbados: IAEA Conference.

Index